The Love Fix

Also By Rachel Thompson

Rough: How violence has found its way into the bedroom and what we can do about it

The Love Fix:

Reclaiming Intimacy, Vulnerability and Care in a Disconnected World

RACHEL THOMPSON

Love (fix)
from
Rachel
xo xo

■ SQUARE PEG

1 3 5 7 9 10 8 6 4 2

Square Peg, an imprint of Vintage, is part of the Penguin Random House
group of companies

Vintage, Penguin Random House UK, One Embassy Gardens,
8 Viaduct Gardens, London sw11 7bw

penguin.co.uk/vintage
global.penguinrandomhouse.com

Penguin
Random House
UK

First published by Square Peg in 2024

Copyright © Rachel Thompson 2024

Rachel Thompson has asserted her right to be identified as the author of
this Work in accordance with the Copyright, Designs and Patents Act 1988

Typeset in 12/14.75pt Dante MT Std by Jouve (UK), Milton Keynes
Printed and bound in Great Britain by Clays Ltd, Elcograf S.p.A.

The authorised representative in the EEA is Penguin Random House Ireland,
Morrison Chambers, 32 Nassau Street, Dublin d02 yh68

A CIP catalogue record for this book is available from the British Library

ISBN 9781529927955

To my parents, Nancy and Gary, who showed me what true love really looks like.

Contents

Introduction

'How's your love life?'

If you've picked up this book, you've probably been asked this question at some point, or a variation of it: 'Are you swiping right now?' or 'Got any dates lined up?' or 'How's Tinder?' or 'Chatting to anyone right now?' The subtext being: Are you still single? (And if so, why?)

In these moments, it's hard to know what to say. Depending on the day, you might go full-frontal honesty, or perhaps change the subject. Sometimes the response is a fun one – heaps of delicious gossip to dish up to a hungry listener. But often, that question hangs heavy in the air as for many people the answer is: Dating is hard. But why? What is really going on for so many of us to feel drained rather than nurtured by our romantic experiences? *The Love Fix* investigates how romantic and sexual relationships have evolved in the past decade – since the advent of Tinder. It unveils the chances of finding 'the one' in a big city; how apps compound but have not created the interpersonal challenges currently plaguing us, and how we have become the first generation to be more likely to meet a partner online than through friends, at work, or at the pub.

In this book, I will explore our love of love, our need for love, and what finding, keeping and being in love could look like if we regained access to vulnerability. My mission is to give you a comforting glimpse into why more than 46 per cent of UK dating app users report having bad experiences,[1] and why so many of us are struggling to find meaningful and lasting connections in the current moment, so that you can better insulate yourself against its challenges. I want to create a critical mass, so that together we can create the romantic landscape so many of us long for, and the care that all of us deserve.

As a journalist working on the relationships and sex desk at *Mashable*, I've been writing about dating and relationships for more than a decade, researching how our dating lives are changing alongside rapidly evolving technology, which in turn is affecting social norms. I've spoken to thousands of people of all orientations, races and genders about their dating dilemmas, their sex lives, their breakups, their heartbreaks, their innermost thoughts about love. I've also interviewed a wide range of experts, from psychologists and researchers to matchmakers and people who work behind the scenes on dating apps. Dating, especially online dating, often feels like a numbers game – with emphasis on 'game'. I want to uncover what it's like for the real people behind the numbers. I've investigated what the mindset behind ghosting is, or why you've got a phone full of matches but not a single chat in sight, or why you keep telling yourself you need to change before you're 'good enough' to go on a date. To write this book, I've spent years trawling through hundreds of studies, stories and stats, to compile a comprehensive guide to navigating modern dating culture. I've sat on the Tube and counted the number of wedding rings and engagement rings I can see on people's fingers, people-watched in bars and pubs, studying happy couples, wondering, how did they do it? Through this research, I have learned about the maths of love, what a spark truly is, why we are becoming more sensitive to rejection, what 'emotional availability' and vulnerability truly mean and look like in real terms. It has been the most demanding work of my life, but I hope it isn't in vain.

Just like singleness itself, doing this work comes with some judgement. In my career, I have encountered countless people who regard the topic of relationships as frivolous. In fact, some academics fear they won't be taken seriously if they research love.[2] But, to be human is to be relational. We're hard-wired to seek out the company of other people and it was once essential to our survival to do so – in fact, it still is. Even academics studying the phenomenon of love come up against this idea: that examining love is an inconsequential endeavour. Elizabeth Reid Boyd, an academic specialising in Love Studies at Edith Cowan University in Australia says the field is regarded as 'still a little cheesy, cringeworthy, intimate – a more intense thing to speculate about'. To dismiss conversations around love and sex as inconsequential overlooks the serious ways in which relationships can – emotionally, psychologically, physically, economically, socially – harm or sustain us. It elides how systems of oppression show up in our dating culture, or conversely, the symbol that a relationship status can bestow upon a person (no matter how unwarranted this is). Love is political. This cannot be overstated enough: Our dating lives are not immune to oppression – in fact, as this book will demonstrate in Part 2, it is often on dating sites that the unsightliness of our worst biases surfaces.

Alongside my work as a journalist, I've also been in the dating trenches with you. I'm in my mid-thirties and I've been single for 15 years. But 'single' is far from the full story. The reality is: I've been dating this entire time, observing these changes both first-hand and professionally. I've experienced most facets of relationships: I've been heartbroken several times over, been embroiled in countless emotionally fraught situationships, had whirlwind romances, workplace dalliances, one-night stands, been ghosted, stood up on dates, unceremoniously dropped. Friendships have blossomed into sex and then into feelings, before withering into painful silence. I've had steamy talking stages that ended with the discovery that he had a girlfriend the whole time. There have been crushes, flings, late-night kisses, excited texting sprees, gushing over brunch with friends. There has also been heartache, rejection, protracted empty periods of longing, moments of thinking I'm unlovable, that I'll never find love, that I need to change myself in order to be worthy of love. Through my singleness, I've learned that sometimes people mean more to you than you mean to them. Sometimes you must teach yourself how to get over someone you never dated. Sometimes you feel things and others don't. And sometimes, despite every good intention, you'll be the bad guy, the rejector, the poor communicator, the ghoster, the person causing someone else's pain. Being on that side of the fence doesn't feel great either! But what's the alternative, staying with the wrong person out of fear of hurting their feelings? More often than not, dating often feels like a no-win game. So why do we keep playing it? Why do we put ourselves through the pain of repeated rejection, the blows to our egos, the feelings of failure, the dashed hope? It can't just be about the serotonin! If you're on your umpteenth redownload of yet another app, I hope what follows helps you to take heart.

In the toughest moments, I have wondered: Do humans need romantic love? So, I asked Professor Michael Banissy – neuroscientist at the University of Bristol – about the neuroscientific case for romantic love: 'We know that having supportive social relationships in our lives is beneficial for our health and our wellbeing. So, people who feel that they have socially supportive relationships tend to live longer, they tend to show benefits through all sorts of day-to-day health, immune system, stress response, things like that. They tend to get benefits in mental health.

'Now, the important word there is socially supportive relationships, right? For one person that may need to be a romantic partner, but for somebody else that could come in a very different space where that could be a family member, that could be a friend,' he says.

Banissy says that the research around socially supportive relationships doesn't focus on the specific person, but rather the nature of the relationship. Those socially supportive relationships manifest in different ways in modern relationships. 'We might have a difficult relationship with our family, but a great romantic relationship, we might have awful luck in the romantic space, but really good supportive friends and family.

'And so in that sense, do we need it [romantic love]? Maybe, maybe not,' says Banissy.

So, here's some reassurance: *The Love Fix* is not a narrative that feeds into compulsory coupledom. Its aim is to centre your sense of agency if you do choose to put yourself out there. While thinking about my own approach to my love life, I stumbled across some words of wisdom in my X feed from *Love In Colour* author Bolu Babalola. 'The best thing I did in my 20s was loving myself more than the idea of a relationship. Make space for the kind of love you seek, establish your standards and the kind of love and friendship you want to pour out and you want poured into you.'[3] You might love being single most days. But if you've ever doubted your lovability, your worth, your value – keep reading. If you've ever felt your body would never be good enough, you're far from alone. If your mental health has ever exacerbated the intensity and emotional pain of dating, if you're neurodivergent and feel like dating culture doesn't cater to you, read on. Dating is really hard right now. If you've ever found yourself swiping endlessly through apps wondering if there was something wrong with you, rest assured, there isn't. If you've stared at those three little dots while your situationship was typing and felt derailed by anxiety, you're far from alone. This book is an offering of the real stories, science and data behind the business of relationships in the conflicting era of both therapy-speak and emotional avoidance. *The Love Fix* is a love letter to people working on their self-esteem. Who feel they need to change something, or everything, about themselves in order to be worthy of another person's love (they don't). For the people who feel insecure about whether they're lovable at all (they are). It's for the anxious babes who just want you to text them back (seriously though). For the person who can't get out of their own head when they're having sex because they're so distracted by negative thoughts about their own body. For the person wondering why they've just been rejected yet again and whether they'll ever be loved. For the person who just wants to feel safe when they're wearing their heart on their sleeve. It's not too much to ask. Love can get better than this.

Part 1

Love, Today

1

First Encounters

When did it get so hard to just *meet someone*? No, you're not imagining it .We're living through an intimacy and communication crisis and it's making dating and relationships feel decidedly joyless and, at times, downright impossible. So why do we even bother? In short: To be human is to connect with others. Touch is a fundamental human need. It is one of our first senses to develop and it's one of the last senses to die out, says Professor Michael Banissy, neuroscientist and author of *When We Touch: Handshakes, hugs, high fives and the new science behind why touch matters*. 'It's right with us even from before we're born right the way through to our final moments,' says Banissy. 'We asked about 40,000 people worldwide what touch means to them, and the most common theme is around comfort, care, and connection.'

If we don't have enough touch in our lives, we can feel lonely and it can impact our mental health. 'Having positive and supportive touch in relationships can lead to more satisfied relationships. It can also lead to physical health benefits. So, touch really has a lot of hidden benefits and we don't always realise, so things like: it can benefit our immune system, it can benefit our stress response.'

Feeling 'touch hungry' means you're not getting the amount or type of physical touch and affection that you desire, explains Banissy. 'Touch deprived' refers to not getting any touch at all.

'There can be negative consequences to being touch hungry – greater incidences of depression, anxiety can increase, you can see changes to things like loneliness, so can have a lot of negative mental health outcomes.'

And so, we swipe. Dating apps are now the number one method to meet new romantic and sexual partners. More than 300 million people use dating apps worldwide. In 2022, Tinder was the most downloaded app, with Bumble coming in second place.[1] The dating app industry is estimated to be worth around $3.06 billion, a figure that's expected to grow to $10.87 billion by 2026.[2] In the past decade, we've seen online dating transform from what was previously a stigmatised, private activity to a mainstream pursuit, shedding the shame it once carried, and radically transforming how society forms new bonds. By 2037, researchers at Imperial University predict that 50 per cent of babies will be born to parents who met online.[3]

In March 2020, all of us entered a period of mass alienation – it hindered our ability to touch, to explore, to be intimate. In the absence of any physical opportunities to meet people, many of us flocked to our phones. Dating app usage surged during this time.[4] Dating apps are notoriously cagey about revealing exact user numbers and they're selective about which data points they release to the public. If we compare Tinder usership before and after the pandemic, we see that in 2019, before the pandemic, Tinder had an estimated 50 million users worldwide,[5] compared with approximately 75 million monthly active users in 2023.[6] 2020 saw astronomical growth for the dating app. On March 29, just as lockdowns and stay-at-home mandates were being rolled out across the world, Tinder's swipe activity hit a new record: 3 billion swipes in a single day. That year, the record was smashed 130 more times.

We also know that the enforced isolation impacted the way

people – Gen Z in particular – feel about interacting with fellow daters. A 2024 survey of 15,000 Hinge users worldwide found that Gen Z singles are 47 per cent more likely than millennials to say the pandemic made them nervous to chat to new people.[7]

Dating is Hard

What is it like to date in our current moment? I asked people to describe the current dating scene in a few words:

'Fucking shitshow, mate.' 'Hellscape.' 'Completely fucked.' 'Bin fire.' 'Lonely.' 'Soul-destroying. Time-wasting. Boring.' 'Bleak.' 'Ghetto, whack, frustrating and unserious.' 'Harrowing.' 'Hell. On. Earth.' 'Absolutely fucking despair.' 'Dysfunctional, disappointing, dehumanising.'

Is it any wonder 79 per cent of Gen Z daters and 80 per cent of millennial daters feel burnt out by dating apps, according to a 2024 study by Forbes Health?[8]

This is unsurprising given that these apps are now engineered to keep people active on these apps for as long as possible. To the apps, you're at your most valuable when you're an active user – trapped in the revolving door of swiping, matching, chatting. Where's the incentive to make dating apps work better, to allow your most valuable assets to break free?

At the very same time, dating apps are clearly working for some people. Take my brother, for instance. In September 2020, he started messaging a woman he'd matched with on Hinge. Granted, it'd taken Alice two weeks to reply to Jamie's initial message. Better late than never, though. Their first date was by all accounts a disaster – my brother messed up the restaurant reservation and they ended up having to scramble for a place to eat; all the while Jamie's shoes were cutting his feet to ribbons. None of that mattered, though. Jamie and Alice fell in love. Two days before Christmas 2022, my brother proposed to Alice in Broadway in the Cotswolds, with both our families waiting at a nearby pub to toast to their happy news. By the time you read this, they'll be married. Other friends I know have similar lockdown love stories, when swiping was literally their only chance of finding someone to go out with (once we were allowed to) – Hinge chats that went on for months before blossoming into real-life connections, evolving into lives built together.

It's easy to get bogged down in the mire of negativity that surrounds dating app culture. But ultimately, most of us aren't on the apps just for the sheer fun of it. We are looking for something – love, sex, friendship, connection, passion, fireworks, life-altering romances, or one-night dalliances.

How the Internet Took Over Our Love Lives

So, how did we get here? Dating is far from a new concept, but the way we seek out connection has seen a seismic shift in the past century. The first use of the word 'date' has been attributed to American columnist George Ade who used the term in 1896 in one of his columns in the *Chicago Record*. Ade told the story of a clerk called Artie whose girlfriend was seeing other men. 'I s'pose the other boy's fillin' all my dates?' Artie asked her.[9] But it was the explosion of dating apps in the 2010s which catapulted online dating into the mainstream, raking in the billions as it did so.

But the big-bucks business of love existed long before the internet. In 1897, W. T. Stead – a newspaper owner and editor who later died on the Titanic – launched *The Wedding Ring*

Circle, which published catalogues of single people in the area, listing their interests and hobbies.[10] People could write to each other via a central intermediary office in London. Nichi Hodgson, journalist and author of *The Curious History of Dating*, tells me that marriage organisations were the precursor to dating agencies. 'Stead thought the answer to all these unmarried women creeping about was to actually just create an organisation where everyone can be matched up with each other,' says Hodgson. Matrimonial advertisements – which were basically lonely hearts ads – were published in newspapers throughout the Regency and Victorian eras and gained popularity towards the middle of the 19th century. These ads – often frowned upon by traditionalists who considered them dangerous – were placed in local or national newspapers. Take this ad published in 1894 in the *Derbyshire Courier*: 'Spinster, middle-aged, lady-like and very affectionate with ample private income. Feeling lonely, wishes to correspond with high principled Christian gentleman (bachelor or widower) of a quiet and sympathetic nature, with a view to marriage.'[11]

Love and technology have been bedfellows for longer than we realise. In 1959, two Stanford University students, Jim Harvey and Phil Fialer used an IBM 650 – the world's first mass-produced computer – and a questionnaire to try and matchmake 49 male and 49 female students. No love matches were made during Harvey and Fialer's project, but a seed was planted. In 1964, British businesswoman Joan Ball started the first commercial computer dating service in 1964, the St James Computer Dating Service.

The 1970s gave way to video dating, the '80s brought telephone dating, and in the '90s, the first modern dating websites launched: In 1994, kiss.com, and then in 1995, match.com. At this point, dating sites began entering mainstream consciousness through pop culture – remember Chandler Bing's foray into internet dating in Season 2 of *Friends*?[12] In 2009, Grindr launched, enabling users to harness their GPS location to browse profiles according to proximity, making it one of the first geosocial apps for gay men. When Tinder launched in 2012, the concept of 'swiping' – invented by Tinder's creators – came into our lives.[13] And with the flick of a finger across our phone screens, our love lives were never the same again. Two years later, in 2014, Tinder claimed more than 2 billion matches had occurred on its app.[14] The app has now been downloaded 530 million times since its launch, with 75 billion matches globally, and approximately 1.5 million Tinder dates happening each week, according to Tinder data shared with me. As Tinder went from strength to strength, we saw newcomers enter the market and find success: Hinge launched in 2013, Bumble was founded in 2014 by former Tinder VP Whitney Wolfe Herd, Her, an app for women loving women, launched in 2014.

Love, Incorporated

In the UK, one in ten adults use online dating services, according to Ofcom figures published in 2024.[15] The explosion of dating apps has revolutionised the way we meet people. In those early days, the gamified elements of swiping had a novelty factor, it was fun to see the dating pool laid out in front of you without having to leave your sofa, and it was even more fun when you matched with someone attractive and interesting. But the novelty appears to have worn off, leaving many of us feeling disillusioned, hopeless, and glued to our phones with limited alternatives. Have we fallen out of love with dating apps? The figures certainly show that something has changed – the number of people paying to use Tinder declined by 8 per cent in 2023, according to its parent company Match Group in its earnings letter to shareholders.[16] Downloads are also dwindling, with 2023 seeing 36 million dating app downloads, a 2 per cent decrease in the number of dating app downloads in America, and a 16 per cent decline from 2020, per figures from analytics company data.ai.[17]

So, what do academics studying the evolution of the digital culture of love say when you ask them, 'What's going on with dating right now?' I interviewed Dr Carolina Bandinelli, associate professor in media and creative industries at Warwick University, and a leading sociologist whose research focuses on digital love. 'It is not too emphatic to say that dating apps have brought about a digital revolution in the field of dating,' she tells me. 'This is what media scholars sometimes call the platformisation of the intimacy of love.'

What this means is: Most aspects of our daily life have moved into the digital realm – the platformisation of life – where apps provide the solutions to the problems we face. Those problems include feeling anxious, not knowing when we'll get our period, getting lost while driving, not having a way to print off tickets. The solutions we're presented with for these problems include meditation apps like Calm and Headspace, period tracking apps like Flo and Clue, apps like Google Maps and Waze, apps like Ticketmaster, AXS, etc. Dating apps are built on the assumption that we cannot find the right person in real life, says Bandinelli, and their solution is to give you access to 'a virtually infinite number of people'.

Problem solved? Not quite. Access isn't the only ingredient that's needed to make a love match a success. That's just the first hurdle to clear. We need more than a match to make a connection – we need to get to know each other too. I wonder: in an age when we look to apps to solve all our problems, are we expecting too much from dating apps? And are dating apps over-promising and under-delivering?

Tinder's solution is 'match, chat, meet', per its tagline. Sounds efficient, simple even! Finally a timesaving solution to the messiness of love. But, as many of us know, the reality is not quite so streamlined, and matching doesn't automatically elicit a bounty of chats or dates, for that matter. Perhaps that explains why only one in five Brits think dating apps are a better option for finding love than meeting in real life.[18]

Hinge's tagline is 'designed to be deleted' – from that you can infer that the app claims to be constructed in a way that makes it succeed in its promise to find love for the user. While this is a catchy slogan, and laudable in principle, it feels disingenuous. 'Hinge is built on the belief that anyone looking for love should be able to find it,' reads its mission statement. An egalitarian utopia of love is not necessarily the experience many users are having – with many claiming the app 'gatekeeps the hottest people' with its Standouts feature. As Merritt Tierce writes in the *Paris Review*, an app that's designed to be deleted 'would not be a great business model. Sure, a lot of people find a partner on the apps, but how many don't?'[19]

So, wait. Do dating apps actually deliver on this promise of streamlining? Statistically speaking, the picture we see tells us that the system isn't entirely broken and that it does work – for some people. Even before the pandemic, online dating had overtaken analogue dating as the primary route to meeting a partner. By 2035, it's estimated that 50 per cent of relationships in the UK will begin online, according to research by Imperial and eharmony, which used ONS data and statistical probabilities.[20] That same research found that almost a third of relationships started between 2015 and 2019 began online.[21] This echoes similar findings from a 2019 paper by Stanford sociologist Michael Rosenfeld, which found that the most popular way heterosexual people in the US meet their partners is online.[22] Since that study, the number of people meeting on apps has remained the same, per Rosenfeld in a 2024 interview.[23] The study found that 39 per cent of straight couples met their partner online, compared to 22 per cent in 2009, when people relied on meeting partners through mutual friends.

2023 data shows that one in five partnered (married, cohabiting, in a committed romantic relationship) adults under the age of 30 met their significant other on a dating app or site, according to Pew Research Center.[24] This number rises among queer people in the US, with a quarter of partnered lesbian, gay and bisexual people meeting their loves online.

'Claiming an app can fix the problem of love is where we get into trouble,' Bandinelli tells me. 'We expect them to work the same way in which I expect Uber to work. So, if it doesn't work, it's a problem. That is where people freak out.'

In the days of analogue dating, there were always multiple variables that could impact your chances of finding love. You lived somewhere with a serious dearth of eligible suitors, perhaps you weren't going to the right bars. Your workplace didn't have anyone remotely fanciable there. You were shy and not good at putting yourself out there in public places (spoken from experience). Now, when dating apps don't yield results, when we don't get matches, we question our desirability. It's never 'Dating apps are broken.' It's always 'I'm [insert biggest insecurity] and I'll die alone.'

This is because dating app culture has shifted our perception of how love finds us.

In analogue days, love was viewed as something mystical and elusive that could strike when you were least expecting it. As a child, my favourite question to ask grown-up couples (often my parents' friends) was 'How did you meet?' As a shy kid, I couldn't wrap my head around the alchemy that brought two strangers into each other's lives and made them fall in love.

In my parents' case, love entered their lives unexpectedly when my dad crashed my mum's dinner party when she was at university. My mum was infuriated because this sudden and unexpected addition to the party meant there was no longer enough spaghetti Bolognese to go around. Of course, my dad isn't the type to go round to strangers' houses and ruin their dinner parties – his friends were playing matchmaker and assured him it'd be okay for him to come along. After the disastrous dinner party, my parents kept running into each other in situations that were being engineered by their friends. But my mum didn't find it cute. To get these persistent friends to stop, she and my dad agreed to go for a drink. And it was during this drink that they discovered that they actually quite liked each other. Six months later, they were engaged. In 2024 they marked 40 years of marriage.

The (Emotional) Labour of Love

Nowadays, the abundance of choice but absence of commitment has become our greatest challenge – we match, exchange a few messages, before contact fizzles and we restart the cycle, rinse and repeat. Dating apps by design hold us hostage in a loop of talking stages which lead to nowhere. This is a symptom of data-driven capitalism. The tech industry prizes active users – aka human beings using a product – as a success metric. Dating apps aren't trying to 'solve' our love lives out of the kindness of their hearts. Apps are a product of platform capitalism. If the app doesn't deliver on its promise, it holds you hostage as an active user for a longer period of time, the ultimate metric for any app. According to Bandinelli, 'An app that works is an app that is financially completely unsustainable. So, the apps need people to return to the app, to be there. We say that the app needs to be sticky, you need to get stuck to it.' While many dating apps market themselves as fun, playful and empowering, the reality is, the longer we use them, the worse we feel, and looking for love online can make us feel bad about ourselves. Dating apps are a breeding ground for body image issues, creating negative perceptions of oneself and an increased internalisation of appearance ideals and comparisons to others, according to research from the University of North Texas published in 2017.[25] And, in particular, people of colour experience fetishism on dating apps, leaving them feeling objectified, minimised to a mere stereotype, and held back from finding real, lasting connections.[26]

But we keep swiping. Because the 'stickiness' Bandinelli described is both addictive for customers and imperative for the dating apps' sustained model. But, there's also a psychological aspect to the state of being 'on the apps' – even if they aren't working that well for you. Simply having Tinder or whatever app you use on your phone, you're saying, 'I'm still in the game,' 'I'm putting myself out there.'

If you think about the way in which we now ask our single friends, 'Are you swiping?' we're asking them whether they're actively putting themselves out there in the dating pool. Swiping, or even just having the apps on our phones, becomes a way for us to keep up the appearance of being an active member of the dating scene. 'When you say, "Yes I'm swiping," you say, "Yes, I'm doing my part, I'm active, I'm doing the labour that I'm supposed to be doing," ' Bandinelli tells me.

Swiping therefore not only acts as the way in which we project the image (be it true or false) of being a person who's 'doing the work' of putting themselves out there, it also feels like labour, like a chore we're being forced to keep up with. Dr Jenny van Hooff, a sociologist at Manchester Metropolitan University, says that in her research into contemporary intimacy among undergraduate students, many told her that dating apps have become 'like a job'. Those surveyed said having an additional time-draining task to complete on their phone made them feel pressured to be 'always on', says van Hooff.

I wanted to find out about other people's experiences of searching for love, connection, sex, fun, whatever it is we're all out there searching for, so I created an anonymous survey designed to understand people's experiences of dating culture, their use of apps, and how the apps make them feel.

One of the people I spoke to to bring this data to life is a young person called Alice, aged 25. Alice identifies as straight and describes dating apps as 'literally the biggest time suck'. Dating in London, she says, is annoying because people aren't willing to take any risks when it comes to vulnerability and putting their hearts on the line. 'People aren't even willing to risk their Tuesday night in case it's not a good date,' she says.

Having dating apps on her phone makes her head feel 'cluttered' and the process of swiping consumes too much of her time. Faced with this frustration, Alice deleted her dating apps. 'When I didn't have them for two months, I was just reading more, I was going to bed earlier. I think it's just too easy to stay up messaging people, scrolling through endless profiles.' Ultimately, Alice felt she wasn't getting a return on investment. 'To be honest, the amount I actually use dating apps, like my screen time on them, I just don't get enough dates out of them.' Even when she's chatting to people, it just fizzles into nothing. 'I feel like both me and the people I'm speaking to never actually commit to go on a date most of the time.'

Alice is not alone in feeling this way. In fact, more than 90 per cent of gen Z daters feel frustrated with dating apps, according to research:[27] Seventeen per cent of Gen Z singles feel sadness while swiping, and 28 per cent feel overwhelmed. Millennials, meanwhile, aren't having a great time either: Eighteen per cent feel depressed by dating apps, and 24 per cent feel inundated by too much choice. Most dating app users have negative emotions while swiping – with only 4 per cent feeling happy while doing so, according to research sent to me by a representative of dating app Mattr. More than a quarter of dating app users feel overwhelmed while swiping, and 17 per cent experience depression while looking for connection.

Is the labour of swiping one that yields a return on investment? On Hinge, one swipe in 500 results in a phone number exchange, data suggests.[28] The average UK Grindr user spends around 6 hours 49 minutes on the app per month, according to 2024 Ofcom figures.[29] Other figures suggest Americans swipe on around 4,000 profiles before finding a partner, spending eight months on the app.[30] So, how much of our day should we spend swiping? Dr Jess Carbino, Bumble's in-house sociologist, says we should only be spending 30 minutes per day on the app, 15 minutes in the morning, and 15 in the evening. 'It shouldn't feel like a job,' says Carbino. 'Dating should feel like something that you're doing in order to meet somebody.'[31] Does this advice match up with daters' experiences, though? Dating app Badoo (owned by the Match group) surveyed its 370 million users worldwide and found that on average people spend about 90 minutes a day swiping.[32] People don't sit for an hour and a half solidly swiping, however. Instead, people log into the app about ten times a day and swipe for nine minutes at a time. That equates to 10.5 hours a week. To give you an idea of what that means, people are legally allowed to work an average 48 hours a week (calculated over a 17-week reference period) – a quarter of that average working week is 12 hours.[33] Based on Badoo's figures, that we're swiping for a period close to a quarter of the working week, is far from negligible. It's like a side-hustle.

Though I'm borrowing from the language of capitalism here, when you think about the return on that temporal invest-ment, you ultimately have very little – if anything at all – to show for it after putting in hours of work. Take the findings from a 2016 study of an unnamed dating app, which showed that 49 per cent of users who message a match never receive a reply.[34] The Pew Research Center in the US looked at the gender breakdown of messaging habits among current or recent dating users and found that 54 per cent of women have felt overwhelmed by the volume of messages they received (compared with a quarter of men), whereas 64 per cent of men reported feeling insecure about the lack of messages they received (only 40 per cent of women said the same).[35]

Of course, that figure only takes into account the people who actually send messages rather than swiping endlessly without contacting anyone.

The reason why we even regard our dating efforts in terms of investment, labour, and profit and loss is because of the effects of living in a capitalist society. As Katherine Angel, author of *Tomorrow Sex Will Be Good Again* explains in an article on selfish dating culture, 'The modern capitalist system we all exist under wants us to optimise our time as much as possible so we have a money-making mindset, which benefits the econ-omy.'[36] When our labour of love doesn't show a return quickly enough – perhaps it's too much of a slow-burn romance – we cut our losses, cease investing any more of our valuable time.

The cost of dating isn't limited to the hours we put in, how-ever. Dating drains our bank balance too. Increasingly, apps are asking their users to pay to access what feels like essential features such as unlimited likes on Bumble or being able to contact 'Standouts' on Hinge. And one in five single people have gone into debt from dating during the cost-of-living crisis, according to research by credit reporting company Experian. With 28 per cent of people using credit cards to fund their dates, this can cost around £78 on average each time. The cost of dating could run up a bill of £1,878 per year, per Experian. So 54 per cent of single people say the cost of dating puts them off, and 53 per cent think dating is now a luxury.[37] (I explore the financial side of dating some more in chapter 7.)

There'll Always be Someone Better

Is there something better out there? In my view, this is a question which dominates the dating mindset. Under capitalism, we grow up with the notion that we should always be wanting more – more money, more possessions, more status symbols, more comfort, more luxury. That mindset of always wanting more, always striving for better is ever-present in our dating culture. It guides some daters' behaviour – some feel they're on the receiving end of being discarded in favour of a more 'enticing' offer, some feel they need to model themselves on an idealised version of perfection to make themselves into the 'more' that someone else craves, and some are trapped in a cycle of swiping until they find the elusive, unattainable match that represents the best they can get.

Decision making can be divided in two groups of people: 'Maximisers' versus 'Satisficers'. Satisficers have a 'this'll do' philosophy when making choices; they tend to choose more quickly with the mindset that one solution cannot usually tick all boxes. The term 'Satisficing' – a portmanteau of 'satisfy' and 'suffice' – was first developed in 1956 by Nobel-Prize winning economist Herbert A. Simon. 'Maximisers' want to literally maximise the outcome of a decision, so they'll spend a great deal of time deliberating to ensure their choice is the right one. One study found that graduates with maximising mentalities earned 20 per cent more than their satisficing counterparts. On the other end of the spectrum, satisficers make their decisions quickly, albeit with slightly worse outcomes and using slightly impulsive means.[38] Lengthy deliberation might sound like the more practical and thoughtful approach, but it has its downsides too. While maximisers might get more out of their decisions they'll likely feel worse about those outcomes. Research has found that they're more likely to experience depression, perfectionism, self-blame and regret.[39]

Looking at dating through the maximiser versus satisficer prism can illuminate our fellow daters' (and our own) behaviours. In the past, I was more of a satisficer on dates, I'd ask myself, 'Can I make it work with this person?' during first encounters. These days, I see maximising tendencies in my decision making, existing in a protracted state of deliberation, weighing up ad nauseum whether the person in front of me would make a good partner. Going forward, I'm going to try and strike a better balance of the two states.

Dr Jenny van Hooff says dating has become akin to shopping for consumer goods. 'You scan through so many photos or profiles so quickly that it's like online shopping. When you're evaluating human beings in that kind of way, I think it really undermines our humanity. Disposability is bred into our consumer culture.' You might have a phone full of matches, but you run into trouble when you attempt to convert that match into a conversation. Perhaps you chat a little bit, but it fizzles out. Well, it's not you – it's a consequence of unlimited choice. According to social psychologist Professor Viren Swami, prominent psychologist and author of *Attraction*

Explained: The Science of How We Form Relationships, 'The first consequence of unlimited choice is that often people don't engage in the relationships, particularly in the early stages . . . because if things go badly, [they] can just go back to the dating app. The idea is you go into a shop and you put all the things that you want in your basket, and then you go home and you check out what you've bought. You look at it and if you don't like it, you go back to the shop, you return what you didn't like, and you pick up some new things. And that's essentially what dating apps offer – the impression of unlimited choice.'

Researchers have dubbed this phenomenon 'relationshopping'. You might have heard the term 'paradox of choice' when we talk about modern dating. The paradox of choice means that when you have a boundless number of options, you can become paralysed by that infinite choice. As psychologist Barry Schwartz wrote in his book *The Paradox of Choice*: 'Learning to choose is hard. Learning to choose well is harder. And learning to choose well in a world of unlimited possibilities is harder still, perhaps too hard.' Regarding yourself as just an option in a limitless bundle of choices can feel dehumanising. While too much choice can give us choice paralysis, it can make us behave selfishly and callously, treating other human beings as disposable commodities, and distancing us from the consequences of such behaviour. This culture of non-commitment gives way to a repertoire of negative digital behaviours like ghosting, breadcrumbing, benching, orbiting – things you probably wouldn't do in 'real life' when face to face with the individual.

Choosing a future partner is not a decision that one takes lightly, so a certain degree of deliberation is to be expected. There's a happy medium, though. Too impulsive and you could end up 'settling' for the wrong person. Too indecisive and you could end up in choice paralysis and unable to settle on a decision. Balancing the two is key.

A New Way to Date

If you're feeling stuck in a revolving door of swiping and matching with very little conversation or in-person dates to show for it, then something isn't working. UK-based relationship counsellor and social psychologist Dr Kathrine Bejanyan says the technology really limits our ability here – that it's impossible to talk to a thousand people and get to know their character. 'I think sometimes people forget why they're on there. They're accumulating more matches than they're actually doing proper dating. They'll spend more time scrolling than actually talking.' Bejanyan suggests limiting your matches to around 10 to 15 people and to engage with each one as much as possible. If this conversation goes well, Bejanyan advises trying 'to get it into real life as soon as possible'. Ask them if they want to meet in person, to go for a coffee, or a walk, or a drink. 'Because we need all of our senses to be able to gauge what's what,' says Bejanyan. 'It's so easy just to get into this rhythm where you feel so connected and you're keeping that conversation going, and then in real life you're not that attracted to one another.'

This is good advice, but there has to be a balance that works for us. Yes, it's important to make sure we aren't using our dating apps as a trophy cabinet full of two-dimensional faces we're collecting. But it's also important to check in with yourself and how you're feeling.

Meeting up as soon as possible does not mean dropping everything and meeting them within hours of matching. If you're messaging someone you've just matched with and they want to meet up that very same day, you won't be betraying yourself or your desire to find love if you say no.

Poorna Bell, an author and journalist who writes about mental health, tweeted that if a match asks to meet up with very little notice, 'don't feel guilty or like you'll miss out on "the one" if you don't. Work to your own timeline.' 'I know it's not as simple as this but the right person will wait,' Bell adds.[40] 'The right person will understand you have a life and aren't egotistical to assume you'd drop everything to meet with a random. And time with yourself even if that's on the sofa with Netflix is as important.'

So, where do we go from here? With dating apps now the most popular way of meeting your partner,[41] I don't think opting out of the dating app marketplace is the answer to all our problems. The onus of fixing dating apps shouldn't be placed on individuals. But when dating apps have very little business incentive to make them work better for us, it's difficult to envisage anything materially changing. So, where does this leave us? I think we have to accept that dating apps are not a fix-all solution. They can provide certain things for us, namely access to more people than ever before. But this 'fix' has given rise to new problems, new digital behaviours that present emotional challenges for us to overcome, while also navigating the difficult emotions that have always come with our quest for love. Bandinelli theorises that we are living through an age of 'post-romantic love' which she defines as 'a culture in which suffering is to be avoided and the ideal self is one that is always in control, always "empowered".'[42]

I think we need to remind ourselves of what being alive really means – to feel, to experience, to love and to grieve. Love cannot be optimised with clinical solutions to make you feel less, to make the sensation more bearable. So, my advice is to use your feelings as your compass through the rocky terrain of love. Feelings aren't always facts, but they can help you realise when you don't feel safe in a romantic or sexual situation, emotions help you see when your needs aren't being met, when a match doesn't feel right. Place more faith in the emotional signals – the discomfort, the nerves, the stress, the euphoria, the joy, the butterflies – and listen to the messages they're sending you.

Take the emotional reaction I had to one man I'd been seeing on and off – he'd sleep with me then ignore my texts for days on end, blowing hot and cold. I would feel so anxious in his presence that I'd throw up after seeing him. When I told my therapist about this, she was stunned. 'Wow,' she said. 'That is an incredibly strong message your body is sending you.' And perhaps I should have listened to that message sooner.

The apps are not the great panacea for our love lives we perhaps initially believed them to be, even if they have become an important part of our dating lives. While we can't control other people's behaviour, we can alter our own habits to change the relationships we have with the apps. Resist the pressure to start relationshopping by limiting the amount of time you spend on the apps and setting a cap on the number of matches you amass without starting a new conversation. So, if you've got five new matches, send messages to those matches and see which of those develop into conversations. Once you're chatting to someone, give yourself a reasonable timeframe for meeting up – perhaps no more than one week (or maybe two) of messaging before going on a date. This will stop you from falling into the penpal trap and help you make better connections through the apps. It's high time we all were more intentional about our swiping and messaging habits.

When we seek to streamline love, as we do with other aspects of our daily lives, to save time, we cut emotional corners. Love is no longer a burning, all-consuming fire that blazes. Instead we seek 'efficiency, controllability, and safety'.

The problem we face, therefore, stems from the inefficiency of the apps. They don't deliver on the promise of hacking your love life and turning it into a well-oiled machine and even if they did, cutting emotional corners diminishes our experience of our love lives. As Jane Austen writes: 'To love is to burn, to be on fire.'

2

Crush

It's not you, it's me. I just didn't feel a spark. I don't see a future here. We're not compatible. I don't feel that way about you.

Getting rejected stings. Sometimes, even when the person rejecting you tries their best to make it as painless as possible, you can still end up feeling pretty sore – a crush is called a 'crush' for a reason. That pain isn't imaginary. And it's certainly not a sign of weakness, either.

The flipside of the choice paradox is that in opening ourselves up to more possibilities of connecting with others, we are now much more likely to be rejected. While rejection on dating apps is now deeply normalised, our reactions to being cast off have not diminished – that's because our neurological responses to rejection are tethered to evolutionary biology, meaning our brains are literally wired to find rejection painful. Neuroscientific research has shown that when a person feels physical pain, the brain releases opioids to limit the impact of that pain and it does exactly the same thing when a person feels rejected by others.[1] That pain makes sense from an evolutionary biological perspective. Our brains are designed to hate the feeling of being excluded or rejected because historically humans needed a community or tribe in order to survive.[2] Those who got lost or excluded simply wouldn't make it.

fMRI studies have found that when we're rejected, the same

parts of our brain are activated as when we're in physical pain.[3] So much so, that one study found that paracetamol reduces the emotional pain that rejection causes.[4] In the study, participants were asked to think about a past painful rejection experience and those taking Tylenol (a brand name for paracetamol) reported significantly less pain than those taking a sugar pill.

Rejection Mindset

Over the past decade since Tinder launched, the dating landscape has transformed dramatically. As of July 2024, the dating app has been downloaded more than 530 million times and 55 billion people have matched. While the opportunities of finding a match are more abundant than ever before, we now have a different problem to contend with: too much choice. This state of overload, in turn, causes a 'rejection mindset', meaning that even though we have almost unlimited access to prospective partners, we're more likely to reject people and we are more pessimistic.[5] Tila Pronk, assistant professor of social psychology at Tilburg University, who coined the term 'rejection mindset', says that people are now more likely to be single and that the rejection mindset is found most often in women. 'The consequence of the rejection mindset is that over time, people "close off" from mating opportunities when online dating,' says Pronk.

This is something many of us well-seasoned online daters can likely relate to. I've been on dating apps for more than a decade, and periodically I find myself getting jaded, bogged down by what feels like fruitless labour, conversations that go nowhere, dud first dates. When the negativity gets the better of me, I notice that my swiping habits reflect that. I either don't bother to begin with, or I mass-reject the profiles in my queue.

My finger gets cramp from swiping left continuously. I know I'm not alone in this.

Faced with the ubiquity of rejection and heartbreak in the digital age, there's now a growing market of breakup apps (Mend, RX Breakup, Halmos, to name a few) as well as subscription boxes and bootcamps, claiming to help people optimise and streamline their own emotional pain. While I'm sceptical about the amount of people using breakup apps, the rise of all these products points towards a shift in the way we're expected to cope with breakups. We have entered an age of breakup optimisation – it no longer suffices to wallow in front of *Sex and the City*, crying into a tub of ice cream, now you must harness your misery into self-improvement, lining someone's pockets while doing so. There's no money to be made in leaving people in peace with their feelings.

In our interactions with potential partners, in our sexual and romantic relationships with others, we are ill equipped to cope with difficult and uncomfortable feelings, to communicate our emotional needs, and to understand the root source of our own reactions. This emotional gap isn't unique to dating and relationships, but forms part of a wider societal issue. In the UK, many children and young people are missing out on learning vital life skills that would help them better regulate their own emotions in adulthood. Social emotional learning (SEL) aims to teach school children self-awareness, self-management, social awareness, relationship skills, and responsible decision-making[6] – but two recent reports by the Cabinet Office and social good organisation NESTA have found that SEL programmes are not being delivered in all schools, meaning only some children and young people are learning these skills.[7] Meanwhile, the country's mental health infrastructure is creaking under the weight of rising demand for help.[8] When we struggle with emotional dysregulation or mental health issues, we face months-long waiting lists to access NHS talk therapy, we hit barriers with cost-prohibitive private therapy, and many people are shut out of valuable ways to gain insights and coping strategies for the difficult emotions we endure. Men are still less likely than women to go for counselling or psychotherapy, with experts stating that masculine stereotypes are one of the biggest obstacles to men seeking mental health support, per the British Association for Counselling and Psychotherapy.[9] A 2022 report found that 27 per cent of men had been to therapy (up from 18 per cent in 2010), compared with 39 per cent of women.

Love Language: The Rise of Therapy Speak in Dating

Running parallel with the mental health crisis is a wave of internet misinformation. People unable to access the support they need instead turn to 60-second videos from unqualified people posing as mental health and relationship experts while imparting platitudes and pseudo-psychology that does more harm than good. TikTok and Instagram ushered in a new era of 'therapy speak', in which everyone online can now co-opt the vocabulary of a person who has (forgive me for this next phrase) done the work.[10] Words like 'triggered', 'trauma', 'boundaries', 'gaslighting', 'narcissism', now roll off the tongue without a moment's pause – and without having spent hours in therapy and years scouring self-help books for insights. Is it then surprising that the Merriam-Webster dictionary named 'gaslighting' its word of the year in 2022, following a 1,740 per cent rise in search interest over the previous 12 months? In Tinder's 2022 report on the dating trends that defined the year, it was revealed that the red flag and gaslighting emojis were trending on the app. According to the research, 58 per cent of young singles aged between 18 and 25 said they were confident they could identify a green or red flag in a partner.

Straight Talking

At the very same time, heterosexual dating culture is at a cross-roads. Millennial and Gen-Z straight women are distancing themselves from their own heterosexuality – a phenomenon academic and writer Asa Seresin, who researches the history of heterosexuality, coined in 2019 as 'heteropessimism', which he describes as 'performative disaffiliations with heterosexuality, usually expressed in the form of regret, embarrassment, or hopelessness about the straight experience'.[11]

While this trend is certainly true of many people's relationships, and it speaks to the systemic issues at play in a patriarchal, white supremacist, capitalist society, viewing all relationships through this lens would be reductive of us, and ultimately disempowering for straight women, to cast all heterosexual relationships into the category of negative. People of all genders have the ability to be unpleasant humans. Much of the online discourse on the topic of 'dating is a hellscape' is centred on the heterosexual experience. Running through much of the writing and discourse surrounding consensual heterosexual relations is a narrative of 'female victimhood', the idea that straight cis women are trapped by ungrateful and neglectful men and treated badly until they make a dash for it. Within this mindset exists the idea that 'All hurt inflicted by a man is abuse on some level, these narratives imply, and all men will hurt you; ergo all men are abusive by nature,' writes journalist Moya Lothian-McLean.[12] But in painting men as villains, as abusers and narcissists when our consensual relations with them turn sour, when our relationships break down for non-abusive reasons, we dilute necessary conversations about male violence and conflate breakup pain with trauma from genuine abuse. If we label all straight cis men as 'trash', where does that leave us in our relations with them?

As the zero-nuance 'all men are trash' and 'women are too picky' narrative rumbles gently on, we're missing the point of what's really going on for heterosexual women in the dating game today. Nearly half of university-educated women in the US report having difficulty finding a partner who meets their expectations (compared with a third of men), according to 2023 research by the American Enterprise Institute which surveyed over 5,000 Americans about dating and relationships.[13] Further insights about this gap in expectations versus reality can be found in the qualitative data in the in-depth interviews conducted with participants, which revealed difficulties with male vulnerability, and straight men being 'limited in their ability and willingness to be fully emotionally present and available'.[14]

Meanwhile, masculinity is in crisis. Far-right figures like Andrew Tate have had incredible traction with young men and boys, with teachers saying his views are fuelling a surge in misogynistic attitudes among teenage boys. Tate gained a huge following as a self-help guru offering advice to young men on how to talk to women. He became one of the most viral people on the internet with incendiary rhetoric like 'women can't drive', 'men can cheat but women can't'.[15] This cartoonish misogyny borders on the ridiculous, but it is being lapped up by young boys who are becoming radicalised. As journalist Ash Sarkar says in an episode of Novara Media's Downstream in January 2023, 'I don't think he'd be able to pedal any of this bullshit if it weren't for real underlying problems that he was able to exploit. Loneliness, resentment, feeling like you're unable to get anywhere in the sexual marketplace, despite being priced at reduced to clear.'[16] 'If these emotions can be leveraged to funnel men towards the far-right then surely we need to take matters of dating, love, and the heart seriously,' Sarkar adds.

2024 research by Kings College London, which polled 3,716 people over the age of 16, found that 61 per cent of young men aged between 16 and 29 feel unfavourable towards Tate, which could suggest his influence is diminishing.[17] And 73 per cent of UK public overall who've heard of Tate find his views on men and women offensive. The result is an increasing sense of mistrust and opposition between men and women.

Is it any wonder then that we're also having less sex? In 2019, the National Surveys of Sexual Attitudes and Lifestyles found that sexual frequency was in decline.[18] Much of the recent discourse on why we're having less sex or bad sex has focused on demonising porn and vilifying casual sex culture. But that's not really what's going on. Sex is having a reckoning. In the years since MeToo in 2017 we've examined the harmful and devastating ways in which systems of oppression manifest in our sexual culture. While writing *Rough: How Violence Has Found Its Way Into The Bedroom And What We Can Do About It*, I heard from more than 50 women and non-binary people, who told me stories of unwanted sex – sex that was technically consensual but not desired, painful sex that they gritted their teeth to bear, microaggressions during sex, fetishisation, and countless other harms and acts of violence. Many people (myself included) are having less sex in order to create space to work through their trauma and try to heal in peace.

We're also living through a sex misinformation crisis, making it harder for young, inexperienced people who want to learn about sex to gain the skills and knowledge they need to have the experiences they want. Big tech's censorship of sexuality on the internet, and the political threat to sex education in the UK and US, are making healthy and positive materials about sex harder to access. Then there's the not-so-small matter of the devastation and suffering we witness daily on our timelines. Social media is full of not only stressful news coverage but also millions of strangers sharing difficult experiences. Faced with such unrelenting destruction, who even has the mental capacity for horniness?

Every single one of these challenges can make finding love and connection feel nigh-on impossible, but there are potential solutions out there. In response to the dating app fatigue we're currently witnessing, a wave of analogue alternatives is now emerging. In fact, I've just signed myself up for a 'Date and Draw' event – a life-drawing class aimed at singles wanting to mingle. Intrepid singletons are flocking to run clubs, which TikTok declared in 2024 'the new dating apps'. There's also Soulmate Social, a service which individually matches people to go on blind dates. After your date, you'll then head to a party venue for a club night where every single person in the room is single and ready to mingle.[19] Then there's the Pear Ring – a social experiment in which single people wear a coloured ring in public to show they're single and open to meeting a beguiling stranger.[20] While this last idea sounds interesting in theory, I've not yet seen a single Pear Ring on any Londoner's finger, so whether it will catch on remains to be seen.

Emotional Intelligence

According to the 2022 'Singles in America' report commissioned by Match in partnership with The Kinsey Institute,[21] a study of a demographically representative sample of 5,000

American men and women aged between 18 and 98 showed that 'Emotional Quotient (EQ)', or emotional intelligence, is extremely high on people's lists of non-negotiables when looking for a partner.[22] Being emotionally intelligent means that you are able to understand and manage your own emotions, communicate effectively, empathise with others and overcome challenges to diffuse conflict. They found that the most sought-after qualities in partners were someone they can trust and confide in (94 per cent), someone who's comfortable communicating their needs (92 per cent), and someone emotionally mature (92 per cent). Surprisingly, a physically attractive partner is lower down the list (86 per cent).

On a similar note, Tinder's 'Future of Dating' dating report in 2023 also shows that young singles want respect over physical attraction. Their in-app survey of Tinder users in the UK, US and Australia found that 78 per cent of Gen Z (18–24-year-old) daters prioritise respect and 79 per cent value loyalty over a partner's looks, which only 56 per cent prioritise.[23]

Let's be clear: the evidence shows that there's sexual and romantic currency in talking about your feelings. With 'therapy speak' entering the mainstream lexicon, finding language to communicate your experiences to others has never been easier. There's more openness around discussing mental health than ever before, and this openness can help us connect with each other. However, daters have conflicting opinions when it comes to therapy speak's infiltration of dating culture. According to the Singles report, one in three singles of all ages and genders think therapy speak can be both useful and detrimental. Younger daters are most likely to feel optimistic, with 40 per cent of Gen Z daters thinking therapy speak helps people have a better understanding of their mental health. While having a better understanding of psychology can help us understand ourselves and each other, the rise of therapy speak has also made it easier for people to sound self-aware and emotionally intelligent, even if they aren't. Data collected by OkCupid in 2022 revealed that daters who claimed to have healthy boundaries had 51 per cent more conversations and garnered 68 per cent more likes than those who didn't, which means that there's a clear incentive for daters to present themselves as having boundless emotional intelligence without having done the introspection and self-reflection that typically would bring those insights.[24]

So how do we go about distinguishing who is actually emotionally intelligent from those who are displaying what I've termed 'performative EQ'?

Firstly, we need to unpack exactly what we mean when we talk about emotional intelligence. What's the definition? And, how can EQ help us in our interpersonal relationships? To make sense of this I spoke to Madalaine Munro, a UK-based somatic attachment and psychosexual therapist. Being emotionally intelligent, according to Munro, comes from an ability to identify emotions as we're feeling them and to understand *why* we feel that way. For example, as she explains in the case of being triggered within a relationship: 'Someone at a younger developmental age would perhaps just feel like, "I feel sad, you are the cause of my sadness," whereas an adult with adult emotional intelligence thinks, "I feel sad" and has the inquiry of "where does this sadness come from?" ' An emotionally intelligent adult knows that a person causing them sadness may be triggering an old wound; they'll ask where this hurt is coming from, what does it stem back to, and they'll think about their childhood and early years to figure out the root trauma.

She also tells me she looks at emotional intelligence through the lens of developmental trauma and looking to our past to understand ourselves as adults. 'What I see with people is that if we don't get our needs met growing up, then we develop coping mechanisms and behaviours in relationships, strategies to get our needs met, strategies to get love,' explains Munro. For example, withdrawing to draw attention to oneself. She adds that these childhood survival mechanisms are carried forward into adulthood and we keep these strategies alive in our relationships in ways that don't always serve us. Munro looks at individuals' developmental ages to gauge emotional intelligence. 'We go through developmental models growing up in terms of attunement, connection, and these get met in a specific order,' Munro explains. In developmental psychology, attunement is a parent's ability to understand and respond to their child's needs. 'And if these aren't met, we're likely to be hindered at a certain stage or age growing up. When I'm working with people, someone may present as a 40-year-old but developmentally they're 15 and then acting out 15-year-old patterns.'

In other words, many people who have yet to get an understanding of their feelings can be emotionally immature well into adulthood. So, what does emotional immaturity look like? Well, it can be messy, draining and painful, causing us to experience miscommunications, feelings of rejection and disappointment, sometimes in similar ways over and over again, until we learn hard lessons in how to improve our communication skills. As Munro says, 'I really believe that everyone that comes into our life is a teacher or a mirror so people are mirroring our own stuff back.'

How do we work on our emotional intelligence? It starts with identifying your own emotions – if you're feeling upset or dysregulated, write down those emotions and what might have caused them. Over time, this will help you build up an understanding of yourself and your inner emotional land-scape. You might begin to see patterns or triggers emerging.

Situationships

Take Nadia's experience. When Nadia, 24 and bisexual, met a guy on a dating app, they quickly began spending all their time together and developed a 'situationship' – a term describing a murky relationship where you're not quite in a relationship with someone, but you're not just sleeping with them either. The word situationship entered our lexicon in 2017 when writer Carina Hsieh wrote a piece after hearing her friend Tony use the word at a party. Tony told Hsieh the word was a 'catch-all term for those relationships sitting at the intersection of "hooking up" and "in a relationship".'[25]

If casual is what you've both mutually agreed upon, then a situationship might be exactly what you want. But situationships can arise when people are having trouble communicating how they feel or what they want or if there's a disconnect in what both individuals' expectations are.

For Nadia, spending a lot of time together led to her feelings growing over time. They'd see each other every day and stay over at each other's places, growing emotionally closer. 'After a year of spending a lot of time together and being intimate, I realised I had developed strong feelings for him, which he said he mostly reciprocated but he did not want a relationship at all due to coming out of a five-year relationship the previous year before we met,' she says.

Six months after this conversation, Nadia was still seeing the guy and she told him more explicitly that she had romantic feelings for him. 'I really let myself just go along with the whole thing and didn't put in strict boundaries or admit how I felt properly, but we live and learn,' she says. When she told him that she loved him, he told her he didn't think she did. He then took her hands and said, 'It will pass' – a moment that mirrored that soul-crushing scene in *Fleabag*. 'I then said I needed to go on dates and get out there a bit and then his mental health massively dipped and he cut contact,' she says.

'The rejection really hit me and massively knocked my confidence overall,' says Nadia. She plummeted into a low ebb and her insecurities reared their heads. She felt – and still feels – unlovable, even though logically she knows that's not true.

But the experience has also taken her on a self-knowledge journey, of the kind Munro mentioned above. Nadia has thought a lot about how her attachment style has impacted her relationships and she recognises that she doesn't cope well with rejection. 'I cling to people and often romanticise or idolise them and then get hurt when they pull away or don't reciprocate it,' she says. 'It's tied to abandonment issues in my childhood and I am currently in therapy to figure this all out and become more stable and make boundaries in relationships.' Because she is anxiously attached and also suffers from anxiety in general, Nadia often looks for signs of rejection or signals that her partner doesn't like her or love her anymore.

'The second I feel a sense of rejection in a relationship or with a partner, I often try to people-please to an extreme in order to make my partner happy and therefore not reject me,' she explains. 'I usually need reassurance and become needy as I will ask my partner numerous times: "Is everything okay?" or "I feel you pulling away, what have I done wrong?"' Nadia explains that rejection often triggers her inner child, making her revert to a scared and insecure person who wants to cling onto people so she doesn't feel abandoned. 'I need a lot of reassurance in relationships which is why I'm taking a break from dating as all of this is very unfair to put on a partner,' she says.

But there's another way to view this situation, and through this lens, perhaps Nadia wasn't personally being rejected. With insights around emotional intelligence, the situation can be reframed as follows: the man she was seeing was emotionally unavailable – he clearly wasn't able to be in a committed relationship. Integrative psychotherapist Steve Leach at Think Therapy psychotherapy practice says emotional availability is 'when someone has the free space and attention to genuinely listen to us without immediately getting triggered by their own stuff. They have worked on themselves and can, to some extent, regulate their emotions and "be there for us" in a moment when we need them.'

When someone is emotionally available to us, we typically feel secure and like our needs are being met. 'When we are with someone who is genuinely emotionally available to us, we feel safe in our "gut" and our nervous systems settle,' says Leach. 'We know where we stand and there isn't frantic guesswork about the relationship.' He says that the sign of an emotionally intelligent *and* available person is consistency. Someone who has done the work and is ready to show up in their relationship for you will bring their emotional intelligence to all areas of their relationship, especially the challenging and difficult parts – they won't turn it on and off. Their actions will be driven by their genuine desire to grow and learn from the tough moments with you.

Reconciling the reality between emotional maturity and availability can be particularly difficult for those of us with a history of mental illness. In Vicky's case (bisexual, 32 years old) she's been on her own learning curve, figuring out what she wants and reconciling that with what she's emotionally able to withstand. In the past year, she's been diagnosed with borderline personality disorder (BPD) (also known as emotionally unstable personality disorder (EUPD)), a mental health condition characterised by unstable relationships with other people, unstable emotions, and an unstable sense of self. Newly single, Vicky decided it would be a good time for her to have some fun and to try and separate sex and emotional attachment. Vicky started using Feeld to find hookups and FWBs and began exploring ENM (ethical non-monogamy). Her hope was that she would be able to keep sex and relationships firmly demarcated. 'Of course, that didn't happen to me because of the BPD,' she says. 'I couldn't separate sex and relationships because BPD warps your perspective of what is reality sometimes and it's so emotion based, the fear of abandonment and rejection is at the forefront always.' If somebody was nice to her, or carried out a small act that made her feel loved or attractive, she'd go all in because her brain told her that these actions meant she was lovable. Everything came to an almighty crescendo when she fell for a guy who was in a polyamorous relationship. She had told him 'I only do hookups' and began seeing him regularly. He would bring her flowers, brought food to her when she had Covid. 'These niceties are kind of [the] bare minimum when you like somebody,' she says. Added up, though, Vicky imbued meaning into them and developed strong feelings for him. When she asked, 'What are we?', the response wasn't the one she'd hoped for. Crushed, she ended things, putting herself in the role of the rejector to try and reclaim some power. He accepted this, 'just let it happen,' and didn't try and change her mind. That felt like a rejection in itself.

We've all been there, right? Imagining a future with someone who doesn't want the same things or who is falling hugely short of what you truly want in the way they treat you. Someone who, in spite of all that, you find yourself wanting with a sense of urgency that makes you feel ever more panicked with each gesture of indifference they throw your way.

When it happened to me, my brain searched for answers, scoured for things I could have done differently. Should I have acted less keen, more aloof? Was my flat too messy when he came round? Was all this because I wasn't thin? Even though he'd told me he liked women with curves? Was I just the curvy girl he fucked before going back to having relationships with thin women? A voice inside my head told me I needed to lose weight and I'd win him back and make him love me. When I discuss this phenomenon with Madalaine Munro, the therapist from earlier in this chapter, she tells me that these kinds of reactions are common in situationships because the nebulous relationship structure doesn't satisfy our core need for safety and security and lacks the clarity and boundaries of a relationship. 'In these situations, we bring it back to our childhood; if our parents don't meet our needs growing up, then our subconscious will choose people that will have the similar wounds in order for us to heal it in ourselves,' Munro explains. In the case of emotional unavailability, people who had absent caretakers during their childhood may choose people in their lives who mimic that childhood wound, says Munro. The mentality there follows the idea that 'if I can make them more available, I'll prove to myself that I can do that in the way I couldn't do for my parent.'

For some people, this can become a fixation, where thoughts turn to 'If I did this, there would be more certainty. I'm trying to win that person over to give me what I need.' But more often than not, the person in question won't be able to meet that core developmental need. 'If we have high self-worth or - awareness, we'll notice this person can't meet me [where I am at], they can't commit, they can't show up for me,' says Munro. 'So what we'll see in someone that has more experience or awareness in this area, if they end up in a situationship, [is that] they'll be like, no, I need boundaries. I need clarity here.' This is a helpful reminder that in order to get the clarity and peace of mind that we deserve, we need to look at ending situationships that make us feel insecure as an essential act of self-love.

Queer Expectations

Of course, the picture of rejection isn't exclusive to heterosexual dating, or cisgendered men. The impact of rejection on self-esteem casts a long shadow. In the dating arena, our oldest emotional wounds can rear their heads. Izzy's first rejection happened when they were in primary school. They asked a boy to 'go out' with them because everyone in class kept saying they both fancied each other. 'He looked *absolutely* disgusted at the thought and it really stuck with me a lot through my teenage years,' they say. Izzy, 22, feels held back by the fear of being rejected and the worry of 'what if'. 'Being queer makes it unmistakably harder because there's the added 'are they also queer?' element, and sometimes it feels like it's more hassle than it's worth to try and figure out if someone's queer, and then if they're into you, and if you're into them, and are they single, and would it work!' Izzy came out as queer when they were very young and didn't realise how much underlying rejection they were dealing with at the time. 'In reality I ended up losing friends, family members, and got a lot of backlash from it. It's becoming more reasonable, but young queer people face rejection early,' they say. 'I recently came out as non-binary and faced a lot of outright rejection from people who didn't want to accept my identity for how I saw it.'

These days, if Izzy senses a rejection is coming, they convince themselves they don't care about the source of the rejection, be it a friend, romantic partner, or a job. 'If it's a job I've applied for, and really wanted, I'll be sure to act as aloof as possible about it to almost 'trick' myself into not caring so the rejection doesn't hurt. Same goes with people; friends, relationships, because I hate the feeling rejection gives me so if I don't care, I don't feel rejected!' 'I read into people's tone far too much, so I overthink the signs rejection is coming – if it seems like it's not going to go my way, I bin it off before I get hurt,' they add.

This idea that we're being rejected because there's something inherently wrong with us is something many of us grapple with. As sex and relationship expert Ruby Payne tells me: 'Dita Von Teese once said, "You can be the ripest, juiciest peach in the world, and there's still going to be somebody who hates peaches." And she was right.' Recently, when I did a book reading at the Feminist Bookshop in Brighton, a woman with three grown-up daughters asked me a question: 'How do we teach young women to have self-worth?' The woman raised a valid question – one that I have often wondered. Self-esteem is how we see ourselves and the value we attach to ourselves. It is connected to beliefs and opinions we have about ourselves, many of which might feel deeply ingrained and impossible to change. But change is actually not impossible – you can challenge the negative views you hold. Bad self-esteem isn't something you should be stuck with for life just because. It's possible to improve it, to turn it around, and to transform your relationship with yourself completely. Through those changes, it's not just how you see yourself that will evolve, but also how you respond to the actions of other people, how you interpret their actions, and the impact they have on you. And those actions include rejection.

If you feel like you need to change things about your physical appearance before you'll be worthy of love or attention, pay close attention to the following piece of advice. 'You have value as you, because you are you, a human being on this planet. Base your confidence on this notion, that you have worth, that you are sufficient as is. Remind yourself of this daily,' Daniel Fryer, a psychotherapist at the Priory Hospital Bristol, tells me. Simply by being a person living in this world, you have value. You are worthy of respect and kindness, just as everyone else is. Of course, it's a lot easier said than done and dismantling long-held negative self-beliefs takes time – we'll talk more about strategies for challenging your inner critic and countering harmful self-talk later in Part 2.

In moments like these, when you feel worthless, the best weapon in your arsenal is self-compassion. Resist the (very natural) urge to reach for the low-hanging fruit of 'I'm ugly, I hate my body, I'm not sexy enough, not successful enough, not smart enough, not cool enough, not chill enough, not stylish enough.' Don't go round in circles wondering 'Why?' 'What did I do wrong?' 'Did I give them the ick?' 'Is it XYZ?' – you'll likely never know the answers to these questions. So, stop torturing yourself, and start nurturing yourself.

On the other end of the spectrum, instead of turning inward with feelings of self-doubt and anxiety, some of us feel angry in the face of rejection. In the heat of the moment, we can end up expressing that anger in ways we come to regret. On this topic, somatic attachment and psychosexual therapist Madalaine Munro explains that often when people spiral after being rejected it's because when we get triggered, the prefrontal cortex in our brain goes offline. 'Therefore we're not even thinking as human beings, our empathy and communication skills are not available. And therefore we look at our systems through fight or flight.' She adds that our brain interprets that rejection as our survival being threatened on a deeper level. I find that when I feel these kinds of emotional reactions in the face of rejection, it can be helpful to step away from the situation. Talking to trusted friends, family members or a therapist can help remind us that what we're feeling in the moment is just part of the equation and that we get to decide how we want to move forward.

We know that a universalising response to rejection can make us question our value or social standing. But, what if we could reframe our perception of rejection as a society? If we could see beyond that initial sting and recognise rejection as nothing more than a person taking care of their own needs? This is a philosophy that's present in consent negotiations at sex parties. It's really common in kinky spaces for conversations about consent to be built into the event, either through the rules shared with attendees on the invitation or organisation website, or even with a consent talk at the start of the event. We all know intuitively that we're not going to be a perfect fit for everyone that we meet – we can prepare ourselves for rejection by reminding ourselves of this fact. We ultimately want the other person to feel safe and confident enough to decline an invitation to something that they don't really want – when seen in this light, a rejection helps you both move on towards experiences that you can fully enjoy with an enthusiastic partner who is enjoying them just as much.

Preparing yourself for nos on dating apps should be a golden rule. And knowing that more often than not, those nos have nothing at all to do with you, your attractiveness, how interesting or cool you are, your value as a human being, is vital.

We also need to be prepared for the fact that sometimes we don't get a clear no. Dating apps are rife with ghosting – a term that refers to when someone stops responding to your messages, disappearing without a warning or a goodbye. In my research for this book, I got to ask myself: What is it about dating apps that makes ghosting so run of the mill? And why do people ghost us? One 2022 study conducted by researchers at Harvard and Wharton found that boredom was often a factor when it comes to ghosting behaviours on dating apps when they spoke to users about their reasons for abruptly cutting contact with matches.[26] 'The most common reason respondents gave for ghosting matches was that their matches became boring,' the study found. This isn't because they were matching with boring people – it was the nature of the conversations that were monotonous. Respondents said they'd open dating apps on their phone when they were at a loose end and in need of diversion, but what they found when they started swiping and chatting was that their boredom only increased. 'Boredom often drives users to initiate texting their matches on dating apps,' the study concluded. 'But when users are bored to begin with, they tend to send boring texts, which creates even more boredom. This heightened boredom, coupled with the inherent unrealness of connections on dating apps, drives ghosting and flaking.' The study found that users then become disheartened by the number of matches they spent time getting to know only to become ghosted, which eventually leads to disillusionment. It's a lose-lose situation. But, what's heartening is that rejection on apps is often not personal, it's just symptomatic of a system that isn't very engaging.

There are all kinds of reasons why a person doesn't return our interest, or merely doesn't respond to a message – most of which have absolutely nothing to do with you. A lack of reply to a message isn't a reflection of your value as a person. Some of the myriad reasons for a person not being interested or engaging with us are: They are having a tough time in their life right now; They don't have the mental energy for messaging right now; They aren't emotionally available; They thought they were ready to date, but turns out they're not; They're unwell; they're on holiday; They are neurodivergent and feeling overstimulated; They are taking time away from their phone to be more present; They haven't yet figured out what they're looking for. The list goes on and on.

If the reason for the lack of reply is due to a lack of interest in you, that also has nothing to do with your value as a person. It is not a commentary on how attractive you are. It is not a sign that you need to alter your body or face. Sometimes, it's just not a match. It doesn't mean you're undesirable, or that there's something wrong with you. It just means this stranger on your screen isn't your person. It's brutal out there. So go easy on yourself.

3

Sparks

When it comes down to the actual in-person, IRL date, there's one thing many daters are looking for: the spark. There's a certain kind of thrill when someone first looks at you like they're *really* looking at you. It's like you're being seen for the very first time in your life. This person just gets you. Like, *really* gets you. They think you're funny, they laugh at all your jokes (even the unfunny ones) and they're looking at you with such warmth, such presence, it's like you've known them all your life. And yet . . . you've only just met. You don't know their middle name, where they went to school, or what they look like naked. In fact, they haven't even touched you. Then there's the electric current that courses through your body when you sense that their body is approaching yours, when you cannot quite believe they're about to lean in and touch you, but you really, really hope they do . . .

If a crush is a potentially unrequited interest in someone else – who you might never even have spoken to or met with – a 'spark' is an initial jolt of attraction upon meeting. Carla, a 29-year-old bisexual woman, says most of her dates find her 'attractive enough', but when it comes down to finding a spark, she runs into trouble. Either her dates don't feel a romantic spark, or Carla doesn't. The issue, she says, comes down to personality and the fast-track nature of modern dating culture, which doesn't allow for a slow reveal of one's true personality over time. 'It's the little quirks about someone you fall in love with – the way they do certain things – on dating apps you're either learning everything about someone too quick or they don't reveal enough for you to be interested in them and vice versa,' Carla continues.

We have all manner of poetic ways of describing this phenomenon, but setting language to one side: What exactly is chemistry or the spark?

The search for romantic chemistry is far from a modern phenomenon, in fact, you can trace its literary origins back to the 16th century. In 1590, English metaphysical poet John Donne wrote about 'love alchemy' in *The Comparison.*[1] Despite the ubiquity of the terms in our dating lexicon, the psychological phenomenon of romantic chemistry or the 'spark' has not been adequately researched.

When we go on a date, many of us want to feel a glimmer of magic, that elusive instant connection with someone. When we don't find that frisson straight away, then it's often a write off. On to the next one! As a 2021 paper states, 'the metaphor of chemistry to describe relationships is pervasive, indelible, and powerful, yet as a psychological construct it remains slippery and elusive.' We all have our own subjective definition of what chemistry or the spark feels like to us – an intense burst of connection, a flutter of attraction – but these definitions are largely intangible and their causes are under-researched. As the paper further states: 'Although chemistry is a well-known, sought-after interpersonal phenomenon, it has remained relatively unexplored in the psychological literature.'[2]

That's not to say that chemistry or the spark isn't real – it's just difficult to put our finger on what these experiences consist of. Furthermore, we can easily confuse similar psychological or physiological symptoms for the spark.

One hurdle in our hunt for the spark is that it's nigh-on impossible to feel chemistry through your phone screen. 'Dating apps can cause us to miss true connections and romantic chemistry because of a profile picture,' says Texas-based therapist Alisha Powell, who has a PhD in social psychology. 'While we may have a type, there's a strong possibility that we could be attracted to someone who may not be our typical type after having a conversation and spending time with them.'[3]

Professor Viren Swami says, 'chemistry isn't a scientific term. It's a layperson's language for how they felt the date went.' Swami, while investigating human attraction for his book *Attraction Explained: The Science of How We Form Relationships*, conducted qualitative research and found that an absence of chemistry 'is often used as a kind of offhand way of saying "I don't like you physically."'

In my experience, saying there was no chemistry after a date has definitely become this kind of shorthand for telling someone, albeit not in so many words, that you didn't like them. Sure, it can mean you didn't fancy them on a physical level, but it can also mean you didn't like their personality, perhaps they exhibited signs that they don't share the same values as you. 'It's become a language tool to say, "I don't want to let you down by saying you're a horrible person" or "I don't want to let you down because I think we're just not going to click for whatever reason that I can't explain." (. . .) it's a catch-all term,' Swami continues.

In this quest to find an immediate thunderbolt from above, we have a tendency to treat dates where we don't feel a spark straight away as disposable. This is where the overabundance of choice provides a kind of safety blanket for us. Didn't feel a surge of magnetism within an almost impossible and arbitrary period of time? No worries! Open up the app again and you'll have an infinite number of alternatives to choose from in your search for the spark.

The Science of Attraction

Another problem with the spark is that we can't rely on it as a source of certainty. What might feel like a spark could in fact just be an adrenaline rush caused by something that has nothing to do with a connection. A study at the University of British Columbia carried out on a rickety bridge (North Vancouver's Capilano Suspension Bridge)[4] in 1974 by researchers Donald Dutton and Arthur Aron showed interesting results.[5] Men crossing an unstable bridge, which was swaying above a 230-foot drop with a river below, were approached by an attractive woman asking them to complete a survey. Once they'd filled out the survey, the woman gave the men her number and said they could call her if they wanted further info about the study. Nearby, men on a sturdy bridge were also approached by another attractive female researcher. This bridge didn't sway and it was only a few feet above a small stream. So, how many of the men surveyed ended up calling the woman? On the safe bridge, only two out of sixteen participants called, but on the rickety bridge, nine out of eighteen called. The researchers behind the study hypothesised that the men interpreted their body's fear response on the bridge as attraction, prompting them to call the woman.[6] This phenomenon is referred to as the 'misattribution of arousal'. Misattribution of arousal essentially means misinterpreting the reason behind a physiological response, such as increase in heart rate, sweating, breathing rate and sexual arousal. It makes you think, 'Oh, I'm attracted to her,' but actually your adrenaline is just really pumping because you're on this rickety bridge. What is actually caused by anxiety or fear is thus mistaken instead as attraction. This can also happen in situations where we might think we're really attracted to someone who holds a particular status in a social group – such as a popular person at our university or the 'cool' person in our friendship group. What we confuse for attraction is actually just excitement at the idea of a person and what they represent.

'When I think back to so many relationships I had when I was younger, I didn't actually enjoy being around that person. I just liked the idea of that person,' explains behavioural scientist turned dating coach Logan Ury in a podcast episode.[7] 'And I would go to bed at night and as I'm falling asleep being like, what am I doing? This doesn't feel good. But on paper, they were great.' Ury stresses that this is why it's important to teach young people that we should date people for 'who they bring out in you' rather than 'who they are on paper'. This is where it's important to ask ourselves the question: How does this person make me feel? Do I like them because all my friends think they're a catch? Or that they're hot? Am I considering how this person makes me feel when I'm with them? As Ury says: 'Some of the best relationships come from a slow burn rather than a spark. The important thing to remember is that its absence doesn't predict failure, and its presence doesn't guarantee success.'[8]

Even if we feel that we have correctly identified the spark and there was no misattribution of arousal, is it as important as we think it is? Dr Kathrine Bejanyan, an independent relationship counsellor in the UK, doesn't want to discredit the significance that the spark can hold for people. 'I know how exciting it is when you're out on a date and then something clicks,' she says, but cautions that we can't rely on the spark alone. 'It's been shown over and over again in lots of studies that that initial spark, while it does a lot for that initial attraction, doesn't strongly correlate with how well a couple does over time . . . [they must also] do the hard work of building the relationship, the intimacy, having awkward, weird, and uncomfortable conversations, expressing their needs, trying to figure out what their partner's needs are.' Bejanyan sees couples that come in and say, 'But it was so amazing in the beginning!' or 'I thought this was meant to be destiny' – they can't understand why they're having the same old conflicts that they've had in previous relationships; they didn't expect it.

This led me to wonder what would happen if we paid less mind to the elusive spark, and looked more closely at a person's attributes, the qualities they hold that could build the foundation for a long-lasting relationship. I asked Dr Benjanyan for her advice on how can we stay out of the spark trap and she says that the green flags we should be looking for are 'a person's ability to have open and honest conversations and their ability to have some level of self-awareness.'

How about those early encounters? What are some other things to look out for? Bejanyan says she'd be concerned about someone being very critical of their exes right off the bat and by a lot of hypersexualised conversations. Rather than focusing on the immediate spark, she recommends that you focus on having fun together. She also says, 'Keep your wits about you, ask significant questions, you want to know how someone's grown up, what their family dynamics are, why past relationships haven't worked out, and how their careers developed. You're trying to get an idea of someone's internal world rather than how excited you feel about them.' One of the reasons we're so keen on finding the spark is because we're hoping it will lead to a wonderful relationship, but we need more than the spark in order to get there.

So, what makes a first date turn into a long-term relationship? Laura, 33 and bisexual, used to believe that a spark was a relationship requisite. But, when she met her current partner, there wasn't a spark straight away, but instead a kind of slow-burn and ease. 'We started out with video call dates during the pandemic. It wasn't so much a spark as I was really intrigued and enjoyed his company. After we met in person and it was going really well, I even considered ending it because it was comfortable straight away rather than flames. So glad I didn't.' Six months later, I followed up with Laura and she told me they're now engaged. 'I felt like he cared and was interested and present right from the start, as well as confident in and comfortable with himself,' she tells me.

Love at First Sight?

Romeo fell in love when he first laid eyes on Juliet in William Shakespeare's 1595 eponymous play. In Jane Austen's 1811 novel *Sense and Sensibility,* Colonel Brandon fell for Marianne when he saw her playing the piano. Biblical interpretations have deemed Isaac's first sight of Rebekah and Jacob's first glance of Rachel as love at first sight. Kylie Minogue sang a (very catchy) song about it. For millennia, we've believed in the alchemy of instant love. And many of us still believe in it to this day. Research by dating site Elite Singles found 61 per cent of women and 72 per cent of men believe in love at first sight.[9]

Logan Ury, behavioural scientist turned dating coach, and the author of *How To Not Die Alone,* says only 11 per cent of people experience love at first sight when they meet their partner.

But what exactly is love at first sight? One study found that what we consider 'love at first sight' is not a distinct form of love. It's actually 'a strong initial attraction' that people label as love at first sight either in the moment or in hindsight.[10] Sorry folks, it's not love, it's physical attraction.

Psychologists have identified two modes of thinking – called 'implicit theories of relationships' – which shape the way we begin and maintain relationships. If you have destiny beliefs, you believe that a relationship is either fatally meant to be, or it's not. It's written in the stars and out of your control. Whereas if you believe that good relationships require work and communication, and that problems can be worked through, then you have growth beliefs.[11] 'Believing in love at first sight, or the idea that you can fall in love instantly when you see someone for the very first time and again, is a form of destiny belief. And destiny beliefs have a negative impact on relationships,' says social psychologist Professor Viren Swami. 'There is a whole body of research which shows that people who hold those kinds of destiny beliefs have more difficulty forming relationships, primarily because they're much more likely to be disappointed at the start of the relationship compared to those who don't hold those beliefs.'

The Soulmate Myth

There are 8.1 billion people on earth and out there in the vast expanse, there's a human that's perfect for you. This is what the notion of soulmates is predicated on.

The idea of soulmates or having 'a person' isn't uncommon – quite the contrary. Around 49 per cent of Brits[12] and 60 per cent of Americans[13] believe in soulmates. The concept itself has been around for millennia, but its first recorded use can be traced back to 1822 in a letter written by poet Samuel Taylor Coleridge, who wrote: 'To be happy in Married Life . . . you must have a Soul-mate'.[14] Whether we're talking about finding 'The One', 'my person', or a 'twin flame', these beliefs are all rooted in a sense of pre-destiny, that there's a little bit of magic at play. In theory, it's deeply romantic and a lovely idea. In practice, hitching your wagon to the concept of a soulmate could be dooming your relationship from the get-go. Bradley Onishi, an associate professor of religion at Skidmore College explains: 'The soulmate myth promises that amidst the dizzying and often confusing landscape of dating apps there is one match out there that will make sense of it all. It promises an anchor to modern life that many find appealing.'[15]

It's lovely to imagine there's a soulmate out there who you're destined to be with and maybe marry and that this relationship will stand the test of time. In fact, when we're in the trenches of terrible dates, it can be comforting to picture that there's someone out there for us. 'The soulmate myth is really good at taking all the bad first dates, the breakups, the dashed hopes and disappointments and putting them into a story that says "someday all of this will fall into place,"' says Onishi.

In reality, these kinds of beliefs are actually more of a hindrance than a help when it comes to having a long-lasting marriage.[16] As psychologist Dr Shauna Springer, author of *Marriage, for Equals: The Successful Joint (Ad)Ventures of Well-Educated Couples*, writes, 'if we are convinced that we have met "the One soulmate" that we were always destined to meet, whenever we discover that this person is not what we first imagined, our sense of disillusionment with them will be much greater and our hopes for the future of the relationship may be quickly squashed.'[17]

Destiny beliefs aren't just detrimental to relationships, they can also put us in danger, causing people to stay in abusive and violent relationships because of the belief that they're destined to stay together. Renae Franiuk, of Aurora University, Illinois, researched implicit theories and relationship satisfaction and longevity and found that 'the longer destiny theorists stayed in relationships with someone who is not the right person, the more they reported violence.'[18]

'They downplay problematic relationships,' Franiuk added. 'They might give someone a longer chance than other people might. Some might see warning signs early and end the relationships, but there will be some who don't believe they are in a relationship with the right person but for economic reasons they remain and their personality traits make them more forgiving, which puts them in dangerous situations.'

One in 526 Chances: Is Dating a Numbers Game?

When we find ourselves habitually fixating on the one person we're talking to, the people in our lives might roll out the old 'dating is a numbers game' line. Content abounds on the benefits of talking to multiple people at once, so you're not focusing your energy on one person.

Mathematically, the odds of falling in love are actually really low. Per research by mathematician Rachel Riley and eharmony, the odds of finding love with someone you're compatible with are one in 562.[19] So, what does that mean exactly? Well, the odds of having twins are 1 in 67 and your chances of becoming a millionaire are 1 in 55. So, how did Riley arrive at this figure? She began by calculating the number of people looking for love in the UK, which she projected at 23 million. 'Out of these [people], only 39 per cent are the right gender and sexual orientation for you, bringing us down to around 9 million,' Riley explains.[20] Then there's the small matter of age appropriateness, which reduces that number by four fifths (based on an average person not wanting to date someone more than six years older or younger than them). 'Our data shows that you're likely to feel mutual physical attraction with 18 per cent of people,' Riley added.

But is there any truth to the idea that adding more numbers to the mix will maximise your chances? Let's take a look at The Secretary Problem – also known as the Fussy Suitor Problem or The Sultan's Dowry Problem – which is based on optimal stopping theory, a mathematical model which examines the right time to take action in order to yield the best result. The theory became popular in 1960 when mathematics writer Martin Gardner penned a piece about it in *Scientific American*. 'This is the mathematically correct way to know when to stop looking and when to choose someone,' Logan Ury explains in an episode of 'The Diary of a CEO' podcast.[21]

Picture this: You're advertising a role for a new secretary. There are 100 candidates and you must go through each of them and one by one eliminate them from the process. After interviewing the first candidate, you tell them yay or nay. And you repeat the process with each candidate with zero chance to turn back and change your mind.

Question is: How do you know when you've found the right person? And how do you know when you should stop looking? As Ury says: 'If you choose too early, you don't know what's out there. But if you choose too late, maybe all the good people have passed you by?'

The magic number? Thirty-seven per cent (or 36.8 per cent to be mathematically precise). Per this theory, if you want to pick the best of the bunch, you should turn down the first 37 people you interview (or in our case, date). When you encounter the next person who's better than the benchmark person, you choose them.

What could possibly go wrong? Well, a few things, according to mathematician Hannah Fry.

'Imagine if your perfect partner appeared during your first 37 per cent. Now, unfortunately, you'd have to reject them,' Fry explains.[22] 'Another risk is, let's imagine instead, that the people you dated in your first 37 per cent are just incredibly dull, boring, terrible people. That's okay, because you're in your rejection phase, so that's fine, you can reject them,' Fry adds. When the next person to come along is 'marginally less boring, dull, and terrible', does that mean they're the person you should be with? 'Now, if you are following the maths, I'm afraid you have to marry them,' jests Fry.

Mathematicians, statisticians and economists have investigated the problem of love and our odds of finding our special someone. Economist Peter Backus investigated his own chances of finding love while studying for his PhD at Warwick University, penning a paper entitled 'Why I don't have a girlfriend: An application of the Drake Equation to love in the UK'. 'In 2008, I was experiencing a period in my life that I would call "the great loneliness". I did not have a girlfriend,' explains Backus.[23]

Backus had a few things he was looking for in a girlfriend: someone who lived nearby, someone age-appropriate, someone degree-educated, someone he'll get along with, someone who's a) attractive and b) finds him attractive. Not a lot to ask for, eh?

Backus calculated that there were 26 women in London who fit his requirements. 'So, on a given night out in London, there is a 0.0000034% chance of meeting one of these special people,' explains Backus. 'That's a 1 in 285,000 chance. Not great.' If it's any consolation, Backus got married in 2013.[24]

Understanding Limerence

Limerence (also known as 'unrequited love') was first coined by psychologist Dorothy Tennov in the 1970s. The defining characteristics of this emotional state include intrusive thoughts about the individual in question – the limerent object – along with one's mood being dependent on the limerent object's behaviour and the level of interest they display. There is also a deep-rooted need for these strong feelings to be returned, and devastation ensues when that doesn't happen. Limerence also causes you to exaggerate and overblow the limerent object's positive qualities, and to ignore the negative traits. The limerent object occupies such a large space in one's mind that all other concerns feel significantly less important – it feels all-consuming. For limerent individuals, there can also be feelings of insecurity or shyness in the physical presence of the limerent object. Referring to someone you're infatuated with as an 'object' might sound a bit jarring, or even dehumanising. The term has certainly met with some uneasiness. Dr L, author of *Living With Limerence* – who runs an online community for limerent individuals – notes that Tennov chose the term 'limerent object' deliberately.

LalalaLetMeExplain, the anonymous relationships expert and author of *Block, Delete, Move On*, describes herself as the 'queen of limerence' and has been educating her community of 246K followers about the emotional state. 'It's incredibly common with limerence to put them on a pedestal, to create those scenarios,' says Lala. 'Often you're not even that into them, what's created this link is the familiarity. I can spot somebody just from their dating profile, I will know this is somebody I could get limerent over.'

Lala tells me that her limerence manifests in creating connections that are tangible at best.

'My birthday is on the 22nd and I'll meet someone whose birthday also happens to be on the 22nd of a different month and I'm like, oh my god, he's born on the 22nd, like that must mean something!' she explains. 'He works as a teacher, that must mean he's gonna be an amazing dad.'

Lala acknowledges that she should regard the limerent object instead as 'a new, real person who I need to slowly get to know'. Non-limerent people, Lala says, 'date really slowly'. 'I have friends who go out on the first date and like someone, and they're like, I've met him once, I can't really like him that much, whereas I'll go out on one date and I'm like, oh my god, I'm just really worried about next Christmas because his parents live in France. So how are we going to manage that?'

Overthinking is a big part of limerence. And with that scrutiny can come a propensity to infer positive meaning from behaviour – a meaning that might not line up with reality. As Lala tells me: 'The most dangerous part of limerence for me is that I start reading positive meaning into things, rather than thinking, oh he's ghosting because he's a prick, [I'll think] he hasn't messaged because I'm so incredible that he's feeling scared to text me because he must think I'm going to reject him because I'm so amazing.'

This is where the stories we tell ourselves about someone can get us into trouble. In my case, I've told myself, he's not texting you because he's having bad mental health or he's intimidated by you and thinks you're too good for him.

Ultimately the only detail I needed to look at was the simple fact of the absence of his communication. If I'd looked at that, and that alone, I'd have noticed that this man wasn't showing up for me in the way I needed. If they're not texting you, that's all you need to know. I didn't need to examine it from every angle to know that this wasn't the man for me.

For Lala, she recognises that limerence can plunge her into a state where she gives herself too much hope. She says she's had a lot of therapy and knows that if someone wants to be in her life, they'll make that very apparent. But she does still feel limerence from time to time, she's just a lot more aware of it these days. 'I won't do the embarrassing shit anymore that I used to do, even like five years ago. But it's hard to control. Do you just pull back and sit there or do you communicate how you're feeling?' she asks. Lala finds that pulling back is best for her when she's feeling limerent and it's clear her feelings aren't reciprocated.

Describing your own experience of limerence can come with a strong sense of embarrassment or shame. Particularly once you're no longer limerent and are looking back on how deeply you fell under the spell of someone with little or no signs of reciprocation. 'Now I also recognise when someone is limerent for me and, upsettingly, it really puts me off,' says Lala. 'It always makes me feel really embarrassed because I feel like this is the energy that I was giving to other people and it's such a horrible feeling when someone is limerent for you. It really highlights to you how much you went into that spiral of madness and you've come out of it and you're like "fuuuuuck, limerence really took over," but when you're in it, even though there's a portion of your brain that's just like stop it, just calm down, there's another portion that's like, no, go and check his mum's Facebook to see if he died.'

Psychologists have subsequently built on Tennov's body of qualitative research, with Albert Wakin and Duyen B. Vo drawing parallels between limerence and obsessive compulsive disorder, in addition to substance use disorders.[25] Per Wakin, professor of psychology at Sacred Heart University and a leading scholar on the subject, who used to work with Dorothy Tennov, limerence is an involuntary and incessant state of 'compulsory longing for another person'.

Limerence is an under-researched mental state and more empirical evidence is needed to build a more thorough picture. There is currently brain-imaging research underway to learn more about this widely misunderstood condition.[26] Prof. Wakin theorises that limerence is a cross between addiction and OCD. After examining scores of case studies, Wakin defines limerence as 'a love variant. It feels like love but it isn't.'

'People think about the other person just about at the expense of everything else,' Wakin tells me. 'The OCD is extreme in strong cases of limerence in the sense that the other person is constantly on their minds. The addiction is extremely compelling as well, because for example, if you're addicted to a substance like alcohol, you don't have to worry about will alcohol be there when you need it? Might alcohol prefer some-body else and leave you? When you're addicted to a person, you're constantly worried about that. So, the combination of feelings of OCD and addiction are extremely powerful. And that's what we see limerence as.' Per Wakin, you can still experience limerence 'without having OCD for anything else or without being addicted to anything else'.

So, what are the main symptoms of limerence? 'In the first several months of a relationship, it is almost impossible to tell whether or not it is evolving into a healthy love relationship or into limerence,' says Wakin. 'Because it is natural in the first period of a relationship to think about the person all the time, to feel elated, to not be able to wait to see them again and stuff.

'What happens in a healthy relationship is those roller-coaster high feelings in the first several months tend to subside a bit, and they're taken over by the deeper feelings of familiar-ity and regular contact and things like that. In limerence, the rollercoaster-type feelings actually increase after the initial few months of the relationship. And sometimes, therefore . . . to the person experiencing it, it feels like a super love.'

What exactly causes limerence? Wakin tells me that more research on limerence is needed. 'What's so fascinating about limerence is that it can happen to a person who might be borderline-adjusted and bounces from one limerence relationship to another. But it can also happen to a person who is very well adjusted, has had very healthy relationships. And then all of a sudden, that person meets someone which triggers something.' Researchers don't know why that happens.

If you're prone to limerence and you keep finding yourself in limerent relationships, what can you do? 'One of the first things to do is to enter into any new relationship very, very cautiously, and monitor it for the first few months. If it begins to ease off and develop into something more steady, fine. If it begins to intensify, then you know the relationship is going in the wrong direction.

'Is the relationship developing into something bigger than life? Is this person going to make my life incredibly happy and wonderful? Is this person not only going to become a part of my life? Is this person going to *become* my life?'

Wakin believes brain imaging research is needed so we can gain more of an understanding of the parts of the brain that are activated during limerence. He'd also like those scans to be compared with those of people with substance misuse disorders and people with OCD. 'Limerence is common enough and it is serious enough so that it definitely warrants further attention and further research,' he says.

If you're in a limerent relationship, Wakin is very clear on what you need to do: 'Unfortunately, one of the first things I tell anybody is that with limerence, you need to completely end the relationship and that sometimes is very hard to do. No contact. You can't be going on to social media and finding out what they're doing or how they're doing or anything like that.' You have to completely cut off ties, he says, which will be extremely difficult at the beginning.

'I think now, because we were in isolation [during Covid], and we're coming out of it, people might be a little hungrier than usual for relationships,' he says. 'So people are more likely to jump into them and/or to look for someone who is going to completely make my life happy, look for someone who is going to come into my life and change it. With this person, I will be able to walk out of the shadows and into the sunlight. And if those are people's goals, for a love relationship, they're setting themselves up to be in a limerent relationship.'

For Lala, noticing when she's experiencing limerence and mentally making note of what's happening has been helpful. 'One of the best things I found for it is mindfulness. As somebody with ADHD, I find calming my mind really hard. If I am in that horrible limerent place and can't stop thinking about them, I usually do some mindfulness techniques to just be like, okay, I'm going to allow this thought to pass. I'm going to imagine myself in a little boat, and I'm going to watch the boat just gently flowing down the river. And in that period of time when I'm thinking about the boat floating down the river, I'm not thinking about my limerent object.'

She also advises breaking contact through whatever means feels best for you. If that means blocking them permanently, or for a finite window of time, go for it. Make plans with friends and find ways to distract yourself.

Love Takes Time

Some people don't experience limerence or the feeling of love at first sight at all; for them, love has a habit of playing the long game. Logan Ury explains in her podcast that this is also completely normal: 'Love can absolutely grow over time. And there's actually something called the "mere exposure effect" where the more we see something, the more it can grow in us. That's why people end up dating somebody from work or dating someone in their apartment building.'[27]

The 'mere exposure effect' theorises that the more exposed you are to something – or rather, someone – you feel neutral about, the more likely you are to develop positive feelings about it. So, attraction might not be felt straight away, but that doesn't mean it can't develop over time.

In fact, multiple studies have found that familiarity breeds attraction. Research shows that people rate faces that are more familiar as more attractive.[28]

The slow-burn romance is something Cara, 35 and heterosexual, wasn't entirely familiar with – until she met her partner. Cara and Charlie matched on Bumble initially but didn't manage to go on a date because Cara met someone else, who she then dated for two years. For three years after that initial match, Cara and Charlie were like ships in the night. Charlie would contact Cara to see if she was single – she was not. When Cara's relationship ended, she matched with Charlie on Hinge, but didn't meet up because, this time, Charlie had started dating someone else. After a years-long will-they-won't -they saga, the stars finally aligned and the pair went on a date in October 2020 – three years after that initial match. 'It was an unusual date for me,' says Cara. Historically, she put a lot of energy and expectation into first dates. 'I've had some pretty wild first dates that have ended up lasting entire weekends.' This date lasted for an hour and a half because they both had plans that evening. They met up for a pint at a pub and just talked for the entirety of the date. 'I remember being initially attracted to him,' she says. 'But there wasn't this full-body spark. I remember thinking that the conversation was easy and felt really natural. I thought he was charming. I thought he was handsome. I thought he was clever.' She came away from the date thinking, 'I'd like to see this person again,' but she didn't feel the infatuation that she'd felt on other first dates. 'It was definitely more of a slow burn,' she says.

'We waited until the third date to sleep with each other which for me is slow. I understand that for others that might not be slow.' Cara and Charlie casually dated over the course of a few months, seeing each other once a week or once every other week, a frequency that Cara found really slow. 'I was used to relationships that had a quick, fast burn, where I'd spend a weekend with someone who I'd just met on a first date,' she says. Her feelings for Charlie came really gradually – something she attributes to the stable, managed way she approached dating him. 'I was definitely excited and looking forward to meeting someone, but it wasn't everything to me. I had recently finished some therapy, which had really helped me de-centre relationships from my life and my perceived purpose in life,' she says.

Around midnight one evening, a distressed Charlie called Cara during a panic attack. 'I remember feeling really protective over him and quite worried about him and like I just wanted to be there and to comfort him and so I took an Uber to his flat, arriving at around one in the morning,' she says. They sat and watched *Modern Family* together and she remembers turning to him, looking at him, and telling him she loved him. She told him he didn't need to say it back because she understood that he was in a heightened, anxious state. 'I remember feeling a real clarity descend when he'd called me and I felt like I needed to mobilise and go to him just to sit there and be with him. But I didn't require anything back from him at that moment,' she says. Charlie didn't say 'I love you' straight away – in fact, it happened a month or so after Cara's initial soul-baring. 'I'd come back to his after quite an intense bottomless brunch, I was really drunk and I was upset because it had been maybe a month or so since I told him that I loved him. And he still hadn't told me and I was crying about it. And he simply looked at me and said, "Of course I love you."' Charlie and Cara are now engaged and expecting their first child together.

With the spark, we often expect it to manifest very early on. Dr Carolina Bandinelli tells me she was recently told a story of a man who went out with a woman he met on Feeld. The woman was in a polyamorous relationship. 'At one point, she told him, "Look, I haven't felt the spark, but if you want we can make out for two minutes and then I'll let you know,"' explains Bandinelli.

Bandinelli says this anecdote demonstrates the ideology of efficiency that's at play in dating app usage. 'I want to know if there is a spark, here's what I think I should do to understand and test the spark. Now, we make out for two minutes and I'll let you know if there's a spark.'

In this case, the woman used kissing as a test to find a spark. Others increasingly use sex as a means of gauging whether a powerful connection exists between them. As Eva Illouz writes in *The End of Love*, 'the body henceforth becomes the only or at least the more reliable source of knowledge'. Illouz hears from one case study, Lena, who says, 'After I meet a woman, if I am attracted to her, I have to go to bed with her. It is the first thing I do, not the restaurants, drinks, and movies bullshit.' Lena explains that her method of ascertaining if she wants a relationship with a woman is exclusively through sex.

Similarly, another case study told Illouz, 'The first test a man has to pass is the one in bed.' This is so she can gauge if they are sexually compatible. 'If he knows how to touch me,' she says, she pursues a relationship, if not, then she doesn't bother.

Looking for fireworks in bed as the definitive sign of compatibility isn't a failsafe strategy. For starters, people experience sexual performance anxiety – research suggests that between 6 and 16 per cent of women and 9 and 25 per cent of men experience it (people can be reluctant to disclose sexual performance anxiety, so those figures are likely to be underreported).[29] People who believe in something called 'sexual destiny beliefs' – that having that instantly mind-blowing sex is a sign of relationship compatibility – experience more volatile relationships, according to a study. Conversely, the research showed that people who hold 'sexual growth beliefs' – that good sex takes some work and can develop in a relationship – are ultimately more satisfied in their relationships.[30]

After speaking to people about their experiences of searching for a spark and finding something else . . . something more substantial, more long-lasting, I feel there's a disconnect in our expectations of what love should look like, and how it feels in reality. People go out looking for fireworks, but instead find a warm glow that feels like home, it feels safe and sustaining, the beginning of something that could warm them for a long time to come. This new outlook makes the experience of being in the dating arena feel lighter, more hopeful. What we can learn from the data and from slow-burn love stories like Cara and Charlie's is that giving ourselves the chance to get to know people slowly can help us find lasting love. If, as Bandinelli and

Illouz's research shows, we're wrong about the importance that physical attraction can have on the success of prospective romantic relationships, then there's also a chance that we've misunderstood the different nuances and roots of our attraction altogether and that we should take the spark with a pinch of salt.

4

Just My Type

With the new evidence presented to me by experts, I start to reevaluate what's been instilled in me, and all of us, about desirability. I imagine the script running through the minds of potential suitors: 'She's a 10, but her desirability has been determined by the systems of oppression that operate in society. She's a 10, but society says her skin tone makes her a 2. She's a 10, but her body isn't small enough, so she's a 4. She's a 10, but she's slept with too many people, so she's "low value".'

What can we do to make online dating less terrible? This is a question I posed in my interviews with psychologists, sociologists and neuroscientists. The answer is pretty unanimous: We must start by fixing the problems we have in our culture. Professor Viren Swami tells me, 'I'm hesitant to put the responsibility on consumers primarily because a lot of what's happening on dating apps is a reflection of wider society. Unless you tackle what's happening in wider society, you don't tackle what's happening within dating apps. It's not an either–or situation. If you don't tackle racism in society, you will get racism on dating apps. If you don't tackle sexism in broader society, you get sexism in dating apps.'

We can't put our love lives on hold while we wait for society to be cured of its ills. So, where does that leave us?

Since we can't instantly remove the systems of oppression within society, what we instead try to do is protect women, femmes, and marginalised people within these structures. The disempowerment they experience can look like: Changing your behaviour or censoring your communication style in order to avoid abuse. Ghosting someone to avoid rejection violence. Pretending to have a partner when someone won't take no for an answer. Sharing your location with friends while on a date. Friends or family telling you to text them once you get home. Consenting to sex we don't want to have because we feel the other person is expecting it. As we navigate dating, we need to be mindful of how our society has created an uneven playing field for us, placing a political layer over our dating lives that affects how safe and empowered we feel and influences who we find attractive.

Desirability politics permeate our culture at large. By this, we mean that we are socially conditioned to regard humanity as a hierarchy of attractiveness, that some people are more deserving of love or sex or attention than others, based on a series of attributes that we have been taught to prize. While this might seem theoretical, the intersections of our identity and the unconscious biases we have as a society have a very real impact on our lives. As Audre Lorde puts it: 'Those of us who stand outside the circle of this society's definition of acceptable women; those of us who have been forged in the crucibles of difference – those of us who are poor, who are lesbians, who are Black, who are older – know that survival is not an academic skill.'[1]

When it comes to dating, the qualities we consider attractive are not a coincidence. Far from it. Many people have ideas about the kind of person they want to date which includes their race, their religion and their socioeconomic class. Melissa A. Fabello PhD, a US-based sex and relationships educator who provides politicised relationship coaching to clients says, 'When you talk to people about these things, they'll say, "Well, that's just my preference."' She adds, 'There's very little critical analysis that people want to do around where their preferences come from. We're not born with our preferences, they're shaped, and you can change them.' Changing them can involve making a concerted effort to date people who look different to what we've been taught is attractive, which is difficult and isn't something a lot of people are eager to do. Fabello says this is because we are still 'coming to terms with the fact that oppression lives inside of us, and we show up in the world in oppressive ways. It's like people don't want to look at themselves'.

So, who possesses 'fuckability', as philosopher Amia Srinivasan puts it? In *The Right to Sex*, Srinivasan frames the concept of fuckability as 'not whose bodies are seen as sexually available (in that sense Black women, trans women and disabled women are all too fuckable), but whose bodies confer status on those who have sex with them'. Srinivasan posits the existence of a sexual hierarchy, under which 'hot blonde sluts' and East Asian women are prized as fuckable, while Black women, Asian men, and disabled, trans and fat people are considered unfuckable, and Black men are both fetishised and feared. Hotness is not separate from politics. Srinivasan points to the 'racism, ableism, transphobia and every other oppressive system that makes its way into the bedroom through the seemingly innocuous mechanism of "personal preference"'.

Those who are able to conform to society's ideals – who are white, thin, cis-gendered, young, non-disabled – hold 'pretty privilege', which can result in markedly different dating experiences to those who do not hold this privilege. Perceived attractiveness has been found to produce a 'halo effect' that creates an irrational bias in favour of the person deemed attractive. One study even found that thin white women were expected by others to become more successful, and have a better personality, than bigger white women.[2]

Systems of power and oppression shape what we think about, what we feel, how we see ourselves, and how we see other people. Whether it's our size, the colour of our skin, our race, being able-bodied or even whether our gender presentation matches the rigid ideas of masculinity and femininity we hold in society, Fabello says, 'It's not a coincidence that when we think about what is attractive, it generally falls exactly on the line of power and oppression.'

Our interactions with others can therefore feed into wider patterns of oppression, even if we don't intend any harm. Because we've been socialised within a culture of internal biases, we can unwittingly commit small harmful acts or say hurtful things – we call these microaggressions. This lack of thoughtfulness can often show up in the choice of words. Statements like 'You're not like other girls,' 'I've never been attracted to Black girls, but I'm attracted to you,' and 'I didn't even know you were trans,' are all microaggressive. Physical microaggressions can include things like speaking more loudly when addressing a blind person or rolling your eyes when someone talks about feeling excluded or invalidated because of their difference. Fabello says that if we're not doing the work to unlearn the things we've been taught by the world, then we're going to continue these oppressive interpersonal behaviours.

Unlearning these harmful biases means examining our so-called 'preferences', reflecting on who we've been taught to regard as 'desirable' and who to view as 'undesirable'. We must also dwell on the consequences of living a lifetime where your societal undesirability is constantly reinforced. Then, while we're dating, we need to be aware of not only how our own identities affect how we move through the world, but also what our dating partners might be experiencing. Dating across difference means making an effort to be sensitive to the other person's experience so that when we inevitably mess up, in spite of our best efforts, we can recognise it, learn from it, and do better next time. It also means knowing that when someone you're dating says or does something insensitive, you deserve to be able to raise it with them because a partner that loves you will want to learn and change. These issues should not be met with defensiveness, dismissiveness, with invalidating sighs of frustration or eyerolls. Romantic relationships should be a safe haven, one where you are not harmed, where your needs are listened to, understood and met. When you belong to a marginalised group, it is not too much to ask to expect your partner to listen and learn. And for a partner to respond with graciousness and a willingness to change.

Sapphic Love

Lucy didn't know she was attracted to women until she was in her late teens. 'I had the age-old cliché of falling in love with my best friend, who unfortunately did not feel the same,' she tells me. She hadn't understood why she felt so attracted to her until they drunkenly kissed one night.

'That was my "turning point",' she says. 'It felt like everything made sense, like the reason why I didn't have boyfriends that stayed long, and why I was not sad when they left.' It broke Lucy's heart that her best friend no longer wanted to be friends with her after she disclosed how she felt. 'I never saw her again after my confession, and to this day I've had no contact since,' she says. Women-loving-women (WLW) dating is by far 'the most heartfelt and heartbreaking experience' Lucy has ever had. The acronym is used to describe women who love women and describes lesbians, bisexual, pansexual, and queer-identifying women.

After her experience with her best friend, Lucy decided to actively try and date women. 'I knew meeting someone organically would be very difficult given my limited experience at 18,' she says. So, she turned to dating apps to try and meet women, and 'very quickly understood the complexity of the WLW world'.

'I think one of the main challenges with WLW is that the dating pool is so much smaller than people realise,' says Lucy. 'The eligible dating pool excludes people who are in the closet, those not acting on their attraction, or being suppressed by external forces (e.g. religion and community).' The reality is, Lucy explains, that finding someone emotionally and sexually available, who also happens to be compatible with you is 'rather slim in the monogamous relationship sense'. The limited size of the dating pool can impact rejection and how deeply it is felt. 'With the reduced dating pool, every rejection feels like your last chance of finding someone,' she says.

It's not only the dating pool size that makes meeting women difficult. Lucy says it's harder to meet other WLW 'in the wild' as many third places like bars, clubs and venues are designed for heterosexual encounters. There are queer spaces out there, but there are fewer than there once were. A recent UCL Urban Laboratory Report commissioned for the Mayor of London found that the number LGBTQ-only venues, such as pubs, clubs, bookstores, bars – areas which once carved out places of belonging for queer people, away from the discrimination, violence, criminalisation that pervades society – fell from 125 to 53 between 2006 and 2017.[3] This trend has also been observed in big cities around the world from New York to Sydney and Vancouver.[4]

The remaining spaces that we do have cater to more than just queer people. Lucy says, 'If I were to try to flirt at a bar with a woman I was interested in, most times they would not be interested in the same way back. Even though there are some queer spaces that exist like gay clubs, oftentimes the women you meet there are straight and are with their straight girlfriends,' she says. Lucy says that cis hetero women come to queer spaces to 'find peace from straight men who would perhaps harass them at a normal club, but in doing so they reduce the chance of meeting other queer women'. The question of whether straight cis people should be able to occupy queer spaces is 'tricky', says Ky Richardson, founder of Lez Hang LDN, a community group for lesbian, gay, bisexual, pansexual, queer+ women and non-binary people. 'Queer spaces that are just for queer people are super important for a variety of reasons,' they say. 'They can give us a little bit of respite from the kind of microaggressions we typically experience in a normative world. They're also important for more serious reasons. Some queer people don't feel safe being around cis men, for example, and that could be tied up in earlier trauma.'[5] At the same time, a straight-presenting person might be questioning and might need access to a queer space, says Richardson. 'We have to be very careful not to assume gender or sexuality.'

Having fewer queer spaces also means that the types of spaces you have access to might not be a perfect fit for you. Riley, 28, is a non-binary and femme-presenting person who feels there's a huge issue with loneliness in WLW dating. 'The dating scene for queer women and femmes is hard because it's a much smaller dating pool and there's a decreasing number of queer dating venues,' says Riley. 'It's quite hard to get an alignment on your sexual preference, your relationship and life goals, especially if you are into kink, because you kind of have to weigh up how important that is to your sexual identity.' They say that there's a huge lesbian kink scene, but that it overlaps with a chemsex scene and a party scene which can be quite hard when you have problems with drugs or alcohol. On a more heartening note, in 2024 we began seeing a resurgence of lesbian bars in the UK, including La Camionera in Hackney and Glastonbury's launch of its lesbian area 'Scissors'. Hopefully this is an indication that we'll continue to see more diverse queer spaces opening up in the years to come.

Regardless of whether you're dating online or IRL, partner preferences can also make the already small queer dating pool feel even smaller. 'It's not as simple as putting two (or more) WLW together,' says Lucy. 'Many sub terms like "masc", "femme", "stem", "butch" (appearance preference), and "top", "bottom", "pillow princess", and "stone top" (sexual preference) exist to make partner preferences tangible and collate dates into categories.' It's commonly understood the opposites of these binaries fit together into well-known relationship structures, such as masc and femme, but this isn't always the case. Lucy explains that this can narrow your options in the dating pool and be quite isolating if you don't fit into these tropes. Lucy is 'femme for femme' but, when she meets other femme women, she's often told she's not masc enough for the women she's attracted to. 'At this point I feel like I have to trade either my femininity to date other WLW, or trade my sexuality to keep being feminine but not have the option to date other femme WLW.' Lucy also finds that when she tries to date online, she also finds it challenging to meet someone with compatible interests. As a woman looking for other women to date monogamously, Lucy has had countless encounters with people looking for threesomes, women looking to experiment and people looking for a third in their open relationships. 'Unicorn hunting' is a term that's used in the ethical non-monogamy (ENM) community to describe, typically, a heterosexual couple who are looking for a third person (often a bisexual or queer woman) to have a threesome or a poly relationship with. 'There is no easy way to filter these people out of your potential matches,' says Lucy.

How Does Orientation Affect the App Experience?

The Pew Research Center found that lesbian, gay and bisexual adults are around twice as likely as straight adults to have used a dating app or site,[6] but now that so much of dating has moved online, it's important to examine how we make online dating inclusive. There is a specific type of alienation that comes with using an app that was not made with you or your community in mind, and most dating apps have initially been created with straight people in mind. 'Nothing in this world is made for marginalised people,' says Fabello. 'As a queer woman, I talk to so many other queer women that are like "the apps suck!" And it's like, yeah, because the apps weren't made for us, so even though we can use them, they weren't made for us, and that is impactful.'

This feeling that the apps are not designed with queer people in mind is echoed by scholars too. 'Structures of power are visible also in the social and cultural genealogy of dating apps,' writes Dr Carolina Bandinelli.[7] 'Most apps (dating and non-dating) were funded in Silicon Valley, in a socio-economic environment marked by a culture that, despite the promotional claims of democracy, is in fact based on strict mechanisms of inclusion and exclusion which benefit certain categories, mostly white middle-class males, while marginalising others, notably women and ethnic minorities.' Queer dating apps, which have been conceived and built by queer people, are a response to oppression, says Fabello. 'The queer dating apps only exist because other dating apps are not useful, particularly to queer people, so we create our own,' she says. 'Even if you're trying to create something that's less oppressive, you're doing it in response to oppression, oppression takes up a lot of space in our lives.'

The dynamics these platforms expect of us don't always work, as on top of that our social scripts for dating are also designed for straight couples. As Lucy says, 'Women aren't taught to flirt with other women, so even if someone feels attracted to another woman, they may not know how to express that.' Our culture teaches straight women that men should make the first move, but doesn't have an answer for what happens when both parties are women. In practice, this can mean that if both WLW women in a conversation expect the other person to make the first move, that move might not happen at all.

Journalist Siân Bradley wrote about the hurdle of learning to flirt after coming out as bisexual, saying, 'I had had enough of secretly admiring women, nonbinary people, and AFAB people from a distance. Now I wanted to actually act on my attraction. But how?'[8] Acting on your queer desire is scary, Bradley added, particularly when many WLW have absorbed heteronormative dating scripts. 'When you've only been with cis men, like I had, dating women feels like a whole other ball game: one where you don't know the rules, let alone who's playing or whether you're allowed on the pitch.' Not only is it difficult to know how to flirt, there's also a hypervigilance that comes with hitting on queer women and femmes because when queer women aren't being treated by straight women as experimentation fodder or a means to attract the male gaze they're contending with the fetishisation of WLW in mainstream culture. 'We are seen as something for men's pleasure only, and not our own entity,' says Lucy. 'It feels shameful sometimes admitting I'm a lesbian to men and seeing the turned-on look in their eyes.' They're always aware that the response they get might be more than a simple rejection. 'We're hyper vigilant about who we can hit on and when,' says Riley. 'A lot of us have really extreme emotional scarring and we really don't trust a lot of questioning women.'

Once the flirting stage has been overcome, there's also the question of how to behave within that relationship. 'Before I started dating women I found it a struggle to imagine how I would behave when it was just me and another woman in a romantic relationship,' says Cassie, a 27-year-old bisexual woman who, for years, only dated men. 'This stopped me pursuing women for the longest time. I think this was because heterosexuality was all I knew. It was shown to us on the TV, in books, in films, on the street. I guess you could say I'm a visual learner, and with no queer representation in sight, I was lost!'

Compulsory heterosexuality – a term coined by feminist scholar Adrienne Rich in 1980 – is society's imposition of heterosexuality as the norm, the false assumption that relationships are between men and women only.[9] Cassie feels there is toxic masculinity at play with some queer cis women. 'Sometimes we feel the need to behave in a certain way in order to fit the roles we've been shown our entire lives,' she says. 'At times it feels like even the people around me, who are supposedly allies, are only happy with me dating a woman as long as one of us is "the woman" and one of us is "the man".'

Lucy echoes this, stating that within the masc and femme labels, there are expectations for behaviour as well as appearance. 'For example, some mascs having to be the financial provider to their femme partners in the same way some women would expect men to romantically treat them (e.g. buying dinner and drinks). This can be perceived to an external audience that the masc replaces the man in the relationship, and that they are not in fact valid women when they are,' she says.

Riley feels that the conversation around how bad it is to date men is 'hugely overhyped' and she really disagrees with it. The idea that straight women are the only people having bad dating experiences is also 'hugely disrespectful' to queer women – and to people of all genders and sexualities. 'The last queer relationship I was in was so bad, it was three years long and extremely codependent. It was so bad that I ended up wanting to explore the 1 per cent of me that is interested in men.' The dichotomy of all men as abusers, all women as victims, is a narrative which characterises a great deal of discourse surrounding how bad straight dating is. Riley says that within WLW dating 'it's harder when there's not an idea of who is the victim and who is the perpetrator. It's a lot harder to draw those boundaries and you accept a lot of unacceptable shit,' they say.

Riley says that a lot of queer women and femmes have an 'arrested development' because they weren't able to be out in their formative years and to lead an uncloseted life when they were teenagers. 'That means that they kind of go through a delayed adolescence, at like 25 years old.'

Lucy hopes to see more positive examples of successful WLW long-term relationships reflected in mainstream culture. She also wishes there was more acknowledgement of the struggles that come with WLW dating. 'I wish it was better accepted that even though rejection texts from women are better than being ghosted, especially when you've been dating a little while, it still hurts the same.'

Twice as Hard

Going into 2023, journalist Kelle Salle, 34 and straight, told herself it was going to be her year. She had high hopes for her love life. 'I'll get a good idea of what is out there because if you don't get the idea of what is out there, how do you know what you want?' What transpired, however, was not what she had envisaged. 'I had the worst dating experiences ever,' she says. The first guy Kelle dated ghosted her. The second guy was 'very dishonest about what he actually wanted'. These experiences made her take a huge step back from dating.[10] 'When I say the world of modern dating hasn't been kind to Black women, there are so many layers to that,' she says.

While these experiences aren't unusual, research shows that modern dating is even harder for Black women than for women of other races. A 2014 survey by OkCupid found that the majority of male users of the site believed that Black women were less attractive than women of other races and ethnicities.[11] The article which published the findings of the survey – alongside an op-ed from OkCupid co-founder Christian Rudder – has since been deleted.[12] After much fruitless research to try to find more up-to-date figures from dating apps, I conclude that not one has released any data about racial preferences since OkCupid's study. Curious? I certainly think so. Could apps be shying away from revealing this data because they're aware of their own role in amplifying sexual racism through dating apps? A 2024 field experiment conducted in Spain looked at the racial preferences of people looking for straight and same-sex relationships. Participants were shown Black and white men and women's profiles. The results showed respondents in all groups favoured white people's profiles.[13] This was echoed by anonymised data from a mainstream US dating app published in *The Dating Divide*, by Celeste Vaughan Curington, Jennifer Hickes Lundquist and Ken-Hou Lin, which showed white, Asian and Latinx straight men and gay women are often unwilling to message Black women on dating apps.[14]

Apryl Williams, author of *Not My Type: Automating Sexual Racism in Online Dating*, explained at a Harvard University event that dating apps use algorithms that aim to calculate attractiveness and attraction, but that these rankings are often 'racially informed' and result in matching its users with people who look like them. 'Dating apps allow sexual racism to flourish because they rely on the white heteronormative standards of attraction, desirability, and gender aesthetics to perform the sorting and matching algorithms that we are so comfortable with these days,' explains Williams. 'But sexual racism existed long before dating platforms came to be. What dating apps do is automate sexual racism, making it hyper efficient and routine to swipe in racially curated sexual marketplaces.'[15]

So, what justification is given by people who see Black women as undesirable? A 2021 study delved into the reasons Black women are least likely to be chosen on dating apps, interviewing white, heterosexual, university-aged students in the US to explain and justify their reasons for swiping left.[16] While a small number responded using 'overtly racist language', the vast majority of people interviewed used 'colorblind racist rhetoric'. This meant that those surveyed cited reasons like cultural incompatibility, used stereotypes and generalisations 'that often conflated race with social class', and 'attributed their racial preferences to family values and regional demographic restrictions'. Researchers concluded that these obfuscatory responses and their lack of honesty 'perpetuates ideologies of colorblind racism'.

Statements like 'that's just my preference!' are rooted in neoliberal ideas around personal choice.[17] Not only are our preferences typically the result of social conditioning, but these kinds of statements serve as a camouflage for overt racism, while normalising racism in the dating marketplace.

According to a statistical analysis by sociologists Ken-Hou Lin, Celeste Curington and Jennifer Lundquist performed in 2021, white heterosexual men are four times more likely to message a white woman than a Black woman, despite those two women having similar attributes.[18] They added that their findings revealed that 'a willingness to date Black women often does not mean an embrace for racial justice. One can "love" Black women without seeing the struggle Black women experience on a daily basis.' As part of their research, they interviewed Nena, a Black woman from Florida who told them about an experience she had matching with a white man on Bumble who claimed to love Black women, and seemed like the type that dates Black women, but told her, 'I don't like when Black people say "Black Lives Matter"; all lives matter.' Nena didn't like the resulting conversation, adding that she told the man that his statement made no sense to her and unmatched him.[19]

The differences between white women's and Black women's experiences on dating apps are markedly different. In Black publication, *Ebony*, writer Meena Anderson wrote about the stark difference between her own dating experiences and that of her white, thin roommate in her second year of university. Anderson recalls her roommate going on daily dates with men who treated her, for the most part, with kindness and respect. 'Meanwhile, on the rare occasion that I did get a response from a man, it often resulted in them divulging their violent sexual fantasies – choking, slapping, kicking and more – and how excited they were to enact them with me.'[20] Her descriptions bring me back to Amia Srinivasan's 'fuckability' spectrum: 'The discrepancies between our interactions with men made me realize that systemic, anti-Black racism is inescapable, even in the digital realm,' writes Anderson. 'In my case, the violent messages I received from men of all races showed that they assumed that I am promiscuous because of my build (thick) and my race (Black).'

Meanwhile, Kelle says that from a young age, she and many other Black British women are 'prepared' and pushed towards a perfectionist ideal with the end goal of landing your dream partner. 'It's like you have to work on yourself until you're good enough for a man. Throughout your life, make sure you've got an education, make sure you've got good grades, make sure you do this, make sure you do that. Then you're going to attract the person of your dreams.' But, this isn't really how life works. Kelle believes that striving for perfection with the belief it will inevitably render you 'worthy' of an ideal partner is a fast-track course to disappointment in the realm of dating. 'We take those thoughts and ideas into dating in adulthood and, you know, it hasn't helped us,' she says.

'I think Black women have always been held to such an unrealistic standard that women from other races are not,' says Kelle. These standards permeate all arenas of life, whether it's Black women and girls being held to white, eurocentric beauty standards,[21] Black schoolgirls facing immense pressures to achieve academic excellence,[22] or the pressure to work twice as hard as your white counterparts in the workplace.[23] The reward is always hard won – if won at all. Despite the expectation to work hard, Black women face career progression barriers in the workplace and are promoted at a significantly lower rate than their white counterparts.[24]

When Kelle tells me 'I've heard so many Black women say when they were growing up, if they were watching TV, their mums would come in and say, "Is this something you're going to do in your husband's house?" I think, "This perfectionism is a consequence of white supremacy and the coping mechanisms that people of colour have had to develop in order to survive an oppressive power structure".' As columnist Alexis Yeboah writes: 'Perfectionism is a survival mechanism for operating in a white supremacist, patriarchal society.'[25]

This creates a cutting double bind. When Black women are socialised to strive for perfection, to then be named as the least desirable community on dating apps sends a clear message: Your best will never be good enough. To say that dating while Black is disheartening would be an understatement. So, how do you navigate such extreme disappointment while hoping to find love and partnership? 'We've been left with no choice but to maintain a sense of neutrality through it all,' says Kelle. 'That is the reality and it's sad to feel like okay, maybe I might go on two dates this year. I might not go on any dates. We just have to prepare ourselves for any outcome, as opposed to approaching dating from a more positive standpoint.' Kelle says that she sees a lot of posts from Black people on social media that say things like, 'I only have one more date or one more relationship left in me.' Kelle finds these kinds of posts quite concerning, 'That's dating burnout right there,' she says.

Dating While Fat

Fatphobia is insidious in the dating realm. Nine in 10 people feel more physically judged in the dating world than in any other area of life, according to research by Bumble.[26] One in four daters say they've been body shamed on a dating app or on social media. Fifty-eight per cent of people under 34 say they've cancelled a date because of their body insecurities. Research by YouGov asked men and women for their specific preferences with regards to weight and height and the survey found that 10 per cent of men prefer 'chubby' women, but 40 per cent are more attracted to slimmer women, indicating that there is a significant preference for slimmer women across men overall.[27] When this preference is repeatedly communicated across the apps, and in the media overall, it can have a negative impact on our dating lives.

On dating apps, this manifests in people explicitly naming

what they don't want. On apps like Grindr, it wouldn't be uncommon to see 'no fats, no fems'. But weight discrimination isn't always as explicit as this. When I see statements like 'Looking for someone active,' I always look closely at it. Sure, on the one hand, that person might be sporty and find pleasure in going to the gym. But the statement could be interpreted as a coded way of saying they want thinness.

It may be one thing for people to screen for body types they're attracted to while swiping on an app, but in practice body-shaming can also arise after matching, even though both parties have already seen photos of each other. Thirty-five-year-old Tae, who is non-binary and pansexual, says, 'I'm plus-size and I do feel some cis-hetero men negatively screen on this . . . More than once I've met someone in real-life after getting along well via text, and been rejected because I was "fatter than expected".' Tae isn't alone in feeling this way. One in six plus-size daters say they've experienced weight discrimination on dating apps.[28]

The fatphobia on dating apps is part of a wider diet culture in our society that positions our fatness – or thinness – as a choice. Diet culture is hinged on the lucrative notion that bodies can and should shrink in order to fit society's idea of 'fuckability'. There's money to be made in the promise of squeezing yourself into society's idea of what's attractive. A lot of money, actually. By 2030, the global weight loss and weight management industry is estimated to be worth around 405.4 billion US dollars.[29] You must be thin, but not 'painfully' skinny, toned but not muscly, you should have a tiny waist and a flat stomach but big boobs and a fat ass. Your big bum can't be saggy or flat though – you must make sure it's pert by doing squats and lunges to keep it perky. If that doesn't work, well there's always a BBL. And if you can't lose weight, well . . . have you thought about Ozempic?

Seeing weight or body shape or size as something that people can easily fix or change shows a fundamental lack of understanding of human biology. But, should this even need to be said? Why should anyone have to justify having a bigger body? Regardless of your body type, you deserve to be treated with respect.

'High value, low body count'

Unfortunately, body-shaming doesn't stop at fatphobia. Society's obsession with 'body counts' – the number of people someone has slept with – has been a longstanding fixture in our conversations about dating. Fortunately, 61 per cent of women and 67 per cent of men say they don't care about other people's body count, according to research by sex toy brand Lovehoney, but that still leaves 33 per cent of women and 39 per cent of men who say they do care. While the figures show that men and women place near-equal amounts of importance on their partners' body counts, there is a societal difference in the way men's and women's body counts are viewed.

To make better sense of this, I interviewed sex journalist Beth Ashley, author of *Sluts*. According to her (and I'm inclined to agree), body counts are 'misogynistic bullshit' and the way they manifest for men and women looks really different because we live in a patriarchy. 'If anything, men are shamed for the opposite, they're encouraged to have a high body count and shamed for having a low sexual desire, or a low body count, where it's the absolute opposite for women.' While we made progress challenging this idea in the 1960s and '70s with the women's liberation movement, unfortunately, there has been a recent resurgence in this discussion – we have Andrew Tate, the manosphere, and 'alpha male' influencers to thank for that.

Conversations about who has more value in the dating market-place have become more explicit with the rise of 'misogyny influencers' and pick-up artists who talk about women's 'body counts' as a metric of their worth as potential partners.

As of July 2024, misogynist influencer Andrew Tate claims to have 169,000 subscribers to his Hustlers University where, for the privilege of $49.99 a month, patrons can get dating 'advice' via his egregiously named Pimpin' Hoes Degree (PHD); he also has 9.5 million followers on X. In 2023, Tate was the fourth most Googled person in the UK and the third most searched person in the world.[30]

Tate's hyperbolic statements on women are well docu-mented (I shared a few in Chapter 2). He has expressed his preference for dating 18- and 19-year-old women because they've 'been through less dick' than women over the age of 25. He has also said that he believes women are their husband's property and that 'a woman is given to the man in marriage', adding 'I believe she belongs to the man.'[31] Tate has also stated that 'A body count is probably the number one most easiest way to judge the value of a female'[32] and that '99 per cent of the world's problems would be solved if females walked through life with their body count [their number of sexual partners] on their forehead.' Not to mention his comments that female rape survivors 'bear some responsibility' for the violence inflicted upon them. The impact of his views cannot be understated. According a YouGov poll in May 2023, 26 per cent of men aged between 18 and 29 in the UK agreed with Andrew Tate's views on women and how they should be treated. Twenty-eight per cent of men between 30 and 39 agree with his views on women.[33] A small kernel of hope can be found in the figures relating to young boys, however. A YouGov poll in September 2023 revealed that while 17 per cent of boys aged between six and 15 have a positive view of Andrew Tate,

56 per cent of boys hold a negative opinion of him – and 63 per cent of 13- to 15-year-olds think negatively of him.[34]

These conversations aren't just taking place in hidden corners of the internet's seedy underbelly. So pervasive is Tate's content, that he has propelled the topic of body count back into the forefront of our collective conversations. On TikTok, videos relating to 'average body count' have racked up over 60 million views, and videos on 'body count meaning' have amassed more than 25.3 million views. TikTok is just one example, but these conversations are happening all over social media. There are scores of Subreddits and Quora posts dedicated to dissecting what people consider a high body count to constitute and whether it carries any weight in a person's value as a partner. Many of these posts announce verdicts like 'All time high is 5. Basically up to 25 years old if ur above 5 people then ur beyond nasty,'[35] 'If you want a loyal girlfriend/wife then it does matter. Cause Real Men dont want a Woman who slept with dozens of guys,' and 'No hymen. No Diamond.'[36]

The pervasiveness of these ideas is alarming. When boys and young men spend their formative years listening to the likes of Andrew Tate loudly proclaiming that a low body count is indicative of a woman's worth, they grow into men whose dating habits reflect these warped views. The generational cycle of misogyny continues and we preserve the toxic dating culture we're so desperate to break free from.

According to Ashley, 'It's just a really scary point that we've reached as a society where even though we had this massive mainstream sex-positive movement and third-wave feminism, women are still at risk of being mistreated at worst, ignored at best, because of sex that happened before they met [their partner] . . . We've all grown up believing that people with high body counts – especially women, and especially women who are minorities – are bad people.'

So where does this belief come from?

Many cultures have historically valued virginity as a way to ensure paternity and uphold patriarchal societal structures. In aggregate, these kinds of beliefs can be called 'purity culture'. In purity cultures, women and girls are positioned as gatekeepers to sex – they must not dress too provocatively or behave immodestly lest they make the men around them too horny, provoking them to sin.[37] Within Christianity, the concept of 'soul ties' – a connection that binds one person's soul to another person's – shapes how people regard sexual behaviour and the consequences thereof. 'There's this idea that if you sleep around, if you sleep with multiple people, you're tied to those people whether you like it or not, and a part of your soul is tied to them,' says Ashley. 'Therefore you are being chipped away with every person that you sleep with. And by the time that you meet "the one", you will be damaged goods. Whether you're religious or not, a lot of us have this belief somewhere in our brains, whether it's at the forefront of our brains like Andrew Tate clearly does, or it's deep in our subconscious because of something we were told at school, something we saw in a film,' says Ashley.

Having more sexual experience should be viewed as exactly that – experience. As Ashley says, 'If I was single and dating, I think I would find it exciting if I met a woman who had a really colourful sexual history, because I'd be like, wow, me next. But a lot of men who are straight just don't seem to feel that way.'

I remember once bumping into a neighbour and discussing modern dating. He asked me my thoughts on the topic of body count and over the course of the conversation said, 'If you were my partner, I'd be looking at you like the future mother of my children, and I wouldn't want to think that you'd been sleeping around with everyone.' I was stunned. Holding heavy shopping bags in one hand, before I could say anything, he said his male best friend had told him that his comments had sounded misogynistic. 'I know it probably sounds that way, but I can't help the way I feel.' But can't he help it? Is there nothing we can do to inoculate ourselves against these toxic beliefs?

How do we deconstruct and dismantle these systems of oppression that underpin the world around us? For people who already hold power and who benefit from the privilege they hold, the comfortable thing to do is nothing. This all harks back to the conversation of emotional intelligence. Breaking down biases is work – but with the alternative being bigotry, action is worth our while.

5

Putting Yourself Out There

For anyone, the idea of opening yourself up to the prospect of meeting someone new can make us feel exposed, as if we've removed the protective armour we usually wear in daily life. We dip our toe into the dating pool, knowing full well that rejection is inevitable, that heartbreak will almost certainly happen, that we might emerge from the depths with a bruised ego. But, when you are carrying the weight of poor body image, the idea of putting yourself out there comes with even more trepidation and fear, which can be debilitating. And is it any wonder? When you grow up hearing pejorative comments about people who look just like you, it doesn't take long before these ideas begin to take root. Over time, those roots become more entrenched, harder to weed out, and they grow bigger and bigger in one's mind.

Body Talk

'I'll start dating again once I've lost weight.' That's a sentence I've said to myself for the past 15 years of my life. Throughout those 15 years, my weight has changed – and I have been a UK size 10, 12, 14 and 16 during that time. But while my weight has been in flux, one thing has remained constant: my belief that my body isn't 'good enough' for dating. I have acted on this belief before, practised disordered eating, deprived myself until I felt dizzy with hunger. And when I reached the 'goal' weight and size, I felt no different. I still had the same old lousy voice in my head telling me I'm not good enough, that men didn't fancy me. I, like so many of us, had ingested the idea that the only way I deserved to be loved was to shrink myself, starve myself into a body type that I can't naturally sustain. Once I get the weight off, I'll date again. Once I feel good about myself, once I get my confidence back, I'll be in my 'slut era'. Once I drop a dress size, I'll meet the love of my life. The world won't be ready for me!

But what about present-day me (or, you)? Does she not deserve to be loved and desired? This 'once I' conditional state had been permanent for me through my teens, twenties and thirties. I've sat with this for so long, mulled it over in years of therapy, talked to best friends over wine about it, thought about it during pensive evenings on my sofa. The right person will accept me, love me for who I am. 'Just as you are,' like Mark Darcy says in *Bridget Jones' Diary* (which is, let's not forget, a film about a woman who weighs 9 stone and is regarded as alarmingly overweight). Do I really want to be with someone who only likes me when I'm two stone lighter than I currently am? What happens when my body inevitably changes? When I age? Will he still love me?

I'm not alone in feeling the way I do. Today, body image concerns have risen considerably among young adults in a culture pervaded by social media.[1] In *Cosmopolitan UK*'s 2021 anonymous sex survey of more than 2,000 people, 30 per cent of respondents said body confidence was standing in their way of having more orgasms.[2] Dating app Pure surveyed 2,000 American adults of all genders and ethnicities and found that more than half of people feel the need to meet unrealistic body standards.[3] Fifty-nine per cent of women backed out of sex due to body insecurities, compared to 20 per cent of men. Being bombarded with images of unrealistic body types from a young age sends a message to girls and women of what we 'should' look like. Unsurprisingly, research suggests that exposure to media depicting thinness as a body ideal causes body image issues in women.[4]

The majority of people surveyed haven't backed out of sex after seeing their partner naked. Eighty-one per cent of people – 78 per cent of women and 64 per cent of men – have never backed out of sex because they felt their partner's body size or shape didn't meet expectations. Of course, the figures show that some people have changed their mind about intimacy, but thankfully those people are in the minority.

When it comes to specific body hang ups, the data is also promising. Stretch marks are one of the top body insecurities. Ninety-four per cent of American people surveyed by Pure don't regard stretch marks as a turn off (fun fact: 90 per cent of people have stretch marks). When it comes to body hair, 73 per cent of the women surveyed and 61 per cent of the men have never been turned off by their partner's body hair.

How Did We Get Here?

Shrinking your body to meet an arbitrary concept of desirability isn't a foolproof 'solution' because body ideals are not static. The goalposts are constantly being moved. If we look at the last 30 years and the body ideals that have defined this era, it's little wonder so many of us have ingested such toxic ideas about how our bodies should look.

Contrary to popular media, women's bodies are not trends. In the '90s, 'heroin chic' was served up by the fashion industry as the goal, characterised by a super-skinny, strung out aesthetic.[5] Some attribute the origins of heroin chic to the world's first supermodel Gia Carangi, who was addicted to heroin, whose tracklines were visible in a *Vogue* cover shoot in 1980, and who died from AIDS-related complications aged 26.[6] The term heroin chic was coined at the funeral of prominent fashion photographer Davide Sorrenti in 1996, who died in his sleep shortly after he began dabbling with the drug. 'This is heroin, this isn't chic,' *Interview* editor Ingrid Sischy said to Sorrenti's mother Francesca Sorrenti during the wake. 'This has got to stop, this heroin chic.'[7]

When the 2000s arrived, the fashion industry 'preferred a "healthier" – but still incredibly skinny – body type.'[8] Low-rise jeans and crop tops were the order of the day – bonus points for visible hip bones, and points deducted if you have any hint of a 'muffin top'. Let's not forget the scene in *Sex and the City: The Movie* (2008) when Samantha Jones' visible midriff is greeted with Anthony's exclamation: 'Mother of god! What's with the gut?!' This was the era in which Kate Moss proclaimed that 'nothing tastes as good as skinny feels' in a 2009 interview with *Women's Wear Daily*.

I was a teenager during this era. During my formative years, I grew up reading celebrity magazines of the time, which relentlessly and scathingly tore apart celebrities' bodies – circling barely visible cellulite or tummy rolls, publishing shots of celebrities walking around with no makeup like it was the worst thing on the planet. In broader pop culture, fatphobia was at every turn. Watching *Friends* would come with endless fatphobic jokes about Monica, Nicole Richie was called 'the fat one' in *The Simple Life* (2003–2007), Anne Hathaway was dubbed 'the smart, fat girl' in *The Devil Wears Prada* (2006), and *Love Actually* (2003) made several jokes at the expense of 'chubby' Natalie (Martine McCutcheon) and her 'thighs the size of tree trunks'.[9] Special shout out to one of the worst lines in rom-com history: 'I thought you said she was thin,' in *Bridget Jones' Diary* (2001).

As McSweeney's editor Lucy Huber tweeted, 'If any Gen Z are wondering why every Millennial woman has an eating disorder it's because in the 2000s a normal thing to say to a teenage girl was "when you think you feel hungry, you're actually thirsty so just drink water and you'll be fine." '[10]

In 2007, *Keeping Up With The Kardashians* landed on TV screens, and the Kardashian sisters' bodies came under constant scrutiny from celebrity magazines and gossip websites. Some argue this ushered in a new era of the 'slim thick' body ideal – a small waist, flat stomach, with a big butt and full thighs, and a large bust.[11] The consequences of this shift to a slim-thick body ideal was even more detrimental to women's body image.[12] This is likely due to the unattainability of having a flat stomach and tiny waist while also having a big butt, big boobs, and curvy thighs, researchers found.

This body ideal gave way to a 'BBL boom'. Surgeries to attain this physique also increased dramatically during the 2010s. The number of Brazilian Butt Lift surgeries (BBLs) – during which liposuction removes fat from the abdomen and injects it into the buttocks to make it bigger – increased by 90.3 per cent between 2015 and 2019, per the American Society for Aesthetic Plastic Surgery. [13]

Researchers have historically focused on what's referred to as 'negative body image', says social psychology professor Viren Swami. 'So, things like body anxiety, body dissatisfaction, essentially forms of psychopathology in the last decade or so, there's been a shift towards understanding more positive elements of body image.' What's interesting is that things like body appreciation, body acceptance, all forms of positive body image are 'not necessarily the polar opposite of negative body image', says Swami. 'So someone could have, for example, body anxiety, but also still have very high body appreciation,' he explains.

Dating With Negative Body Image

So, how does body image impact dating?

In a survey of 100 people, I posed the following question: Does dating make you feel good about yourself? Thirty-one per cent said no, 49.4 per cent said they have good days and bad, and 8.2 per cent answered yes. The survey yielded interesting results when I asked the next question: Does the current dating scene make you feel pressured to change your appearance in order to attract a partner? 'I worry that I'm too fat to find love,' says Shani, a 33-year-old bisexual woman. 'I feel I need to lose weight,' says 31-year-old Moya, who is greysexual (someone who experiences limited sexual attraction). Hanna, a 31-year-old bisexual woman, says, 'I've lost quite a lot of weight since I became single and I think that's probably subconsciously about wanting to look a certain way to date.' Meanwhile, Jasmine, a 27-year-old straight woman says: 'I feel pressured to be thinner and prettier to get better matches.' Dan, a 23-year-old bisexual man says, 'I wish I was less fat.' Noelle, a 38-year-old straight woman says, 'I am trying to get in better shape.' And 43-year-old Tahlia, a straight woman, says she feels skinny and blonde is straight men's preference on dating apps.

When you ask people on dating apps how they feel about their bodies, this appearance pressure is at the forefront of their minds. Swami says that dating, particularly for younger people, is 'heavily appearance potent'. 'The main reason for that is that we often make judgements about other people in the absence of full information about that person. So, a very simple example: the first time you saw my face, you would have made an implicit judgement about my appearance and what that means to you.'

The reason for that judgement is due to the lack of information we hold about people when we first encounter them, Swami explains. 'You've got very little information about what I'm like, what my personality is like, what my sense of humour is like.' On dating apps, that appearance potency is heightened, he says, because dating apps are 'forcing people to make decisions based on my appearance, primarily through photographs, sometimes through videos'.

The way that apps are constructed to centre around an individual's photographs of themselves means we regard physical appearance as the summation of a person's identity. Human beings are, of course, so much more than the way they look and our physical appearance is not representative of our interiority, our personality, our talents and qualities.

Because the dating app process is 'short-circuited to focus on appearance', a culture has emerged where we place importance on appearance above everything else. This leads us to feel we must present the best physical representation of ourselves.

'Studies also actually suggest that most people using dating apps tend to focus on appearance primarily before they focus on other things,' Swami adds. 'If you look at eye tracking studies, for example, they will show you that people tend to focus about 60 to 70 per cent of the time on the photographs that are placed on dating apps rather than the textual information. So we're biased in those senses.'

When it comes to moving into a real-life context and going on a date, the pressure doesn't ease off. 'During the dating face-to-face scenario, the first thing you see is a person's appearance and you make assumptions,' says Swami. 'On a first date, for example, you will make a judgement about "how closely does this person's appearance match what I think I thought of them prior to meeting?"' This phenomenon is something that is affecting us all now that we are increasingly meeting online before we meet in real life.

Men's Body Image

Viren Swami says that 'Although historically women have been under greater pressure to attain appearance ideals, and they've been punished for not doing so, increasingly, men are experiencing the same issues as well.' His research has found that several studies have shown that dating app use in particular has a more negative impact 'on men's body image compared to women. What the research doesn't tell us, is why. Maybe it's because it is one of the few areas where men are being judged primarily for their appearance?'

Among heterosexual men, the body image pressures from dating apps feel all too real. For straight guys, insecurities largely centre around height, hair, weight and visible muscle definition. During my research for this book, I questioned 25 men about their bodies and their dating lives, and their responses took on a clear pattern:

'I feel I have to work out,' says Joe, a 44-year-old cis straight male.

'I should probably get in better physical shape,' says Dave, a 34-year-old straight man.

'Pictures are the primary decision-maker for people on dating apps which is my primary way of meeting people, so my lack of engagement there makes me want to start losing weight (not that I'm obese, but I'm not skinny either),' says Kai, a 26-year-old straight man.

'I wish I was more toned and muscular,' says Ade, a 30-year-old straight man.

'I am overweight and it feels as if there's a standard one needs to meet. Not necessarily from other app users themselves, but the sites themselves and their algorithms,' says Connor, a 33-year-old straight man.

'If people are using a few pictures to gauge whether or not they want to date me and using how hot I look when they first lay eyes on me on the date, I feel a lot of pressure to work out and have my body looking good and to have my hair look okay,' says Andy, a 29-year-old heterosexual man. 'I always feel more of an urge to get a tattoo (I still have none) when I'm on the apps because part of me thinks it'll help me attract the women I'm into (who usually have tattoos themselves),' he adds.

This has a real impact on their lives beyond dating and affects men of all sexual orientations. Muscle dysmorphia is on the rise for men overall.[14] Twenty-two per cent of men aged between 18 and 24 reported muscularity-orientated disordered eating, per a study published in 2019.[15] 'Over the past decades, the idealised male body image has got bigger and bulkier,' Dr Jason Nagata of the University of California, San Francisco, the lead researcher of the study, told *Guardian* journalist Sirin Kale. 'The drive for a bigger, more muscular body is becoming very prevalent.'

This pressure to be muscular is far from implicit on gay dating apps. Sean, a 30-year-old gay man, has experienced a huge amount of body shaming within the queer community. He says, 'I came out when I was about 23 and a half stone and I've since lost nearly nine stone,' he says. 'So I've seen things from a point where I was of a plus size body to being of an average shape body.' Sean talks about the way in which body types and certain aesthetics are organised into subcultures in the gay community. 'You have your daddies, your twinks, your jocks, your otters, your bears. There are all these different sub-divisions which men categorise themselves into,' says Sean. But, where do you belong if your body doesn't necessarily fit the definition of any of these subcultures? These categories are appearance based and centre on body shape, hairiness, muscularity, and whether a man is masculine or feminine presenting. 'And if you don't necessarily feel like you fit within one of those subcultures, it's very hard to navigate dating,' says Sean.

When people on the apps state they're looking for a twink – a young, thin man with little to no body hair – Sean doesn't feel he ticks every box. 'I have bleach blonde hair, I'm under 30, but I'm also very tall and I'm not your traditional skinny person. I lost a lot of weight, so I have chubby bits. They're not necessarily what you would deem twink-worthy so I don't class myself in that way,' he says. Sean also doesn't feel like he fits into the bear or otter labels either. 'In the past I've messaged guys on these apps and received responses back saying, 'sorry, I'm not into feminine guys' or 'sorry, I'm more into skinny guys or muscular guys' or whatever it may be,' he says. When Sean was plus-size, he found it very difficult to date. He didn't fit the bear or otter body types. 'It felt very hard to find a community within the LGBT community that actually valued my appearance and how I looked at the time.' Since losing nine stone, he's received much more attention from men.

On gay dating apps, it's not uncommon to see the words 'no fats, no femmes', in people's profiles. Research has shown that Grindr impacts users' body image in three specific ways: through sexual objectification, weight stigma and social comparison.[16] But Sean also sees bios which state things like 'please don't be lazy and actually go to the gym' or 'please be in good shape'. Sean says that reading this can make you feel bad if you're not muscular and makes him feel like he's lazy or 'some kind of slob' for not working out. The message he gets is: 'I am not good enough for these guy.'

Sean has had experiences where he's been talking to someone on an app and they've exchanged photos, but once they've met up in person, he's been rejected by them in the worst possible moment. 'They've seen me naked and they have literally said to my face, "Sorry, I'm not into you anymore. I don't actually fancy you. I'm not interested."' This has happened after speaking to someone for weeks, after they've seen multiple photos of him, including nudes. 'But when they see my body in real life, they leave,' he says.

Forty-eight hours after an encounter in which someone backed out of having sex with him after seeing him naked, Sean went out to a gay bar and overheard a group of people making fun of his stretch marks. 'That's something I can't change about myself. To hear not one but multiple people think it's acceptable to talk about my body like that can be really detrimental,' says Sean. 'Luckily, I'm quite a confident person and I have good body confidence which has taken years to develop because of situations like this within dating within the queer community. I didn't let it affect me too much, but it's definitely prevalent and it's quite toxic.' He adds: 'And it's not like these events are uncommon – these both occurred within the same weekend.'

When Sean takes too long to reply to a message, or if he rejects someone, he's found that his appearance is the first thing to come under fire. 'A guy messaged me once on Grindr, and he was like, 'how are you today, handsome? what are you up to?'' Sean was out shopping at the time, so was slow to respond. 'Because I took over an hour to reply, the next message I received from him was along the lines of "who the fuck do you think you are, you fat balding ginger cunt",' Sean recalls. 'It was amazing how quickly I went from being desired by this guy to when I didn't give him what he wanted, he wanted to make me feel insecure and inferior about my body and my looks.'

It strikes me then just how much the toxic masculinity that many women experience when dating straight men can be re-created in the queer community, and how it isn't purely about orientation – a lot of these biases carry across sexual orientations. Historically, research into eating disorders has focused on young, white, thin women,[17] but recent research shows that gay men experience the highest levels of eating disorder symptoms out of a study sample of straight, gay and bisexual men.[18] Gay and bisexual men are more likely to engage in unhealthy weight control behaviours (including purging, fasting, and the misuse of laxatives and diet pills) than straight men, per two studies.[19,20] 'Gay men experience a pressure to be simultaneously lean (devoid of fat) and muscular,' reads one research paper into disordered eating and gay men.[21]

Six-packs, toned abs, and a muscular physique seem to be the gold standard on gay dating apps. But why exactly does muscularity matter so much to gay men?

'Historically gay men, for example, in the '60s were often stereotyped as being femme. And one of the ways to counteract that within the gay community was to straight act, to go to the gym, to bulk up, to become more muscular, and that became much more important during the AIDS pandemic when demonstrating your non-frailty became so important,' says Swami.

'So one of the reasons why gay men often focus on muscularity is a form of "protest muscularity" – protesting against the kind of stereotypical depictions of gay men as femme.[22] He also described how this form of protest muscularity against the effeminate stereotype has become so entrenched in gay culture that it's become part of how gay men relate to each other. He says, 'That's why you see much more explicit forms of discrimination on gay dating apps,' Swami continues. 'No Asians,' has also become a popular 'preference' stated on Grindr. Swami says this is because 'being Asian is often coded language for being femme'.

The context of these pressures is important in helping you separate the hurtful comments of others from your sense of self. We can't control other people's actions, but we can remind ourselves that not everyone has done the inner work to disentangle themselves from harmful ideas about bodies. Dating apps also have a responsibility to ramp up their protections to ensure fatphobic or body negative language is filtered and blocked so that it never reaches people's inboxes.

'I'm going to get rejected because of my appearance'

'Part of any motivation for me to lose weight is because I perceive that as an obstacle for my dating,' says Rohan, a 28-year-old gay man. Rohan's not alone – throughout my interviews with people of all genders, I've encountered a repeated pattern of people feeling their body size is standing in their way of finding love. There's a pressure to attain a certain physique or aesthetic that our culture deems most 'dateable'.

Appearance rejection sensitivity (ARS) is a term describing a tendency to expect to be rejected because of one's physical appearance. A person with appearance rejection sensitivity will overreact to perceived rejection and consider rejection an inevitability due to their concerns over their own appearance.[23]

The idea that rejection is almost certainly going to happen

because of a perceived shortcoming in our looks isn't exactly helpful when you're trying to put yourself out there. But, is this idea grounded in reality? Is it rational? Or, is it all in our head?

As Swami tells me, this appearance-based rejection sensitivity is essentially a cognitive bias. A cognitive bias is a thought process that doesn't match up with 'the tenets of logic, probability reasoning, and plausibility'.[24] That's not to say that no one in the history of dating has ever been rejected because of the way they look – that's obviously not the case (sorry!) – 'It's that the importance of appearance is often overblown,' Swami explains. 'If you actually look at studies of people who have gone online dating, what you typically find is that their own ratings of the importance of appearance of a partner are greater prior to the date compared to after.' Essentially, the fact that appearance is important prior to the date makes people think it is going to be important forever, but the data shows that once people are on the date, it actually has less of an impact on the date itself than you might think.

The problem is that we don't get that feedback in real life. 'We don't get told, "I don't like you because of your personality," or "I don't like you because I don't think we gelled," and so people come away thinking, well if my appearance was the most important thing going into the date then it must have been the most important reason why I was rejected as well.' Charles T. Hill, PhD, a professor of psychology at Whittier College, echoes this, saying that his research also shows that 'Physical attractiveness is not as important as people think . . . It plays a role in initial meeting, but so does intelligence and especially personality.'[25]

Wouldn't it be nice if we could just tell our brains to stop? It's not difficult to see that our own thoughts about our bodies don't appear out of thin air. These thoughts and pressures derive from the societal ideals that continue to evolve around us. What we're witnessing are the real-world, emotional and psychological consequences of existing in a profoundly fatphobic, racist society. Not only that, many of these issues are also born out of internalised homophobia – a direct consequence of overt homophobia – as well as capitalism and diet culture. So what can we do?

'Modern society doesn't really equip us with the skills to understand our inner selves. It instead equips us with the skills of consumerism,' writes Jessica Defino in her advice column in the *Guardian* to a woman who no longer feels attractive after having a baby and is mourning her 'old, pretty self'.[26] We constantly receive messages that conflate the self with the body. As Defino writes, 'People say you "let yourself go" when you gain weight or go grey.' So, we're told, we must constantly bend and break to ensure our self is preserved, that we're not losing sight of ourselves. Defino explains the need to do 'the hard work of separating who you are from what you look like'. She did that by questioning what she felt beauty provided for her and to incorporate that into her life instead. She realised that she had believed that physical beauty was a form of expression: 'I've since realized there are many ways to express my thoughts and feelings that don't involve manipulating my face or body (or cost money, for that matter),' says Defino. 'I sing, I dance, I paint, I write, I have two-hour phone conversations with my sister while making soup.'

I was so struck by Defino's words. I think they hold the key to helping us move beyond our rejection sensitivity. Ask yourself the question: 'What does expression look like for me?' For me, it's writing, gardening, decorating, and soon – once I get round to getting started – watercolour painting. For my mother, it's crafting, sewing, quilting, watercolour painting and gardening. Even if you've told yourself you're 'not creative' or 'not artistic', find a creative outlet or a means of expressing yourself. For you, that could mean trying a pottery class, tending to houseplants, creating a garden and growing things from seed, learning to draw, learning to sew or knit. You could try learning a new language. It could also mean finding a community that shares your love for something – gaming, books, films, poetry, writing, quizzes. Find something you love and lean into it.

And, if you can bear it, identify and challenge your cognitive distortions about yourself, and others. Our preferences in the realm of love and sex are inextricably linked to the oppressive forces at play in society. So, if you belong to a marginalised group and feel that this is impacting your romantic or sexual experiences, let me say it: It's not just in your head. There are dynamics and situations you face that those who fit the so-called norm do not. But your person is – or people are – out there. And if you've ever found yourself approaching a prospective partner's difference through a negative lens, let me say this: You are missing out. Love and care take many forms, and one of the joys of life is you never know who you could fall for, if you forsake the deep programming and shame that is often instilled in us from early on. Thankfully, it's never too late to do the work – the delight and connection you might find on the other side of bias is yours, if you can earn it.

6

DTR (Defining the Relationship)

Trapped in a talking stage? Perhaps you've had a series of casual flings that have fizzled into nothingness, ghosted and gone forever, just like that. Maybe you've not had a long-term relationship in years, but you'd need several hands to count the number of situationships you've had. If so, you're not alone.

Dr Jenny van Hooff, a sociologist at Manchester Metropolitan University, has found in her research that young daters are finding it difficult to progress relationships beyond casual dating or the 'talking stage' despite wanting more serious relationships. So, what's causing the failure to launch? Van Hooff identified an emotional roadblock – the 'emotional stalemate' – among Gen Z daters in particular for a research paper co-authored with fellow researcher Alicia Denby. They spoke to UK-based heterosexual dating app users aged between 18 and 25, who 'were very liberalised when it comes to sex'. 'They were very open sexually, but emotionally, emotions are shameful, and showing any kind of vulnerability means you're the weaker party in a relationship,' says van Hooff. 'We called the paper 'An Emotional Stalemate' because relationships just weren't progressing because nobody was able to make that jump. It was just easier to pop back on the app and look for someone else rather than actually put the work in.' However, anecdotally, this phenomenon seems to apply to millennials too.

'Emotional attachment is rarely articulated, and is seen as a sign of weakness in the early stages of a relationship,' write Denby and van Hooff in the paper. 'For our participants, emotions become bargaining chips, with the "winner" being the party with the least to lose, the least invested and the least emotionally attached.'[1]

The findings demonstrated a gendered difference in power in intimate relationships. 'The trust is completely gone and you can't develop intimacy unless you have some kind of idea of trust.' Whereas 'women were scared of rejection or just being ghosted or hurt, or lied to. So you've got this arena where nobody's trusting each other. Nobody's making themselves vulnerable because the stakes are so high and it's just easier to "see" people [casually],' van Hooff explains. She adds that she doesn't know how anyone makes the leap from chatting, casual dating, or hooking up into a serious relationship – the jump seems huge.

The question of how we clear that hurdle is something I've often wondered myself, particularly when, in my own love life, I feel unable to cross that line. Could it be our reticence to admit we care about someone? The discomfort of the intense vulnerability that comes with laying your cards on the table? Or perhaps the pressure that comes with *deciding* on a person, taking one path, and taking a chance to see where it leads?

Van Hoof's study found that most connections remained suspended in what they identified as the 'failed talking stage'. The data is clear that this is the point where most relationships end before they begin. Hinge's survey of 15,000 of its users worldwide revealed that 56 per cent of Gen Z daters feel that worrying about rejection has made them hold back from pursuing a relationship with someone. The survey also found that 57 per cent of Gen Z Hinge daters have decided against telling someone how they feel because they feared it'd put them off.[2]

To me, it seems the hurdle that's most difficult to clear is the one that separates talking from a more established relationship. Taking that step requires uncomfortable conversations where we feel exposed, vulnerable, we wear our heart on our sleeve knowing full well someone could break it. All too often, it feels we're being told that vulnerability is weakness, we can't 'give away our power', we don't want to seem desperate or uncool. What would happen if we started regarding vulnerability as one of the biggest signs of strength? As a way of standing in your own power? What could be braver than asking for what you want and daring to lose it all?

Dr Rachel Katz, a digital media sociologist with a research specialty in dating apps at the University of Salford says dating has always been difficult, but things have become all the more challenging in recent years. 'I do think things are harder now than they used to be,' says Katz, 'because historically, our social roles in courtship were very defined. In the 1960s, for example, it was clear when you were "going steady" with somebody based on certain courtship rituals, like you would take them out on a date and then you would officially ask them to be your girlfriend and things like that.' Another example she shared were Victorian calling cards – only a few generations ago you couldn't even be introduced to somebody without there being an external social structure codifying how it happened. These days, the absence of clearly defined rules has created a free-for-all.

The strict rules of engagement that previously reigned

supreme in the realm of courtship and dating are now entirely fluid. 'People are having to figure out for themselves, in real life and online, where they stand with another person in terms of what sociologists would call the "relational trajectory" or the "interactional trajectory",' explains Katz. This leaves things really open ended. When we match with someone, we don't know if the connection we've made is going to be a one-night stand, a relationship, or even a friends-with-benefits arrangement or hookup partnership.

Then there's the added complication of people's desires not always being entirely set in stone. 'Sometimes people want different things at different moments,' says Katz. 'So it's not that easy to just say to every single person you want a particular thing. I think people struggle to communicate that. In my previous research on Tinder users, people would say they were on there looking for a relationship overall. But when I asked them, "Did you express this on your profile?" most of them said, "Oh, no, definitely not." Because they were concerned about how they would come off to the other person – maybe they'd be too eager. But also it was a way to protect themselves in case the other person was not a good fit for them. They could have a way out of that relationship or an opportunity to see where things went.'

In my interviews with frustrated daters, this disconnect shone through. There's an idea that communicating what you want – whether that's more broadly in your dating goals, or in relation to a specific person – is cringe and a bit uncool. This needs to change, because, as my granny used to say, 'Don't ask, don't get.' People aren't mind readers and we can't expect them to know what we want if we don't tell them. I also think we need to assume good intentions – the vast majority of people aren't monsters. If you tell someone you like them, they won't laugh in your face or sneer with derision. Chances are, even if they don't feel the same, they'll respond kindly, they may be flattered, and they'll understand the courage it took to say how you feel.

Katz's current research looks into individuals' reasons for being on dating apps and has found that people's motivations shift from moment to moment. Even when someone downloaded the app because they ultimately want to find a relationship, they'll have moments when they might be looking for something else. For example, while travelling they might be looking for a recommendation from a local or a fun date or hookup while they're on holiday.

Another example of this happened during the Covid-19 lockdowns, when people would use the apps to combat loneliness or chat even though they couldn't meet in real life. The COVID Sex Lives Report – a collaboration between the University of Salford, Newcastle University, King's College London and Birmingham City University – shows some fascinating insights into the sex lives of men who have sex with men (MSM) in the UK. Seventy-nine per cent of respondents used dating or hookup apps during the pandemic, but, interestingly, not all contacts made on these apps turned into sexual interactions. The report found that people also used these apps for 'nonsexual connections and to reduce loneliness and isolation'.[3]

So, overcoming the talking stage means that not only will we have to be vulnerable with each other about expressing what we want from our dating lives, it also means that we'll have to be honest with ourselves about why we're using the apps to begin with. Are we keeping someone in a holding pattern because we're not sure what we want from them? Ask yourself if that's fair on them. Are you stuck in the talking stage because neither of you is saying how you feel? Perhaps it's time to break the silence. Are you in a talking stage because you have mismatched expectations about what you want from this connection? Talk about it.

Being honest, vulnerable and authentic – and looking for those traits in our matches – is key.

'I'm looking for someone authentic'

Tinder's 2023 'Future of Dating' report hailed 'authenticity' as top of the list when it comes to what Gen Z singles are looking for.[4] Research by Plenty of Fish found that 84 per cent of single people would rather someone present an accurate version of their identity rather than 'an exaggerated positive version of themselves'.[5] These data suggest that singles are not interested in seeing an idealised depiction of potential dating partners through edited photos and unrealistic positive self-descriptions. Clinical psychologist Dr Cortney S. Warren commented on the Plenty of Fish findings, saying, 'If the goal is to find a long-lasting relationship, starting with a more realistic, authentic picture of who each person is will not only be refreshing but also likely lead to more meaningful connections.'[6]

As appealing as that sounds, I cannot help but be cynical here: is true authenticity even possible on the internet? Let's not forget when BeReal first took off, the social media app promised to be a rare destination for genuineness online. But it quickly cemented the reality that authenticity on social media doesn't exist.[7] Even in moments when we want to faithfully represent our realest selves, we rarely, if ever, show the warts-n-all truth.

Dating apps are urging us to 'be yourself!' and to be authentic. But what does that really mean? And what does authenticity even look like? Katz says: 'Sometimes people will say, I want to look authentic in my Tinder profile. So they'll have these staged photos that look authentic, which some might say is not so authentic.'

How do you curate your profile in such a way that appears effortlessly authentic while also showing the best version of yourself to maximise your chances of finding love with someone who's right for you? When you think about it, it's a lot of pressure.

'I truly believe that it's impossible,' says Melissa A. Fabello, PhD, a sex and relationships educator. 'And it's not because we are inauthentic or disingenuous people.' Fabello likens it to when a person is sitting talking and someone takes out their camera and starts filming them. 'You change. There's a shift,' she says. 'I see it in my five-year-old daughter. If I take out a phone, she'll change her voice. I don't call her out on it because I'm just trying to let her figure this out for herself, but she makes her voice higher, she changes her posture.' This phenomenon is called the 'audience effect' – when a person's behaviour alters because they feel that someone's watching them.[8]

Authenticity is a complicated thing when we try to practise it in real life. Katz explains that from a sociological perspective, humans are always performing in a certain way based on whatever social situation we happen to be in. So that means there's not really a 'constant authentic self' that you can communicate via the confines of your dating app profile.

It's not inauthentic to want to put your best foot forward on a dating app profile. Just because people say they're looking for authenticity doesn't mean you have to show what you look like first thing in the morning before you've washed your face. We have private and public selves and, as Katz tells me, just because those two facets are different doesn't mean they're any less authentic.

'People in my dating app profile picture research, they would say, "Oh, I don't like selfies," for example,' says Katz. 'And that was a sign that somebody was too focused on themselves or it was a negative cue that they could put on their profile. Having someone else take your photo indicated you had friends.'

But, what if you aren't someone whose life gets documented by others? Here, the 'Instagram boyfriend' memo springs to mind. For me, authenticity looks like this: showing my personality and sense of humour through the messages I send to matches. In those early messages, I talk to matches like I would a friend (albeit a friend I think is kinda hot). I try not to over-think my photos – I want to look like a well-rounded individual, someone with friends, but I also want to look nice! It's not vain to post hot pics of yourself. Personally, I am pro-selfie and think it's time to stop judging people who take photos of themselves. At the end of the day, life is short, and if we constantly let other people's opinions of us dictate what we do, then we'd hold ourselves back. I don't want to look back in 40 years and wish I had more photos of my life.

Dr Stefanie Duguay, associate professor in Communication Studies at Concordia University, has researched the concept of authenticity in relation to Tinder use and found that it boils down to users trying to find ways to both express who they are and demonstrate a certain degree of trustworthiness.[9] She thinks that the latter is actually more important where your dating app is concerned. She says that rather than worry about whether the photos in your profile look artfully unstaged enough, 'what I want to know is: are you safe to meet up with and are you telling me things that I can see consistently in your behaviour and in your actions?' The pressure to be authentic leads us into shaky territory. And if we start to perform our idea of what authenticity is like, we're in danger of shaping ourselves into more desirable versions of ourselves for the sake of attracting others.

So, when it comes to authenticity, look for it in people's words. Does the conversation feel free-flowing, relaxed, and easy? Does it feel like talking to a friend you happen to fancy?

Is what they're saying matching up with their actions and how they're portraying themselves? Likewise, when it comes to putting your best foot forward online, don't feel like you need to fit yourself into a box, or to hide parts of yourselves to be more palatable or desirable to others. Speak to people as if you're already friends and use your profile to show off your personality in all its glory – after all, having a great dating life isn't about amassing as many matches as possible, it's about clicking with the people that will really like you for who you are.

Vulnerability in an Age of Disconnection

When I asked single people to describe the emotional challenges they face while dating, vulnerability kept cropping up in their responses.

Caleb, a 41-year-old straight man, struggles with self-doubt and the 'vulnerable loneliness of trying to feel secure in my singleness while being roundly rejected'. He doesn't have high hopes to begin with when it comes to dating but ends up getting even more dissuaded by the experience. He has 'first dates that are nice', but ultimately, his matches don't feel the spark.

Hallie, a 33-year-old straight woman describes dating as 'an emotional rollercoaster' which 'requires you to be vulnerable and open while simultaneously protecting yourself from getting hurt. I've also found the apps to be full of people who are emotionally unavailable despite saying that they would like to meet someone, it's also time consuming, requires drinking more alcohol than I would generally like to, and it costs money,' says Hallie.

Ruby, a 26-year-old straight woman, says her challenge is 'knowing to maintain the balance of being open and vulnerable while also having a bit of a guard up to protect yourself'. 'A lot of my mental health is centred around how much I internalise things and find it difficult to talk openly about my emotions.' Ruby adds, 'I have my guard up so much that often dating feels so surface level and not for any other reason than I find it difficult to be open even with friends, let alone with a romantic partner. Dating is harder because you might be seeing someone new every couple of weeks or months, it's hard to keep being vulnerable with new people.'

Much like authenticity, vulnerability has become a buzzword that's often thrown around when we talk about the prerequisite ingredients needed when finding love. But, what does vulnerability actually mean? Brené Brown defines vulnerability as 'uncertainty, risk, and emotional exposure'. 'But vulnerability is not weakness; it's our most accurate measure of courage. When the barrier is our belief about vulnerability, the question becomes: "Are we willing to show up and be seen when we can't control the outcome?"' [10]

In a romantic context, vulnerability means accepting and acknowledging your emotions, particularly those which cause pain or discomfort, such as shame, anger, anxiety, loneliness.

Franki Cookney, a sex and relationships journalist, says that vulnerability, like authenticity, has been a real buzzword for quite a long time now. She says, 'Something that I realised that I need to watch out for in myself is trying to embrace vulnerability, trying to lean into vulnerability, but slightly missing the mark and ending up kind of performing vulnerability, as opposed to actually being vulnerable.' She walked me through an example: 'Let's say I just want to ask you out for a drink. The truly vulnerable thing to do would be to be like, "Hey, Rachel, do you fancy getting a drink sometime?" Because that way, I've just put it out there and I don't know what you're going to say back and I'm preparing myself to deal with whatever the response is. But if I start going, "Oh, gosh, this is so awkward, but like, I don't know if you want to go for a drink, but probably not and like, it's totally cool if not," then I'm coming across as if I'm vulnerable, but actually what I'm doing is putting the onus on you to make me feel okay about it,' she says. In her scenario, caveating the question with insecurity isn't actually vulnerability. She calls it self-protection and says that realistically, it's saying, 'I need you to be really, really kind to me about this because I'm scared.' It's not that letting people know how you're feeling in these moments is a bad thing, but genuinely embracing vulnerability means something a little different. She adds, 'Embracing vulnerability is being like, I'm gonna ask Rachel out for a drink and she might say no, that's it, and I accept that. And I am emotionally prepared to deal with that eventuality.' In order to truly be vulnerable, we need to express ourselves confidently without shying away from the risk that we might face rejection.

The Problem with Viral Dating App Screenshots

Screenshots of dating app conversations have also entered our social media feeds over recent years. Originally, these were posted to highlight the more egregious examples of dating app opening lines or troubling messages. But we've reached a saturation point now, with people posting entirely innocuous screenshots that are patently just for clout.

This habit, while it may seem light-hearted and harmless, erodes people's trust in others on dating apps. Can you truly let your guard down if you're not sure that your conversation will remain private? Sociologist Dr Jenny van Hooff has encountered this topic in her research into heterosexual young men and women. 'Men were really scared of rejection or humiliation and there was a fear about having your DMs posted on social media,' says van Hooff. 'I think I really liked that trend at first, you know, when it was She Rates Dogs and things like that, but I think some of it has got a little bit almost like they are looking for content, and they're shaming people.' The downside of these trends is that it has made it harder for people to trust each other on dating apps and social media. The women she interviewed in the research were also scared of rejection or being hurt or lied to, and seeing this content all day made that worse. 'So, you've got this kind of arena where nobody's trusting each other. Nobody's making themselves vulnerable because the stakes are so high,' she says.

So, what does vulnerability look like when put into practice? Vulnerability can look like this: Telling someone on a first date that you're nervous; Asking for clarity when you're feeling confused by someone's behaviour; Expressing what you need from someone or a situation. It may feel unnatural, at odds with dating advice that preaches being the cool girl/boy, advises against oversharing, or coming on too strong, but it really does help. I have always battled the inner voice that told me not to 'give my power away' by telling someone how I felt about them, by opening up about my emotions and what I need, but in overriding these messages, I have found strength in vulnerability. Putting up a front is a form of self-abandonment. There is power in asking for what we really need, and freedom in finally getting it.

7

It's Raining Men!

'God, it's a lot of pressure on a guy.' This is a comment sex educator Dr Caroline West often says in consent workshops at universities in Ireland. When she says these words, she sees relief appearing on men's faces in the audience. The rules of dating are by and large informed by the wider rules of gender, and even straight men experience negative impacts from rigid gender norms. It's important to remember that everyone – people of all genders – suffers under the patriarchy and our dating culture won't improve until we dismantle systems of oppression.

After acknowledging the pressure straight men face, she continues. ' "You have to know everything about sex. You've got to initiate it. You've got to check in with them. You've got to make sure it's all good or else they'll go off and tell your friends that you're crap in bed, or that you haven't got this giant 15-inch penis." I can literally see relief going across their faces like they've never heard that before: That they don't have to know everything,' says West. 'It shows me that they're not hearing this message a lot, that they don't have to be this alpha male type thing.'

The very same gender roles that position women as the gatekeepers of sex place men as the initiators of sex, the ones in the driving seat, the ones who do the 'asking out', the providers. They must be masculine, strong, powerful, competitive and emotionless. In the realm of dating, heterosexual scripts are still at play, so they face additional pressure to risk rejection more often without being emotionally vulnerable about how hard it is to do that. Particularly with the rise of 'high-value dating' and hypergamy in our dating discourse, they also feel that they have to be wealthy and successful men in order to find love.

George, a 32-year-old straight guy, says he feels pressure to subtly demonstrate signs of being 'high value' through his photo choices on his dating app profile. 'You almost have to tailor your profile pictures to display forms of success and wealth to interest women, to be honest,' he says.

'If you're a guy, there's an expectation that you'd be in good shape, like a gym bod.' There's also a pressure to have a six pack, which George says 'is an extremely difficult thing to achieve unless you're going to the gym every day and focusing on that alone'. On dates, George felt he needed to present himself as a confident, extroverted person, but felt out of his comfort zone because, deep down, he's an introvert. 'That's not who I am,' he says.

In order to be deemed attractive, George feels the need to present himself as 'someone who invests a lot of time and effort in their appearance and body, someone who spends a lot of time at work to be successful, someone who spends a lot of time going out and being fun, someone who spends a lot of time travelling the world to get new experiences.' But achieving that 'total package' feels unattainable, he says. He feels that dating is akin to playing Top Trumps. 'What's your wealth score out of 100? What's your image score of 100? What's your outgoing score?'

Great Heights

Lewis, 37, tells me women would ask him his height as their opening line to him and then unmatch when he revealed he's 5'10". 'I felt that was confirmation that we weren't right,' he says. 'If they'd dismiss everything I am simply because of something I have no influence over.' Lewis told me he felt 'dismissed, ruled out, disbarred', because of his height.

If you swipe through profiles of men who date women, you'll notice men listing their heights in their bio 'because it seems to be important'. Tinder, Bumble and Hinge users can add their height to their profiles so it shows up alongside other essential info like age, location, and whether or not they have children. Six feet appears to be the sweet spot in height preference, though it can vary from person to person. George, 33 and straight, says: 'I have actually had people say to me on dates, "I don't date anyone less than six foot." '

David, 39, is 5'8" – 'a very average height', he feels, and has had a 'mixed' bag of dating experiences. He's dated women who were taller than him and it's been fine, he says, but he's also had some negative interactions because of his height. 'Secure as I am (or think I am) it has felt weird at times,' he says.

'Normally it's early where you'll match with someone and you'll get a message saying, "I just realised how tall you are, sorry," or you'll be messaging for a while and they'll ask about height when a meet-up is suggested and they'll say it's an issue for them,' he says. 'I've only ever had one encounter when someone was unnecessarily rude over messages about it but most of the time people have been really polite and lovely.'

He's also brought it up a few times ahead of an imminent date, just to make sure the person is aware and still happy to meet up. 'I've also met someone where we didn't discuss height and it turned out they were much taller than I am, and showed up in heels, but we had quite a nice date in the end but the height thing was why she didn't want to meet again,' he adds.

Being able to list your height on the app is a positive thing, in David's mind. 'The ability to add all these details about yourself, and then to filter or be filtered out is ultimately a good thing,' he says. 'I think it's one of the good things about how dating apps have evolved . . . Though part of me thinks these things shouldn't matter, though rightly or wrongly they do for lots of people. On the flip side, it's one of the most toxic things about online dating, as it just fuels the desire to find perfection.'

David has been disappointed before, particularly when he's really liked someone, and his height has been an issue for them. For him, it's been upsetting, just as any other form of rejection would be. 'Rejection does hit me hard (good investment in several years of therapy has helped there) but it's never been a source of real insecurity for me,' he adds.

'If I'm honest, you'd be hard pushed to find a man who hasn't rejected a woman because of something physical they haven't liked,' says David. 'I know I have, and I don't think it's a bad thing, so long as you do it respectfully and politely but also so long as you are comfortable being judged by the same standards that you judge others.'

David doesn't feel men are unfairly judged for their height, however. 'I'm willing to bet money that a lot of men who scream about height being an unfair standard, and something they cannot control, are the same men who comment on women's weight or breast size or complexion or whatever the thing might be they don't like.'

So, why is height so revered on the apps? Research by the University of Edinburgh found that our genes play a considerable role in making us seek out partners of a similar height to us. Benjamin G. Voyer – a psychology and behavioural science professor at London School of Economics – says, 'Height is a sign of health, and we are looking for health characteristics when we look for potential romantic partners.'[1] Despite its importance on dating apps, height is an under-researched aspect of men's body dissatisfaction. While there are evolutionary elements to seeking tall partners, we must acknowledge the societal impact in positioning height as a masculine ideal. Research by the University of St Andrews found that men who are taller are perceived as more masculine.[2]

The importance placed on height in the dating realm has also prompted a rise in surgical interventions to increase height. Hundreds of people each year undergo leg-lengthening surgery to add a few inches to their height. This highly painful procedure, which carries enormous risks, involves having a hole drilled into your leg bones, which are then broken before a metal rod is surgically fitted inside. That rod is slowly lengthened by 1mm per day until the patient reaches the desired height.[3]

Eimear Draper, known as The Straight Talking Dating Coach, says height is something that comes up a lot with her clients. 'As both a dating coach and someone married to a 5'7" man I met on Tinder, I can confirm there is definitely heightism in dating,' says Draper. 'It's something I talk to clients about a lot, often women saying they want a man bigger or taller than them, which comes back to their own body insecurities.' 'Many guys lie about their height on dating apps, purely to get past the first hurdle of the filters,' she adds. Research by OkCupid also found that 'almost universally guys like to add a couple inches to their height'.[4] The same research also found that women six feet or taller receive fewer messages than those who are under six feet.

These insecurities don't appear out of nowhere – within straight dating, there is a stereotype that dictates women should be physically smaller than their male partners.

In Draper's own experience, in those early stages of dating her now-husband, she had two moments when his height seemed like a big deal. But when she took a closer look at what was going on in those two moments, she realised her issue with his height revealed more about how she felt about her body.

Ahead of their fourth date, she was planning her outfit to go to a jazz club. It was the first time they'd got 'proper dressed up' for a date together. 'I always wear skyscraper heels. I have a huge collection of shoes,' says Draper. 'And I was like, do I wear heels or not wear heels? Because I'm going to be taller than him if I wear the heels. But if I don't wear heels, I look fatter.

'I said oh fuck it, I'll wear the heels because I look better. He literally didn't give a shit, he didn't care. I'm not sure he even noticed the heels. I was sitting down for most of the night because we were in a jazz club so it literally didn't matter, but it gave me the confidence that I usually get from wearing heels when I walked into the bar.'

About six months into the relationship, they went to a wedding together for the first time.

'At Irish weddings, you've got the handbags, the shoes, the hat, they all have to match. We go all out. And again I was like, what am I going to do? I always wear big heels, I always wear a big hat. Do I not wear those because then I'll look a lot bigger than him.'

Again, Draper's partner told her he didn't care. 'That was a real turning point for me. I realised: it's you. It's your insecurities, feeling fat, people thinking that you're going to look bigger than the guy you're with. That's your problem. It's not his height.'

Lad Culture

Gender roles start from a very young age. Children begin understanding gender roles at two or three years old.[5] In adolescence, boys now face a unique set of pressures from their peers, according to researchers specialising in masculinity. Boys and young men in group chats with their male friends feel pressured to be seen to be going out with girls and having sex, and feel judged if they aren't doing so. Dr Craig Haslop, a senior lecturer at the University of Liverpool, conducted research into young people's experiences of social media spaces and the various ways in which masculinity manifests in those spaces. In focus groups with young men aged between 18 and 25, Haslop and researchers found that men would talk about their sexual exploits quite a lot in their WhatsApp group chats with their friends.

In these group chats, they found that people would have conversations that might not be acceptable in other forums. 'The focus group sessions with the young men revealed what kinds of conversations they'd have with their male friends in group chats – specifically pertaining to the women they knew. They talked about rating women's bodies, so that happened quite a lot. They talked about how they shared lots of images that they shouldn't have been sharing of girls they'd met when they were younger. That was something that seemed to happen a lot more at school.' Haslop caveats that there may have been some 'management' of the truth, and that the veracity of whether they no longer share intimate images in the group chats is unknown.

It's worth noting that the non-consensual sharing of a person's nudes or partial nudes in group chats with friends is a crime. The distribution of intimate images of adults without consent is illegal in England and Wales under the Criminal Justice and Courts Act 2015.[6] Changes made to this in 2023 mean that survivors no longer have to prove that perpetrators intended to cause distress.[7] Distributing intimate images of someone who's under 18 is illegal under Protection of Children Act 1978 and the Sexual Offences Act 2003.[8]

In these conversations with the young men, Haslop noticed that there was a clear disconnect between not wanting to be misogynistic or 'that guy' and their actual behaviour in group chats with their mates. The men would tell the researchers, 'We're mindful, we don't want to be misogynistic.' They repeatedly made claims that 'they were really mindful of it, that they wanted to do their best, they understood that this was an area where there's been a lot of discussion and where it's important for them to try to change as men.' However, Haslop says, 'But then when they talked about what's going on in the groups, there was a mismatch. Some guys were like, "We're aware of the fact that some of these things weren't appropriate."'

The young men would talk about being in group chats with male friends who they knew from work or school but they didn't see particularly often. They would witness these friends rating women's bodies in the group chats, but wouldn't say anything because 'they didn't want to rock the boat' and they wanted to fit in.

The young men would also discuss laddish behaviour on nights out, with one group chat discussing a 'shag a heifer' challenge – a term referring to laddish or hypermasculine men who deliberately target fat women with the aim of having sex with them as a dare. This humiliating violation has been termed 'hogging' or 'pull a pig' and academics view it as symptomatic of societal misogyny and fatphobia.[9]

'Men are navigating quite a complicated set of pressures and expectations now post #MeToo,' says Haslop. 'There is a more general understanding of how the symptoms of misogyny are quite embedded in culture and concerns about it, and not wanting to be seen to be "that guy". But at the same time, there are what we would call homosocial or friend group pressures, male friend group pressures, which are still about proving heterosexual masculinity.'

There's a clear discrepancy in young men's behaviour. On the one hand, they see misogyny as inherently bad and that men should treat women with respect. On the other hand, they feel they must perform a certain type of masculinity in front of their male friends to prove that they're a 'lad', that they are romantically and sexually successful. But in demonstrating their own masculinity, they engage in behaviour that is misogynistic and, at times, illegal.

So, how do you address these behaviours and tackle the mismatch in young men's deeds and words? Haslop and Dr Fiona O'Rourke launched the #Men4change toolkit to critically examine gendered norms and tackle and transform harmful behaviour.[10] The kit is aimed at youth leaders and activists and provides a structured framework for workshops with young men, where they tackle and address questions such as: 'Sexist banter – where do you draw the line?' 'What kind of man do you want to be?' 'What does the word "gender" mean to you? What words come to mind?'

The toolkit, which can be downloaded free of charge online, encourages young men to examine the gender stereotypes at play in society. The workshop leader asks: 'Do these gender stereotypes position one gendered group as more dominant than the other?' and 'What effect do you think these gendered stereotypes have on people who are subjected to them?'

Participants will also be asked what they feel 'be a man' means? 'How are boys and men expected to behave when they're told to "be a man"?' reads the toolkit. The workshop facilitator then asks if the participants have ever been told to 'be a man', and whether they'd like to discuss their experiences. Then they are asked: 'Do you think these messages have had an impact on how you think you should behave as a man?'

They're then asked if men and boys should step outside of these expectations. And if they believe they should, what actions do they plan to take in order to move away from these expectations to 'develop and practise positive and inclusive forms of masculinity'?

Crucially, the toolkit addresses how men can confront their friends when their behaviour is misogynistic or abusive. They also provide scenarios where you can address a friend who appears to be radicalised by far-right and extreme misogynist 'influencers'.

One scenario provided in the toolkit reads as follows: 'A mate of yours tells you he's started to "like" and follow an online influencer who says women often say they don't want to have sex, when they do really. He's encouraging you to "like" and "follow" them too. What do you do?'

The toolkit says that being a good friend constitutes 'the willingness to call out a friend if their behaviour is inappropriate, risky or potentially dangerous, as long as it's safe to do so'. An example message to send a friend: 'Hey mate, about last night. I think you crossed the line.' Advice is provided for tackling rape jokes, sexist jokes and harmful banter. 'Ask questions that show you disapprove. "What do you mean by that?" or

"How was that funny? I don't really get it." "Doesn't it have to be funny to be a joke?" ' The advice also states that you should not laugh and that you can also directly express your disapproval through explicit comments: 'Hey, I don't think that's appropriate.'

More broadly, we should be thinking about the pressures and expectations men face as a consequence of patriarchy and the prescribed roles that exist under such a power structure. The tangible consequences of traditional masculinity ideology cannot be underestimated.

Seventy-four per cent of suicides in England and Wales were men in 2021.[11] Men aged 50 to 54 have the highest suicide rate.[12] Dr Natasha Bijlani, a consultant psychiatrist at Priory Hospital Roehampton, says that 'traditionally, men have been less likely to seek support for mental health issues. This is probably for a number of reasons including stigma and the traditional "strong male" stereotype still prevalent in our society – the idea that expressing emotion is a sign of weakness.'[13]

As long as the stereotype that men should be strong, emotionless, stoic and unfazed continues, the risk to men's mental health will carry on. The stakes for dismantling these roles could not be higher: it's quite literally a matter of life and death.

8

The Rules of Love

No sex on the first date (and second, if we're being honest). If they're not chasing you, then they're just not that into you. Don't double text (no, wait . . . DO double text). If you're straight, make sure the guy pays for dinner. Oh, and if he's paying for dinner, make sure he pays for your travel too. Don't mention your ex, don't overshare, don't DTR too soon. If he wanted to he would, and if he likes you, you'll know . . . and on and on it goes.

Are the rules we date by fit for purpose? Should we abolish all dating rules, or shift our expectations of romance to bring them into line with modern life?

On social media, rules are rife. TikTok is full of 'experts' claiming to teach you 'how to get into your feminine energy' – nurturing, intuitive, 'go with the flow', allowing yourself to be 'catered to' and 'taken care of' – and finding a man in his 'masculine energy', or vice-versa. Then there's the videos on how to snag a 'high-value man' or how to be a 'high-value woman' – wealthy, successful, attractive – essentially 'good on paper'. There are videos extolling the virtues of hypergamy – dating someone with more money and socioeconomic status than yourself – and you'll find videos telling you 'how to be toxic' when someone isn't treating you well, content on 'how to make a man obsessed with you', and even advice on what kind of eye contact to make in order to trick someone to fall in love with you. Then you've got the oh-so-glorious dating advice one-liners like 'if he wanted to, he would,' (more on that later!) 'there's no such thing as mixed signals,' 'if he likes you, you'll know, if he doesn't you'll be confused.' Generalisations that have the capacity to a) mislead you and b) upset you when your dating experiences aren't going well.

Playing by the (Dating) Rules

Picture this: Your phone flashes and you've got a text from the person you like. You turn your phone over. Must wait at least 15 minutes before replying, you tell yourself. Can't appear too keen. When it comes to the first date, you mentally prepare for the night ahead. Do not, under any circumstances, have sex with them. Hold out for as long as possible. After several dates, you start fretting. What's going on? What does he want from me? Are they looking for a relationship? You want to ask for clarity, but something internal tells you to hold fire. Don't have the DTR conversation yet. They'll think you're too much. If you're a woman or femme, chances are you'll have absorbed some of these 'dating rules' during your lifetime. But these dating rules aren't actually rules at all. They're coping strategies for living under systems of oppression.

A rules-based approach to dating can be traced to the hugely popular self-help literature that defined the 1990s and 2000s, including the likes of *Men Are from Mars, Women Are from Venus* (1992), *The Rules: Time-tested Secrets for Capturing the Heart of Mr. Right* (1995), and *He's Just Not That Into You* (2004). Society and dating have evolved dramatically since these books and their ilk were published 30 years ago, but in 2023, TikTok creators began posting videos of themselves reading extracts from these books and framing it as dating advice.[1]

Instead of dismantling patriarchy, society has instead developed survival mechanisms for women and marginalised genders. If we rebrand oppressive, dehumanising diktats as dating rules they sound a lot less depressing! One rule that still has its clutches in hetero dating culture is: No sex on the first date. The 'three-date rule' – no sex until the third date – emerged in the late 1980s or early '90s and was popularised by *Sex and the City*.[2] Much has changed societally, relationally, sexually, technologically, in the past 30-odd years, and yet this sex-negative rule lingers like a bad smell.

Beth Ashley, author of *Sluts*, says this rule comes from a combination of purity culture and patriarchy. 'In my book I say that patriarchy is a Kraken and that slut shaming and purity culture is one of its tentacles,' says Ashley. The no sex on the first date rule is a popular topic of conversation among Manosphere and alpha male influencers. 'There's this idea that's prevalent on TikTok and YouTube that if you have sex on the first date, if you're a woman and you're dating a man, you are introducing yourself as a "low-value woman" and marketing yourself as someone who is to be slept with, not loved.' If we follow this line of thinking, if a woman goes on to be dumped, ghosted, treated badly in some way, we excuse the man's bad behaviour and blame the woman for 'letting him' sleep with her.

Rape culture rhetoric also wields the stigma of 'first-date sex' in perpetuating the permissibility of sexual violence. Just like 'boys will be boys' and 'she was asking for it', 'you did sleep with him on the first date' is a stock phrase that places the blame of violence on women, rather than the perpetrators. 'We think it's self-preservation to say, "hey, don't do that," but it's similar to when we tell people to cover up. It's not actually helping anything. It doesn't protect anyone,' says Ashley.

Women are positioned as the gatekeepers to sex, and once

we unlock that gate, we give away the only power we ever had. Double standards prevail as straight men are expected to have more frequent sexual activity to prove their masculinity. One meta-analysis from 2020 suggests that these sexual double standards – particularly those pertaining to hetero casual sex – are still prevalent, but there's a glimmer of hope. The study also revealed that these double standards were less prevalent in countries with higher levels of gender equality.[3] Given the close connection these double standards share with inequality, it's clear that 'dating rules' aren't as harmless as they might sound, they're closely linked to patriarchy and other systems of oppression. Abandoning a rules-based dating model is necessary in creating a more level playing field.

Who Should Pay for the First Date?

Many dating 'rules' are actually heteronormative dating scripts.[4] Many of these dating scripts originated from a time when marriage was a critical economic transaction, especially for women who had fewer opportunities available to them than men. A prime example is the still-prevalent expectation that a man should pay for dinner on the first date with a woman.

The rise of 'all-expenses-paid' dates in 2023 brought the question of 'who should pay' to the fore once more. The discourse began when a clip from the 'Laid Bare' podcast, hosted by influencer Oloni, went viral on X, gaining 8.6 million views, and dividing opinions in the process.[5] During the clip, Oloni relayed a WhatsApp conversation between a female friend and a man she was going on a date with. 'Will you be picking me up or getting me an Uber?' Oloni's friend asked. The man replied: 'I'm not able to do any of those. Get a cab, train or bus for yourself. Will find my way there too.'[6] The replies to the clip make for an interesting read. 'Eh?! I'm a grown woman, I know how to get to places. Why would I ask to be picked up? I'm hyper independent so this feels uncomfortable for me,' wrote one commenter. Meanwhile, others felt that requesting transport to be paid and provided was entirely justified. One commenter wrote: 'She wasn't wrong. A real gentleman is happy 2 pay.'

Throughout my interviews for this book, cis heterosexual women told me they believed that men should be providers. That the man needs to love the woman more than she loves him. Similar sentiments are spread on TikTok and Instagram with dating coaches telling women that under no circumstances should they be paying for dinner on the first date, nor should she be 'settling' for a coffee date. The idea that men should pay for women's dinner on dates is born out of benevolent sexism, which stereotypes women as weak, fragile, and in need of male protection and provision,[7] but it has become adopted by women as a strategy for vetting men. The justification they often give for wanting the man to pay is that women, under patriarchy, are judged by their physical appearance, so it's only fair that men are, in turn, judged by their bank balances. According to a video by TikTokker @sistalkswithsahar: 'The only reason you're having a problem with it now is because we're doing to you what you did to women for ages – you valued us off our looks and our bodies and now we're valuing you off your ability to provide.'[8]

Take the dating doctrine of YouTuber SheraSeven, who encourages women over 25 to find older, wealthy men to date and to shun low-income men, whom she calls 'dusties', as an example. 'Stop hyping up these broke dudes that aren't doing anything for you,' Shera tells her followers. 'The more you hype them up, the more they're going to think it's okay to stay broke.'[9] Shera's videos have been reposted on TikTok (despite her not having an account on the app) and racked up over 20 billion views.[10] Shera advises women to not sleep with men before they have 'done anything for you' because this means you're 'giving it up free'. She informs her followers that men like toxic women and encourages women to play games and use reverse psychology to manipulate men into transactional relationships. 'I'm not bringing nothing to the table, baby,' Shera says in one video. ''Cause if I bring something to the table, you're gonna be mad 'cause it's gonna be another man, who's not gonna ask me to bring something to the table. He's gonna take care of the bill, them kids, and everybody else, and you if you look broke. That's how I roll.'[11]

This concept of levelling up your socioeconomic status through marriage is nothing new. 'Dating up' or 'marrying up', also known as hypergamy, is the act of marrying or partnering with someone who is from a higher social echelon or wealth bracket than their own. Some experts say the practice of hypergamy can be traced back to 3,000 years ago.[12] But of course we need to take that with a pinch of salt because historically choosing a partner that could guarantee financial stability could mean life or death in a time when women had limited economic agency (not to mention this choice was not made by the women alone – their families were usually quite involved). The topic of women's supposed hypergamy in modern times has attracted the attention of the Reddit Red Pill community – part of the Manosphere – they believe straight women's hypergamy is the root of men's loneliness. On TikTok, 'hypergamy' has 231 million views, while 'high-value dating' has 136.6 million views, and 'high-value woman' has 106 million.[13] 'Marry rich' might sound like the instructions handed to the heroine of a 19th-century novel, but in 2024 the words 'marry rich' have 115.9 million tagged videos.

It's concerning, but if we turn our attention to our economic conditions, we may gain an insight into the source of these trends. A report from 2023 found that house price affordability in the UK hasn't been this poor since 1876 – when Queen Victoria was on the throne and Benjamin Disraeli was Prime Minister.[14] As housing correspondent Vicky Spratt writes, 'On paper, in every way millennial and Gen Z women are the most socially and economically liberated in history,' but despite this, they are looking to secure financially advantageous matches. Spratt says this is because 'Most young women don't feel economically liberated. So the reasons for the return of a Jane Austen-style dating market – student debt and high housing costs – ought to be causing more concern than young women's response to them.'[15]

The return of old-fashioned dating ideas isn't limited to money, however. If we isolate the specific behaviours that purported dating 'experts' wax lyrical about and insist are fundamental in romantic contexts, we see a series of 'scripts' – ideas and stereotypes about how dating should work. Heteronormative dating scripts are essentially the expectation that men and women should play different roles within the realm of heterosexual dating. These scripts not only revolve around men's role as the bill payer, but also that men should initiate romantic interactions and ask the woman out on a date, that men should occupy a dominant role in driving the relationship forward, that men should buy the engagement ring and propose marriage, that women should take men's surnames upon marriage.

A 2023 study examined why, despite the progress made towards gender equality in society, these attitudes and expectations still prevail, and crucially what made women more likely to endorse these views.[16] 'Despite evidence that attitudes are shifting towards greater support for gender equality in the public sphere, gender relations appear stubbornly inegalitarian in the private sphere of intimate relationships between women and men,' reads the paper. Women who had stronger beliefs in benevolent sexism, hostile sexism, lower feminist identity, and a preference for dominant men, were more likely to endorse heteronormative dating scripts. Hostile sexism is defined as antagonism towards anyone viewed as challenging or subverting traditional gender roles. This is because hostile sexists regard feminism as a direct attack on masculinity. What's alarming is that 2022 research found that half the UK population holds sexist views, be they benevolent sexist attitudes (such as 'men should be women's protectors') or hostile sexist views ('women are manipulative and controlling').[17] When dating is transactional in this way, the expectation may fall on women to 'put out' after a meal has been paid for. In my book *Rough,* I wrote about 'unwanted sex' which is sex that's consensual, but not wanted or desired.[18] Women I spoke to told me they felt they 'owed' men sex and that there was an expectation of sexual intimacy after he had paid for something. This pressure is referred to by social scientists as a transaction script – the feeling that you should pay someone back with sex without actually desiring physical intimacy.

Changing our economic conditions is a task that requires the attention of policy makers and is a bigger problem than any of us can solve individually. What I will say, however, is that while the idea of having everything in life paid for by somebody else can, at times, have its appeal, in reality, by buying into this system, we perpetuate the centuries-old cycle of making patriarchy work for women, manipulating an oppressive power structure for our own benefit. 'So what?' you might think. 'Isn't that what men do every day? Maybe it's time we reaped the benefits too.' But if we continue that line of thinking, we should also know that upholding patriarchy means buying into a system of permissibility. We cannot pick and choose which parts of the patriarchy we'd like to hang onto. By ensuring its survival, we accept misogyny and its violent, oppressive and fatal consequences. In doing so, we uphold these very power structures we claim to vehemently oppose.

So, what can we do? I firmly believe in interrogating the relationship values you hold (and their source). If you think it's slutty to fuck on the first date, consider where this view came from, and whether this attitude really serves you and the people in your life. Does upholding this view harm others?

What about wielding your physical beauty to attain financial security? What happens if/when your appearance changes or your financially advantageous relationship breaks down? Might the future version of yourself regret not securing your own wealth outside the confines of a relationship?

'Well, it's my choice,' is often an argument I hear in conversations about relationship values. While it's true that at this moment in history, Western society enjoys more sexual freedoms than ever before, and if you're feeling horny one evening, you can scroll through Feeld or Grindr or Tinder and find someone to have sex with that very night, these freedoms come with a responsibility to make decisions that reflect your values and the kind of life you want to lead.

You could choose to only date people based on how much money they make in the hope of landing a more comfortable situation in life, or you could keep meeting new people and ghosting them as soon as your connection with them gets serious. But let's not pretend that the choices we make exist in a vacuum. In a neoliberal individualist society, those who subscribe to the school of choice feminism may think any decision that a woman or femme makes is inherently a good choice (even if it harms others, even if it's steeped in misogyny, and even if it upholds the patriarchy), but ultimately how we date impacts other people and contributes to a dating landscape that influences how other people treat us. While there is freedom to be found in abandoning the rules – especially the toxic ones – it pays to take the time to think about the bigger picture. Do what you want (within reason), as long as it really is what *you* want.

Part 2

The Love Fix

9

Endings – Reframing Rejection

'If he wanted to he would.' These may well be my least favourite six words. I've had this aphorism uttered to me over gin and tonics with friends, I've seen influencers parroting this line to their followers as if it's a one-size-fits-all maxim. Is this really a truth universally acknowledged that can be blanket-applied to all situations? Certainly not. Advice like this is at its worst when it strikes you in the throes of dating uncertainty or anxiety, when you're wading through the depths of mixed signals or feeling stuck in a situationship you don't remember signing up for. Hearing lines like this makes you feel worse – like it's your fault for not being wanted enough, not being desirable enough to create a sense of urgency or need in the person you're dating. Kick me while I'm down, why don't you!

It's difficult to not feel like you've done something wrong when you hear dating 'advice' like this. What if the person did want to, but they couldn't right now? Maybe they desired you, but knew they weren't emotionally available. They fancied you but their mental health wasn't where they wanted it to be. I've been in a situationship with a man who started out acting keen, who showered me with comments like 'I've wanted this for a long time,' before he began to up drawbridge and ghost me. Hearing the words 'if he wanted to, he would' only exacerbated the pain I was feeling. The words 'if he wanted to' only served to reinforce the feeling that I wasn't enough to make this man put in the effort, and that he didn't want me. It added to the feelings of rejection that I was experiencing keenly. Though my friends had the best intentions, these words were wounding, and I found them cruel. In a bid to protect myself, I've found it helpful to be more selective with the people I turn to for advice. Just because I'm going through something doesn't mean I need to share that with every person in my life. I've learned the hard way after opening up to certain people in my life, only to come away feeling ten times worse than I did before.

Eharmony's relationship expert Rachael Lloyd tells me: 'What is problematic about the line "If he wanted to, he would," is that it generalises problems within relationships and it can also be applied the other way around. There could be a genuinely benign reason behind why a man isn't putting enough energy into the relationship which could come down to self-confidence, not knowing how to approach the situation or not wanting to appear eager.'

As we feel our way in the darkness, it's easy to get drawn into these empty stock phrases.

Sayings like 'If he likes you, you'll know. If he doesn't you'll be confused,' and 'There's no such thing as mixed signals,' are prime examples of this. They lull us into the false sense of having clarity when human beings aren't actually quite that simple.

Relationship expert James Preece, aka The Dating Guru, says it's important to remember that sometimes life gets in the way for people. 'We are all becoming much more susceptible to stress and burn out, meaning our focus can be on other things,' said Preece. 'Phone batteries can die, work can pile up and family members can genuinely become sick. It has nothing to do with you.'

Granted, it takes a few seconds to send a text. But again, it's not always as simple as that. 'Quite often singles want to play it cool,' says Preece. 'They know that if they show they are too keen they might end up getting rejected. So, they hold back and try to act disinterested instead.'

Mixed signals do exist. Human beings routinely misunderstand one another in all contexts of life, not just dating. When I first moved to London during my twenties, I started my first full-time job in journalism and tried to settle into city life. I felt desperately lonely and struggled to admit that to myself for a very long time. Previously I had been close to a friend who was living back home in the midlands, where I'd previously been living, but we lost touch for reasons I couldn't put my finger on. In 2020, I reflected on some of the friendship losses I'd gone through in the past decade and I decided to reach out to that friend to apologise for any drop-off in contact. We had a candid chat about our friendship and what had gone wrong. She thought that I didn't need her anymore after I moved to London and that I was ditching her. I was taken aback by this. That assessment was very far from my lived experience; in actual fact, I was very isolated and spent most nights watching Netflix alone and waiting for my housemates to return home so I'd have someone to talk to. It was not a happy time.

Mixed signals are likely to crop up when you're in the very nascent stages of dating someone. Psychology professor turned podcast host Karin Anderson Abrell PhD says, 'You're just getting to know each other. As you gather information, you may respond in the moment or pull back to process what you've learned.' She says that mixed signals could be interpreted as 'a thoughtful, reflective effort to get to know the other person'.[1] All of this is not to say that we should turn a blind eye to someone who is very obviously pulling away from us and, through their behaviour, making it clear that they're not all that fussed about us. If you feel you've been the only one ever initiating the conversation, it might be worth taking a step back. If you feel strongly enough, you could try and bring it up tactfully – if they are interested, then they'll make it clear. Mean platitudes aside, how do you reframe romantic rejection as a gift, rather than interpreting it as a commentary on your value as a person?

Getting Over Someone You Didn't Even Date

Rejection in the early stages of dating, or a situationship, is a pain that often gets very little attention. Research has found, however, that even in the early dating stages, romantic rejection causes cardiac deceleration. And being deemed 'undateable' even by someone you don't fancy is painful.[2]

As our dating culture evolves, so too does the lexicon of love. And with it, daters are recognising the more nebulous and casual connections as valid relationships. Tinder users say that situationships are a valid relationship status.[3] An in-app survey of Gen Z Tinder users in the UK, US and Australia found that 1 in 10 people prefer situationships as 'a way to develop a relationship with less pressure'.

But while attitudes are shifting around what 'counts' as a valid relationship, we also need to acknowledge that when these situationships or talking stages end, we also experience pain. And that emotional distress shouldn't be downplayed as invalid.

I've gone through this kind of experience a few times and often felt like my pain wasn't valid because I'd not been in a 'real relationship' – whatever that means.

In the days leading up to my 30th birthday in 2018, I should have been excited for my party and entering this new decade of my life. Instead, I was embroiled in a protracted talking stage over email with a man who only seemed to want to have a pen pal. We worked in the same office. I hadn't really noticed him when the company I worked for first got acquired and we moved into an office full of unfamiliar faces. He wasn't the type of guy I'd usually go for and I wasn't attracted to him at first.

It all started when I bumped into him on the tube on the way to work one day and got chatting to him and thought he seemed interesting. That's when we started emailing each other. It was a strange office flirtation that bubbled over into a crush, on my part at least. I'd feel myself blushing as I talked to him. I'd feel self-conscious when he walked past my desk on the way to the lifts.

When we followed each other on Instagram, I started reading into every single interaction in granular detail. He was consistently the first viewer every single time I posted a story – a detail I imbued with more meaning than it actually held. The reality was, when we hung out in person, his behaviour was confusing. His keyboard flirtation did not translate into the real world. One night, after several drinks, we were alone at the very end of an empty train platform. I stood in front of him and looked at his face, hoping he'd kiss me. He didn't.

Instead, a few weeks later, he kissed my friend. I didn't find out about it for many months – a colleague and good friend of his let it slip during work drinks one night. I'd already felt a bit bruised and rejected before I'd even found out about this, but knowing that he'd kissed my friend and that she'd kept it from me only compounded the feelings of inadequacy I felt. Why hadn't I been good enough? Had I misconstrued this entire situation?

Talking to his friend made me realise it hadn't been in my

head. 'No, he's weird with women,' he said. 'Like he'll just text them and won't act on it.'

Getting over someone I hadn't even dated felt strange. Why had this rejection run so deep? Why had I given this man so much power over my sense of self? These questions ultimately led me to seek therapy.

Because we tend to focus on the socially legitimised pain of people emerging from breakups in long-term relationships, the painful experiences of people in short-term romances are ignored and even invalidated. Given we're now living through an age when we participate in a broad spectrum of relationship types and durations, it feels out of place, outmoded even, to consider long-term monogamous relationships the only valid source of heartbreak. Rachael Lloyd, relationship expert at eharmony, says, 'all too often we are presented with the narrative that "breakup blues" are only valid if you've been with a partner for years, experienced significant milestones or if the relationship ended badly'.[4] Take it from me, queen of the situationship, your pain is valid, no matter the length or type of relationship. Match's dating expert, Hayley Quinn, says: 'Modern dating often means that commitment takes time to form, and it's often found that by the time you have "the conversation" about what you are, you're already attached – even if someone doesn't want the same level of relationship as you do.'[5]

Psychologist Dr Darcey N. Powell, associate professor at Roanoke College, who specialises in romantic relationship terminologies, has conducted research into the 'talking stage' – a descriptor that defines the period of time between matching on an app and meeting up when you're texting and getting to know each other.[6] These stages can last days, weeks, and sometimes months. As I write this, I happen to be three weeks into a talking stage with someone I like a lot. 'Talking' as opposed to 'dating' is, according to Powell, 'like a label without a label. It's I don't want to say we're dating because then it might hurt more. But it's probably going to hurt when it ends regardless of the label you put on it or not.' Talking stages are 'a balancing act of trying to protect oneself because you're unsure of what's going to happen, but people aren't good at breaking up with each other or being rejected,' Powell adds.

Even if you don't have a label for your relationship, ending it is going to feel like a breakup. 'Baumeister years ago referred to the fact that romantic rejection and some other forms of rejection are scriptless,' says Powell. There are no good scripts for ending the talking stage.

One of the challenges of having an ever-evolving set of new relationship terms is not having an agreed consensus on the rules and expectations. In Powell's research, she found huge differences in people's understanding of what a talking stage means. People were able to identify that talking stages are different from dating and different from being friends with benefits. 'But the idea of what are your expected behaviours and how are you supposed to be communicating and why people talk are all over the board,' says Powell. 'There's a lack of clarity on what it means to be talking and because people don't agree on what that term means, then there's misunderstandings and violated expectations about who's supposed to be doing what and how.'

If we're in a talking stage with someone, does that mean we're allowed to talk to other people? 'One of the analyses we did was whether or not you expected the other person to only be talking to you, compared to your behaviour if you were only talking to that person,' explains Powell. 'People were like, "Well, I'd like them to only be talking to me, but I'd like to leave the door open to be able to be talking to other people." Because of that, people understandably get upset and they're not necessarily talking about their expectations.'

Why Ghosting Hurts so Much

Ghosting is a modern term for a breakup method that involves cutting ties with no explanation. Any subsequent contact attempts by the ghostee (person who's been ghosted) are ignored and not responded to. Figures vary when it comes to figuring out how prevalent ghosting is. One 2018 study of 1,300 people found 20 per cent had been ghosted, and 25 per cent had ghosted others.[7]

'Ghosting has existed since people delivered messages on horseback,' says Powell. 'That message would go unreceived and you'd be ghosted. But it's the new term that people use because of the fact that there's so much communication that happens through technology.'

So, why does it hurt so bad? Powell says it's the uncertainty that makes it painful. 'The other person, the ghoster, has unilaterally decided that they are ending this interaction, this relationship, whatever the level of it was, and they're communicating that by not communicating,' says Powell. 'Once an individual realises they've been ghosted, there's often a lot of questioning why they were ghosted. What did they do to deserve the ghosting? Why didn't the person feel like they could tell them explicitly, or maybe whether or not they could have worked it out?'

That uncertainty can make our inner critic go into overdrive – am I not attractive enough? Am I too boring? Not successful enough? Did they find someone better? Did they find me annoying? Was I too much? Not enough? All of those questions will go unanswered.

When we're ghosted, it's easy to wonder why the person didn't opt for honesty. And many of us look for clarity and try to understand the reasons why the relationship didn't work out. But, do honesty and directness actually help? Research seems to suggest that it actually doesn't make a difference. 'A study by Kessler and colleagues compared the emotional distress felt by people who were broken up with more explicitly versus being ghosted. The emotional distress felt on being on the receiving end didn't differ,' Powell explains. 'They had similar levels of emotional distress and negative effect from that experience.'

Powell adds that the individuals who were doing the breaking up, who delivered the more explicit breakup communication, felt more distressed than those who ghosted.

Another study measured the psychological consequences of ghosting using voodoo dolls (yes!).[8] Participants reflected on being rejected in the last five years and stuck pins in the dolls. 'The people who reflected on being rejected in the last five years stuck more of those aggressive pins than people who had been ghosted,' Powell explains.

Are you a bad person for ghosting someone?

Much discussion has been dedicated to the morality of ghosting. Are you a bad person for ghosting? What do you owe people in the dating realm? Is ghosting just part of modern dating culture? Are there legitimate reasons for ghosting?

Sociologist Eva Illouz made an interesting observation in *The End of Love* regarding ghosting in the context of consent culture. 'Ghosting is a prerogative of the freedom to exit sexual-romantic contracts at any point,' says Illouz. 'Because the ethics of consent is the main and almost exclusive moral discourse regulating love and relationship, consent makes it legitimate to withdraw from a relationship at any point, as soon as one's emotions change,' Illouz continues.

Ghosting, regardless of where we stand on the ethical and moral implications, plunges the ghostee into a state of uncertainty and ambiguity, whereby they must come to their own conclusion as to why they're being rejected. In the absence of any concrete facts, we fill in the blanks.[9]

Rejection is a universally painful experience. Social psychologist Dr Gili Freedman researches the two-sided nature of rejection and examines how and why people reject others and the consequences for both parties. 'There's been a lot of research on this idea that the need to belong is a really fundamental human motivation,' says Freedman, assistant professor of psychology at St. Mary's College of Maryland. 'So when we're rejected, we're denied that need, and that's just a kind of universally painful experience.'

'One of the things that researchers in this field talk about is this idea of "hurt" feelings and how it's interesting that that's the hallmark emotion associated with rejection, or social exclusion,' she adds. Freedman clarifies that when we talk about our feelings being hurt, we indicate that it's a painful thing. And the reason it's painful is because you're being denied something everyone wants: to feel as though you belong.

As she explains: 'There's also work showing that "ostracism", which is the silent treatment, threatens not just belongingness, but also your sense of control, your self-esteem, and your sense of meaningful existence.'

Ostracism is a term used by psychologists to describe the act of giving the silent treatment to another individual. It means being ignored and excluded. Ghosting and ostracism aren't exactly the same thing, but they overlap and share qualities with one another. 'Because ghosting and ostracism both involve refusing to communicate, it is possible that ghosting may lead to negative consequences similar to those produced by ostracism,' according to Freedman's research.[10]

Those negative consequences include: 'It is detected as pain, threatens fundamental human needs (e.g. belonging, self-esteem, control, and meaningful existence), and increases anger and sadness. Being the target of ostracism has also been linked to interpersonal problems including aggression.'[11]

So, why do we ghost?

One 2020 study, by Erasmus University Rotterdam in the Netherlands, delved into the reasons why people ghost their matches on dating apps. Interestingly, the researchers asked people who'd been on the receiving end of ghosting why they believed they'd been rejected in this way. A large number of respondents (59 per cent) blamed the other person for ghosting them, with many saying they believed the ghoster was talking to or dating someone else. Others felt the ghoster might have had trouble with commitment.[12] Meanwhile, 37 per cent blamed themselves for being ghosted. Respondents believed they weren't good enough for the ghoster, describing themselves as not interesting enough, not attractive enough, 'too boring, too fat, ugly, not tall, or muscular enough'. Other respondents wondered what they'd done wrong, or if they'd said something that the other person didn't like.

Researchers asked ghosters to explain their reasons for ghosting people on dating apps. Five themes emerged in their responses. Sixty-seven per cent of the respondents ghosted because of the other person – with some citing 'undesirable actions and behaviours' – 'being pushy, disrespectful, racist, withholding important information, or sending unsolicited sexual content'.

Some respondents said the ghostee had refused to accept

their reasons for rejection and therefore they felt they had no alternative but to cut ties. A difference in motives for using dating apps also cropped up as a reason; essentially they were both looking for different things. One of the respondents, Tina (31, heterosexual), told the researchers: 'If I had the feeling that we were in contact because of different motives and the other person was not honest about that, I would immediately cut off all contact.' Disappointing or unpleasant in-person dates were also cited as a reason for ghosting. Some said their reason for ghosting was because of the ghostee's unattractive appearance. For 44 per cent, the reason for ghosting someone else was self-related – wanting to protect themselves, not feeling emotionally ready to date, fear of not meeting others' expectations, and a worry that another person was trying to change them. Some people were chatting to other people and simply forgot about the ghostee. Others said they were just too busy to continue the conversation.

Twenty-nine per cent blamed the app for ghosting. Some said they were overloaded with potential partners and ghosted the ones they were less interested in. Many people said they felt they didn't owe the other person anything and said that ghosting is just 'part of mobile dating use'. One respondent, Melanie (27, heterosexual) told researchers: 'I don't owe the other person an explanation given that I did not meet this person face-to-face.' For women and marginalised people, the looming threat of violence can be a motivating factor in choosing to abruptly cut ties with someone. Freedman researched the role of safety concerns in people's decisions to ghost others. 'This research started because we noticed this pattern we saw anecdotally on online forums where often heterosexual men were saying, "I don't understand why women are ghosting me, they should have the decency to just tell me to my face, right, to explicitly say no." And women are responding saying, "I am afraid to say no, because when I do explicitly say no you harass me," ' Freedman explains.

Women have been killed for refusing men's advances. As author Laura Bates writes: 'For certain groups in particular, including trans women, women of colour and sex workers, it is well documented that refusing unwanted advances can result in aggression, physical or sexual violence, or even murder.'[13] This fear of how another person might take our 'no' informs our breakup method. By choosing an evasive, non-confrontational method, we attempt to swerve being harmed. If we have a gut feeling that someone will react aggressively to a rejection, ghosting is a risk-mitigation strategy. A way to exit a situation that could become dangerous. 'We did find that people are more likely to ghost when they have concerns about safety if the target is a man. But when we did this with a group of bisexual participants, we didn't see that same pattern. What we saw instead was just in general, when people have safety concerns, they're more willing to ghost,' she explains. 'What I think is interesting about that is: does it actually help with safety concerns? Because there's other research showing that when you're ostracised, which is a similar process, sometimes people respond aggressively to that. So, does ignoring some-one actually make them less likely to lash out? Or is it the opposite?'

When we think of people who ghost, we typically don't have good things to say about them. In the dating world, they're our mortal enemies. We see them as cowards, too craven to say the harsh truth to our faces. But is that image correct?

One study conducted by Freedman spoke to people who have both ghosted and been ghosted. 'People, when they wrote about being ghosted, talked about: sadness, hurt, feelings, things like that. Whereas the folks who, when they talked about engaging in ghosting, they talked about things like guilt, but also relief.' Freedman said that both ghosting and being ghosted involved negative emotions, just in different ways. 'That was interesting because I think we often have this picture that when people ghost, it's easy for them. They have no feelings. And people getting ghosted are the only people being impacted, but I think what the research shows is, both sides feel some type of negative emotion in response. And so it's not a great situation for anyone.'

How Do We Reframe Rejection?

Getting rejected – whatever form it takes – is not fun. And we all have our own way of dealing with it. Sometimes, those coping strategies are less helpful than others.

Take Jenny, one of my interviewees who didn't reveal her age or orientation. Her coping strategy for dealing with romantic rejection is: 'Don't try at all because that way you can't be rejected.' 'It does affect my self-worth because it's been so ingrained in us that being romantically attractive is the *only* way to be worthy and therefore have self-esteem,' Jenny tells me. 'Obviously I logically don't believe that to be true. I feel like I'm letting myself down and missing out on my "youth" by not trying harder to have these romantic experiences that I'm so scared of and therefore avoid.' Jenny isn't alone in feeling this way. The prospect of getting rejected can put us off making ourselves vulnerable. We protect ourselves from harm by removing ourselves from situations that could hurt us.

But what if we gave rejection less power in this situation? What if we feared it less? Sometimes a conversation just needs to end. And it's not any deeper than that. It's not a match. I'm not the gal for you. You're not the guy for me. Simple as that. Have a nice life.

If you remove romance from this situation for a minute and think about the sheer number of people you come across in your lifetime, you'll know that you haven't clicked with every single person you've ever met. Every time you meet a new person – whether that's at work, at a wedding or party, through friends, through family, whatever – you don't always connect on a deep level that makes you want to get to know them any better. If you did, you'd literally be best friends with every human you ever came into contact with – think how exhausting that would be.

'So when someone "rejects" you, not only is that saving you precious time, but it's also the universe ushering you towards potential mates who are worthy of you, your time and your love,' says Sam Owen, Hinge UK relationship expert. 'Thus, rejection is rewarding: it both teaches us something and it nudges us towards our goals and happiness.'

Sara, 32, who describes herself as 'straight-ish', tells me her rejection coping strategy is to remind herself of all the times she's thought someone was 'lovely and fit' despite not fancying them. 'Rejection stings (obviously) but I really do find it helpful to remind myself of people who've expressed interest in me over the years who I just . . . haven't fancied,' Sara says. 'And it doesn't mean they were physically or spiritually repellent! They were often wonderful people! "It" just wasn't there for me, and the "it" is often quite intangible. Of course there have also been people who I've rejected because I did think they were awful, but I choose to believe that no one who has rejected me ever did so because of that,' she adds.

As I've already mentioned, you aren't attracted to every person you meet in life – no one is. If they were, things would be pretty chaotic. According to eharmony research, 18 per cent of people we're attracted to will feel the same way. The very nature of seeking out partnership where there's mutual attraction comes with a high risk of rejection.

How Should We Reject People?

In the age of online dating, knowing how to break off a relationship – whatever its duration – feels like a minefield. If it's a talking stage and you haven't yet met in person, ending things in person would be strange and unnecessary, right? But, if it's a simple case of not really feeling it, blocking the person feels unkind, cruel even.

Ghosting, as we discussed, has its uses in instances where we fear for our safety or if we're in an abusive relationship, but we also have a whole host of stock phrases in our arsenals that we can pull out when looking for a way to politely phrase a rejection: 'I just want to be friends,' or 'I don't feel a spark,' or 'It's not you, it's me,' or 'It doesn't feel like a good match.' The possibilities are well and truly endless. But the problem with these hackneyed phrases is that we're all so familiar with them that we see straight through them. When someone says, 'I don't feel a spark,' to me, I know they've leaned on a well-used phrase to help them communicate something uncomfortable. That's when my brain starts to unpick their message: Is it that they didn't feel a 'spark' or did they find me unattractive?

Social psychologist Dr Gili Freedman, who researches rejection and social exclusion, talked to me about 'scriptlessness' in romantic contexts.[14] Romantic scriptlessness, she explains, is 'the idea that we don't have good scripts or things we should say for rejections.' She says that even when we genuinely feel that 'it's not you, it's me' or you genuinely want to just be friends, it risks sounding like you're reaching for an easy-to-use cliché.

While they weren't able to find a script for breakups that would alleviate the pain, her team did find that when you're breaking up with someone, apologies don't help. This is because when we receive an apology, our instinct is to say 'that's okay' or to offer absolution, explains Freedman. 'But if I've just rejected you, you might not feel forgiveness in that moment. You might think "Wow, that person is kind of a jerk." So, if you feel obligated to say, "Oh, that's okay," now, I've rejected you and made you tell me that it's okay that I did that. And so that might not make you feel great.'

Turning to stock phrases can be the lesser of many evils. Psychologist Dr Darcey N. Powell says people are only so truthful when rejecting people because they don't want to hurt them. 'People are rarely like, "These are all the terrible things I hate about you," because why would you?' she says. 'Maybe the stock statement seems a little cliché, or redundant, or not very helpful. But then when people do often give critical feedback, it tends not to be received well anyways. So I don't blame people for maybe being like, "It's not you, it's me," and "I don't feel a spark." '

So, what can we learn from this? Sometimes the time-tested scripts for breakups can help us through a difficult conversation, but we should know that they might come across as cliché and disingenuous. Sometimes, when we turn to a stock phrase, the lack of originality gives rise to the recipient imbuing their own meaning with an insecurity they might have. When you're on the receiving end of a stock phrase, it's not helpful to amplify the pain by inserting your own narrative. For the sake of my own sanity, I've told myself to take people's words at face value. Without any more information, you can't fill in the blanks and you'll torture yourself trying to. When you're in the role of the rejector, do not expect absolution to relieve yourself of the inevitable guilt that comes with ending things. It's uncomfortable, but that discomfort will pass. The kindest thing we can do is allow space for the other person to process their feelings without pushing them into forgiving you by apologising or asking them to be friends right away. Rejection is painful, but we must regard it as a means to redirect us to what's truly meant for us. Without this necessary pivot, we wouldn't be free to steer our attention, love and energy towards new experiences and connections. Plant your seeds in fertile ground.

10

Too Sensitive

Beyond our common understanding of the word, neuroscientists and psychotherapists define being sensitive, commonly known as a 'highly sensitive person' (HSP) as involving 'greater sensitivity and responsivity to environmental and social stimuli'.[1] But do these definitions tell the full story of sensitivity? In my mind, being sensitive means having a capacity to feel things intensely, to pay close attention to your own emotions, to feel pain acutely, and to be finely attuned to the moods and feelings of other people. It is in my interactions with other people that I feel most sensitive. And dating and sex really bring out a side of me that feels highly attuned to even the most subtle of shifts. My ability to overthink every interaction in a dating context, to figure out if something is proof of a man's disinterest, a warning sign of an impending rejection, feels debilitating. Dating is a minefield for sensitive folk. So, how do we navigate it? I've tried abstaining from dating to avoid the vulnerability it takes to be open to possibilities. But humans are relational beings. Interaction is inevitable, so too is the opportunity for my sensitivity to come into play, bringing with it the possibility of hurt. Being open to love necessitates vulnerability. You need to lower your guard to let love in. But the very nature of being so exposed comes with the full knowledge that it's fully possible our feelings will be hurt, our egos bruised, our hearts shattered.

Clinical psychologist Jenny Yip says that a person who is highly sensitive will question the motives behind other people's actions or words and draw negative conclusions. 'People who are emotionally sensitive tend to personalize, blame, and be self-critical, and judgmental,' says Dr Yip. 'They can often have a lot of social anxiety about being perceived in a negative light.'[2] The feeling of not being understood is something sensitive people are accustomed to. Genevieve von Lob, a clinical psychologist who works with many highly sensitive people, says 'society tends to view it as a weakness, and they can get these labels like "fragile" or "overemotional".' She adds that sensitive people can often feel lonely, misunderstood, and 'not normal'. 'It's not surprising that they struggle to accept themselves and they struggle to value their gifts because of the messages they have received,' von Lob adds.[3]

Thin Skinned

Rose, 36 and bisexual, is sensitive and describes the feeling as 'walking around with one less layer of skin' than non-sensitive folks. Rose's sensitivity rears its head most often when communicating with people in her life. 'I pick up on delivery of the way people say things perhaps more than other people might and then I will stew on their reactions and worry about the implications of what they might have said,' Rose says. She will then try to come to conclusions about what their words might mean, or what their tone conveys, and she'll find herself getting more and more stressed about it. 'In that sense, for me words are my main sensitivity – the things people say and how they say them to me.'

When people tell Rose to 'just let it go' she finds it difficult. 'I just feel like I'm more reactive to things that other people would just be like "Oh who cares,"' she says. Rose has always envied people who've been able to brush things off and say 'whatever'. 'If I have a fight with someone, if I've fallen out with someone, if someone gets upset with me, it takes me ages to process it, understand it, and if there's any level of injustice I find it really hard to let go of it,' she says. If someone made a comment that she construed as a dig, she'd find it hard to get away from it, and she would grow increasingly upset. 'Your brain collects those little attacks,' she says. 'I just wish I was the kind of person that could be like, okay that was yesterday, and just forget about it.'

In her twenties, Rose struggled with feeling slighted and misunderstood. As she's got older, she has learned to manage her sensitivity better. She's gone through five years of therapy and figured out how to separate 'other people's stuff' from her own. 'I'm not a water-off-a-duck's-back kind of person. I do get over things, it just takes me more time,' she says. 'I wish other people were more in tune with what it feels like to be walking around with one less layer of skin, so you feel everything a bit more. Which means you have to look after yourself a bit more emotionally and you have to get really good at boundaries.' Rose feels things would be much better if others weren't so quick to dismiss those who are more sensitive.

The Psychology of Sensitivity

Why are sensitive people the way they are? What makes us thin skinned to the point where wounding us feels inevitable? What does it mean to be sensitive? One study suggests that sensitivity is a characteristic that's held by a significant proportion of the population. Psychologist Elaine Aron came up with the Highly Sensitive Person (HSP) theory and has been researching sensitivity since 1991. HSPs are believed to have higher central nervous system sensitivity to all kinds of stimuli, be it emotional, social or physical. Aron's hypothesis estimates that the highly sensitive trait is found in 15 to 20 per cent of the population – which makes it too prevalent to be considered a disorder, but not widespread enough to be understood by non-sensitive folks. 'You are more aware than others of subtleties,' says Aron. 'This is mainly because your brain processes information and reflects on it more deeply. So even if you wear glasses, for example, you see more than others by noticing more.'[4]

Sensory Processing Sensitivity (SPS) is the scientific term for being highly sensitive. Neuropsychologist Nawal Mustafa says 'many HSPs consider this sensory processing sensitivity to be something they hate about themselves because most cultures or communities do not value sensitivity or emotions.' She adds: 'Being told "Stop crying" and "You're overreacting" can make HSPs feel like something is wrong with them and potentially lead to low self-esteem, self-doubt, feelings of being misunderstood.'[5] According to these theories, sensitivity is a temperament, but it's also caused by the conditions we've grown up in or the events that have shaped our lives. As Dr Yip says, 'it's also due to environmental factors that have reinforced your sensitivity.' So, what is going on inside your head? Several studies have used MRI scanning to explore what goes on in the brains of highly sensitive people – and crucially the areas of the brain that are most active during moments of sensitivity. One 2021 study used MRI imaging to examine brain activity in highly sensitive people at rest after being shown descriptions of happy, sad or neutral events, and then corresponding emotional faces of their romantic partners and of strangers.[6] Bianca Acevedo, a researcher in UC Santa Barbara's Department of

Psychological and Brain Sciences who led the study, says, 'What we found was a pattern that suggested that during this rest, after doing something that was emotionally evocative, their brain showed activity that suggested depth of processing, and this depth of processing is a cardinal feature of high sensitivity.' While some may say 'you're too sensitive' as if it's an accusation, or a piece of advice that's intended to make you change this about yourself, you're not actually in control of the reasons why you are the way you are. For example, if you've been in an abusive relationship, or had neglectful parents, or experienced trauma, those factors might have contributed to your sensitivity. Simply put, your sensitivity is not something you can turn off like a switch.

When it comes to partnership, sensitivity plays an integral role in how we love others. In Aron's book *The Highly Sensitive Person,* she writes that HSPs 'fall in love harder than others'.[7] That fact is something of a double-edged sword. On the one hand, if that love is reciprocated, the relationship healthy and fulfilling, then the intensity of this love is a gift. Other times, when the love is not returned, or things fall apart, you might wish you didn't fall in love quite so intensely. Unrequited intense love can happen to anyone, but it seems to happen more often to HSPs, writes Aron. 'The failure to be loved back can be the very cause of the intensity,' she explains. 'If a real relationship could develop, the absurd idealisation would cool as one came to know the beloved better, warts and all.'

Sensitivity when combined with an insecure attachment style can produce the conducive conditions for an intense, but impossible love to bloom. But there's another factor that can also bring it about. Another source of insecurity comes in the form of questioning one's self-worth, according to Aron. 'HSPs are prone to low self-esteem because they are not our culture's ideal. So sometimes they consider themselves lucky if someone wants them at all.' Love, when it happens on these terms, can often go wrong and the faller-in-love may go on to realise that the person they gave their heart away to wasn't good enough for them, or wasn't well suited to them, Aron explains. The solution? Work on your self-esteem, try to build your confidence and self-worth. Reflect on what you want from a partner and look beyond the requirement of being with someone just because they like you. Are you attracted to them? Are they kind? Do they make you feel safe and secure? Do you make each other laugh? Do they make you feel good? Easier said than done (believe me, I know), but we'll go into the 'how' in more detail later on.

How can we get close to people without it hurting us? How do we live meaningful, open lives without building walls around our hearts to protect ourselves? Accept that opening yourself up to love and the possibility of a relationship carries a risk of getting hurt. It may hurt, yes. But closing yourself off to protect your heart will bring a different kind of pain.

In my case, knowing that the fervour of love I experience does not make me 'abnormal' – that it actually goes hand in hand with being sensitive – is a real source of comfort. For too long, I have railed against my own sensitivity, wished I was different, thicker skinned and better equipped to handle life's harsh realities, the rejection that comes with dating and looking for love, the harshness that sometimes comes with interpersonal relationships with non-sensitive humans. Other people haven't helped, though. I've had my sensitivity weaponised against me, used as a way of deflecting blame in moments of conflict. It's been whipped out when someone refused to be held accountable for their own shitty behaviour and instead claimed that my reaction to their cruelty was the problem. It's tiring. In an ideal world, my galaxy-brained plan looks like this: The world acknowledges and accepts sensitive people for who they are. Instead of trying to force sensitive folks to change, why not just stop being a dickhead? How about showing kindness and compassion? What about being empathetic? Just an idea.

Rose talked about not being a 'water-off-a-duck's-back' type of person. So, is it possible to stop being so permeable to other people's opinions of us? Yes! There's a lot of things you can do to undo approval-seeking tendencies. The first step is: Identify where these feelings come from. Don't beat yourself up about what you find – humans are hardwired towards inclusion and it's natural to seek acceptance from others. Journaling can also help you pay close attention to triggers and sensitive areas and give you a dedicated space to reflect.

How do I live through rejection without interpreting it as a commentary on my own self-worth? Turn rejection into a positive. It is course-correction to set you on the right path in life and to ensure you don't go too far down the wrong trajectory. Remember that it's not personal (even if it feels it!) – you aren't being rejected, the relationship is. Once the sting has worn off, you'll be back on your way and heading in the direction of something (someone) infinitely better suited to you.

Self-Esteem

'Rachel, where is your self-worth!?' These are the words my friend cried out over the phone after I finally admitted that I'd let someone back into my life who frankly didn't deserve it.

This wasn't the first time my low self-esteem had collided

with my love life, making me feel like I didn't deserve to be treated well. I had been chasing after someone who didn't want me, without asking myself if I was actually into them.

Throughout my journalistic career, I have talked to thousands of people about falling in love.

During that time, I've heard people talk about themselves in a way that betrays a deep lack of self-worth.

'Who would want me?'

'I'm just very hard to love.'

'It's just not going to happen for me.'

In many of these cases, the people who admitted the way they felt about themselves had been made to feel that way because of how others had treated them. Feeling undeserving of love can make us feel we should stay in relationships or situations in which we aren't treated well, or that become abusive. This perceived unworthiness can lead us to not set boundaries with people because we don't consider ourselves to be worthy of respect.

Having low self-esteem can play a massive role in our love lives – from the choices we make, the behaviours we tolerate from others, and how we respond and cope with the more difficult emotions that love and sex bring up.

Rachael Lloyd, eharmony's in-house relationship expert, says romantic rejection is one of the most painful types of rejection. 'It literally cuts to the very heart of who we are and how attractive we deem ourselves to be,' says Lloyd. 'And no one is exempt. A recent report by eharmony and Relate found over 60 per cent of men fear rejection, particularly in terms of their age and appearance. This echoes what women tell us.'

Low self-esteem can make romantic rejection feel really hard. 'Thankfully, most people can weather their way through the painful feelings by leaning on good friends or family. But those of us who already have low self-esteem and carry hidden reserves of childhood trauma can find ourselves derailed for months, in some cases years,' adds Lloyd.

Dr Becky Spelman, psychologist and founder at Private Therapy Clinic, says that low self-esteem can have a significant impact on people's dating experiences. It can lead to self-doubt, fear of rejection, and difficulty in forming and maintaining relationships. 'People with low self-esteem may struggle with negative self-talk and have a tendency to settle for less than they deserve,' says Spelman. 'They may find it challenging to believe in their own worthiness of love and affection.

'I pretend that I'm protecting my peace'

Erin, heterosexual and 45 years old, has life-long low self-esteem which, she feels, stems from her upbringing as the only daughter in a religious, Catholic family in Ireland in the 1980s. Erin remembers witnessing her mum on a 'constant diet' when she was a child, skipping meals to ensure she kept her size eight figure. She tells me she was brought up to feel like she had to find a partner and that if she existed without one, she was somehow 'less than'. She was recently asked by a colleague why she didn't just move back in with her mother, which made her feel that her life as a single woman isn't valid.

'I also feel that we aren't told that being single is a choice. It isn't a booby prize for not being in a relationship and we should be encouraged to make a conscious choice about being single or dating. It's that *Bridget Jones* scene where they act like she's somehow half human because she's on her own,' she says. The societal pressure to 'settle down' has left Erin feeling like a fail-ure. In her 30s, she panicked and tolerated 'really terrible behaviour' because she worried that time was running out.

Despite the pressure being off, Erin can't help but feel she's missed out on something. 'It feels like it's a daily reminder of not having been chosen, of what I don't have, that most of the people I know have had kids by my age (or chose not to, or had fertility issues that prevented them from having kids).'

Erin's feelings of inadequacy because she didn't follow the trajectory many of us grew up believing was the norm are relatable. But life isn't a script that we all follow to the letter. We are all doing things in our own way, on our own timelines and, crucially, on our terms. There is power in letting go of the weight of other people's expectations of you, and the pressures we put on ourselves because of familial or community expectations. It is painful to grieve the life you thought you'd have. But there is much joy to be found in honouring the person you have grown into, the blessings you have in your life, whatever shape they take. Celebrate the fact you've forged your own path and done things differently. It takes courage to do so!

You're lovable just as you are

Author and life coach Maria Liviero says that having high self-esteem makes you less likely to tolerate disrespectful or inappropriate behaviour from a date. 'You won't laugh off uncomfortable situations to please them or avoid confrontation. Instead, you will have the courage to speak up and assert yourself, ultimately earning you more respect and admiration from your date,' says Liviero. 'So, if you're worried about being accepted by your date, remember that having self-esteem is key. It shows that you respect yourself and are worthy of respect from others. Don't compromise your self-worth to please someone else in the short term.'

As Dr Becky Spelman says, 'It's important to remember that you are inherently worthy of love and acceptance just as you are. You don't have to change yourself in order to be loved.

The right person will love you for the person you are right now. Focus on building your self-confidence and self-compassion, and embrace all the things that make you unique and wonderful. Surround yourself with family, friends and other supportive people. Therapy or counselling can help you to work through any underlying issues and to gain a healthier perspective on self-worth.'

Time after time I find myself returning to the words of artist Caroline Caldwell: 'In a society that profits from your self-doubt, loving yourself is an act of rebellion.'

How to build self-worth

Psychologist Dr Ravi Gill says low self-esteem impacts people's dating experiences by making people doubt their self-worth, leading to insecurities and a fear of rejection. 'The dating process itself can also be quite triggering and can exacerbate feelings of rejection, disappointment and not feeling "good enough". It's important to be mindful of such emotions and find ways to recognize your own worth,' says Gill.

Gill says that when we experience low self-esteem, the anxiety and self-doubt that come with that can make it harder to communicate with our partners, establish connection and express our needs, which is why building our self-esteem is not just key to our own happiness, it's also essential for healthy relationships. 'Building healthy relationships often requires a foundation of self-confidence and positive self-image. People with low self-esteem might take feedback very personally,' says Gill. 'For example, in early dating situations if one person is always messaging the other and yet not receiving a response; the person with low self-esteem may take that as a signal of lack of interest.

'Thinking "If only I were different, this person would love

me," is destructive and ineffective. Your partner should love you for who you already are at your core. Your core self isn't something that can change to make a relationship work. 'But what *can* change – and what often needs to change – is how you interact with your partner and how you think about yourself in the world,' says Gill.

Our self-esteem isn't static – we all have moments where our self-esteem is lower than usual, and it's OK to have these low moments. What matters is that we pay attention to when and how it changes so that we can identify what can boost our self-esteem.

'If I tell them it's too soon to sext, will they still like me?'

Recently, after matching with someone who seemed great at first, he launched into sexting just a few hours after matching, which really rubbed me up the wrong way. How could we go from talking about wanting a serious relationship one minute to asking to see a photo of my boobs?

When I'm on dating apps, and it's clearly marked on my profile that I'm looking for something serious, I find it really grating when people find out what I do for a living and think it's open season to go straight for sexting right away.

If it's someone I felt I had a good connection with (up until that point, at least), I find it difficult to know what to do. Do I just end the conversation right there and then? Should I set a boundary with them? What if they don't like me once I set that boundary?

That last question might resonate with anyone who struggles with their self-esteem. Setting boundaries in the early stages of dating can feel really stressful, particularly if you're a

woman or femme and you've been socially conditioned to prioritise other people's needs, to not be a 'difficult woman', to
just go with the flow and be the 'cool girl'. The question we
should be asking ourselves (and frankly, we should be encouraged from a very early age to ask this) is: What about my needs?
How do I assert those needs and ensure that I'm being treated
with respect?

Frustrated by the fact that this keeps happening, I sent a
voice note to my friend Gigi Engle, who is a certified sex therapist and author of *All The F*cking Mistakes*.

Over voice note, Engle advised against shutting it down
and suggested a response that I could use if this situation continues to arise:

'I'm very open to conversations about sex, but I do think
that you and I aren't really at a place yet where I'm comfortable
having those kinds of conversations with you. And, as I've
made clear, I'm really looking for something that's more serious. Maybe this isn't the impression you mean to give but I'm
just letting you know how it comes off to me is that this is
moving very quickly to a physical place when you and I have
had no chance of connecting in any emotional way. So these
conversations aren't something I'm not open to having, I would
just like to get to know you better.'

If the person you send this (or a variation on the above message) to reacts badly, if they don't honour the boundary you're
setting, if they stop talking to you, that person isn't for you.

As Engle said to me over voice note: 'And honestly, if someone isn't cool with that then fuck them because they just did
you a massive favour. I think being really honest about your
boundaries right away doesn't make you a prude.'

Setting boundaries is an essential step in setting the guide-
lines for how you (and your partner) want to be treated.

If the person reacts well to the initial boundary being set, but later goes on to cross that boundary, then it's worth taking a step back. This violation of boundaries could be seen as a red flag. As Neil Wilkie, founder of online couples therapy platform The Relationship Paradigm, tells me: 'If they are breaking the boundaries and don't want to engage in conversation about it, question if they are right for me?'[8]

Changing your mindset when you've felt trapped in a cycle of negative self-talk can feel like a Sisyphean task. There have been times in my life when I've wondered if I'll ever be able to love myself. I found that small, achievable changes in my behaviour had a transformative impact on how I see myself in the world.

Take a Break From the Online Attention Economy

Research has found that people use dating apps to enhance their self-esteem.[9] It suggests that incessant swiping on dating apps can be explained by reward seeking whereby matches become a form of gratification. Messaging those matches introduces a risk of rejection or negative interactions. In contrast, swiping endlessly and collecting matches (with no intention of talking to them) allows you to collect validation without the risk of rejection.[10]

A study by New York University in 2021 found that our use of social media, particularly our attempt to garner as many 'likes' as possible is because of 'reward learning'.[11] This is when rewards are used to positively reinforce a good or desired action; those rewards make it more likely that the behaviour will be repeated in the future.[12] Human beings on social media mirror the behaviour of rats in a box who, discovering that pressing a lever resulted in food being dispensed, repeated the action over and over again to elicit the same outcome, as established by psychologist B. F. Skinner in his theory of operant conditioning.[13]

'These findings may help us understand why social media comes to dominate daily life for many people and provide clues, borrowed from research on reward learning and addiction, to how troubling online engagement may be addressed,' explains David Amodio, professor at New York University and the University of Amsterdam, one of the authors of the study on social media use and reward learning.[14] As essayist Jia Tolentino wrote in *Trick Mirror: Reflections on Self-Delusion*: 'That is what keeps us scrolling, scrolling, pressing our lever over and over in the hopes of getting some fleeting sensation – some momentary rush of recognition, flattery or rage.' Setting digital boundaries with yourself is an important step in breaking this cycle. Set hard limits on your social media usage – you can alter your settings so your app will shut off after a certain timeframe, for instance, after an hour of use. You can change your Instagram settings so your like count on posts is hidden, and turn off your notifications so you aren't being drip-fed droplets of validation on your phone screen. Of course, you already know this. But now it's clear why doing it can have an astonishing, positive impact. Ria, 27 and heterosexual, turned off almost all her phone notifications a year ago and found the move to be transformative. On dating apps, she has notifications turned off, which she's found helpful. 'Don't get me wrong, I still feel aggy if I think I've been left on read lol,' she says. 'But I never actually know so what I don't know can't hurt me.' I ask her if she goes into the apps to check them once a day: 'Sometimes not even that,' she says. 'I've become that person who's like "sorry for the delay! I'm not on here much. I don't feel the need to be readily available to others and don't expect the same back."'

On dating apps, set limits on the time you spend swiping. Establish a rule whereby after amassing five or ten matches – or whatever number feels right – you initiate conversations with those matches or remove any matches you don't want to interact with. Try slowing down your swiping to a more intentional practice – take a little longer to look through the profile of a person you're considering.

Know When it's Time to Say Goodbye

There was the friend-with-benefits in my hometown who I hooked up with when I first moved home after university. Unfortunately, the FWB arrangement wasn't quite as casual in my mind and I developed feelings for the guy. Being in my early twenties at the time, the idea of communicating this seemed like the worst thing in the world. (Vulnerability? What's that?) Nonetheless, the man's behaviour towards me wasn't particularly respectful. He'd ignore my texts for days, sometimes weeks. He'd only get in touch with me when he was horny. He'd pick me up and drop me whenever he felt like it. And whenever he texted me, I'd come running. If he sent me a message asking me to come over, I'd spring into action, frantically shaving my legs and moisturising my entire body. When he went quiet after we'd hooked up again, it affected me deeply. But I'd come running back for more the moment he got back in touch. Over the course of nine months, the cycle repeated itself over and over until I felt I had nothing left to give. One day, when his car broke down when we had plans to see each other, I suggested he take a bus to come see me. 'Nah sorry, don't feel like it,' he said. And that was that. 'I don't know what to say to that,' I replied. But I did know what to say, I was just too afraid to end things definitively. The message, however opaque, got through, however. We cut ties. For the time being at least.

I wish it had ended there. But a few months later, he started messaging again. Everyone around me warned me against it. He'd already hurt me so much. How could I possibly let him back in? I couldn't explain it. But each time I replied to a text, I knew I was betraying myself. I didn't tell my friends that I was responding. Not long after he got back in touch, I found out that he was expecting a baby with a woman he'd been seeing while texting me. I was floored by the news. I felt stupid for going back after cutting ties, I felt I'd been made a fool of. That perhaps I'd been labouring under a misapprehension.

In 2019, I decided to approach a therapist to help me make sense of my tendency to not let go of relationships that were no longer serving me. Perhaps I thought I could make him like me, turn this FWB into a boyfriend who loved and respected me. It was like I needed to prove it to myself that I could turn someone's behaviour around. I could turn a withholding person into someone who was obsessed with me. But that fantasy never came true. I never figured out the alchemy of transforming indifference into affection. I started interpreting someone's disinterest in me as an 'ick'. Instead of processing someone's disinterested behaviour towards me as a reflection on my worth, I saw their bad behaviour towards me as unattractive qualities that made me like them less. Inconsistency in their behaviour and communication? Unattractive. Repeatedly cancelling plans on me? Unattractive. Don't want to be with me? Unattractive. That mindset shift made me look not just at the physical and personality attributes that made a person appealing to me – I looked at their behaviour towards me and how those actions made me feel.

A man who communicates how he feels, what he's looking

for, and how he wants us to treat one another? Deeply attractive. Someone who is consistent and makes their interest in you known? Hot. A person who brings up small details from past conversations and shows that they're not only listening, but they're actively thinking about what you've said? Sexy as hell.

Knowing when it's time to walk away is a skill. Exiting a situation that's unworthy of you is an act of self-love. It exudes self-worth. It sends a message to others and to yourself that you deserve more. By communicating boundaries and expectations, we set the bar for how people should behave towards us and let them know when their actions fall short. Sarah Griffiths, a specialist trauma and abuse therapist, advises asking for change when something happens that violates a boundary, for example if someone talks to you in a harsh tone. 'With tone of voice, if you decide that contempt, impatience and irritation is not acceptable, the next time it happens, simply say, "Please don't talk to me like that," and just be firm and don't engage when someone is speaking to you in a tone that is unacceptable to you,' she says. 'Another good one is to ask, "Why are you speaking to me like that?" "What is your motivation for what you just said?" or "Why did you just say / do that?" '

Feelings Aren't Facts

When our inner critic hits the self-sabotage button, we can fall into a pattern of negative self-talk. This means talking to yourself in a negative and destructive way. It's important to challenge these negative thoughts – to tell yourself that this is simply your inner critic speaking, that these statements are not based on reality. If X were true, why would Y and Z have happened? If I'm unlovable, then how come all these wonderful people love me? If I'm ugly, why did X tell me I'm pretty? If I'm not smart, how did I do X?

Daniel Fryer, a psychotherapist at the Priory Hospital Bristol, advises disputing your negative thoughts. 'Every time you think or say something negative about yourself, dispute it by reminding yourself of something you did well or succeeded in,' says Fryer. 'That way, you will be replacing self-criticism with self-compassion.'[15]

Ask Yourself if You Actually Like Them

Do you fancy them? Or are you just worried that they'll reject you? Does the idea of not being liked fill you with fear?

'What if he doesn't fancy me?' I said to my mum over the phone one evening. 'I just can't stop worrying about this date. I feel like he's not going to like me.' It was a moment when my low self-esteem reared its very annoying head and convinced me that my date wasn't going to like me.

'Who cares?' my mum said. 'What matters is: do *you* like him? What matters is: how he makes *you* feel.' It was the strong dose of reality I needed in that moment.

I went on that date and, yes, I was racked with nerves as I sat nursing a pint in a brewery taproom in south London. The guy arrived and we chatted for several hours and I thought he was a nice enough guy, but it wasn't a good fit.

I was thinking about how to extricate myself from the date when he sat down beside me and told me he was very attracted to me and kissed me. 'You might not want to do this on a first date,' he said. 'But do you want to come home with me?' I politely declined and called myself an Uber.

I'd been so focused on whether my dates liked me that I'd neglected to think of my own feelings and whether I was into them. And I wasn't. My mother was right. (She'll be thrilled to have this statement in writing.)

Human beings want to be liked. We care about what other people think about us. And we seek approval. The state of being alone can bring discomfort. Perhaps because we are wired to seek community, but it's worth sitting in that discomfort, overriding those instincts, and asking yourself: Is this what I deserve? Is this the right person for me?

What's Attachment Theory and Why is Everyone Talking About it?

Attachment theory was pioneered in the 1960s by British psychologist and psychiatrist John Bowlby and later expanded upon by Canadian-American psychologist Mary Ainsworth. The idea behind this theory is that humans are, essentially, programmed to behave in certain ways during romantic relationships based on our upbringing. Bowlby defined attachment as 'lasting psychological connectedness between human beings'.[16] You might be familiar with the three main attachment styles: secure, anxious and avoidant. These three styles were identified by Ainsworth, who noticed distinctions between infants and their caregivers: secure, avoidant and ambivalent. Later, researchers added a fourth type – disorganised – to refer to infants who had problems coping with stressful situations. This fourth style is known as anxious-avoidant, sometimes known as fearful-avoidant or disorganised. Attachment theory is hinged on the idea that it is essential for children's emotional and social development that they form a relationship with at least one primary caregiver. How those caregivers interact with their children goes on to shape the child's relationships throughout their lives, resulting in adult attachment styles.

Securely attached people feel comfortable with intimacy, they have more long-lasting and satisfying relationships compared to folks with other attachment styles. 'They have a positive view of themselves, their attachments and relationships,' says psychotherapist Neil Wilkie, creator of online therapy platform The Relationship Paradigm.[17] Anxious types crave intimacy and approval and may become clinging or dependent on a partner. They're afraid of their partner leaving them or being abandoned. Avoidant types tend to evade closeness and hide their emotions, prioritising independence. They feel stifled by intimacy and long-term relationships. Anxious-avoidant types might begin a relationship feeling emotionally available, but as things progress and more commitment is needed, they can become anxious, distant, or uncomfortable with emotional closeness. Anxiously attached folks are more likely to have 'anxiety-driven "solace sex"', according to sex educator Emily Nagoski in her book *Come As You Are*. That means 'using sex as an attachment behaviour – which can make sex intense without making it pleasurable', according to Nagoski. Secure attachers have the most satisfying sex lives, according to a 2012 review of research[18] cited by Nagoski. 'Secure attachers have more positive emotions during sex, more frequent sex, higher levels of arousal and orgasm, and better communication about sex,' she writes. Meanwhile, avoidant attachers, she says, start having sex later in life and typically have sex less frequently. 'Avoidant attachers experience sex as less connected with their lives and with their relationships.'

Is it really that simple? Attachment theory's role in understanding humans' early social development cannot be understated but can we really expect a psychological theory, developed in the mid-twentieth century – long before the mass adoption of smartphones and the dating app revolution – to be the sole lens through which we judge interpersonal relationships and dating habits?

As journalist Vicky Spratt writes in *Refinery29*, 'attachment theory has entered mainstream discourse to become the framework through which increasing numbers of people conceptualise dating and their approach to relationships, with mixed results.'[19]

In prizing secure types as the state to aspire to, you feel slightly pathologised in your behaviour as an anxious or avoidant type. As Spratt writes: 'The implication here, of course, is a hierarchy of personalities. A secure person exhibits the gold standard of behaviour in their relationships. Anxious people are hurt and damaged while avoidants are cold fishes. Can people in all of their complexity really be so neatly categorised?'

Spratt questions whether attachment theory has gone too far. 'Is someone "avoidant" because they don't text you back immediately? Or are they busy and showing their respect for you by staying on top of their professional obligations so that you can build a life together? Are you "anxious" because you've freaked out slightly that you're falling in love and starting to feel vulnerable? Or is it normal to feel exposed as you reveal your soft underbelly to another?' she asks. 'Most of us, I am sure, have been on both sides of each scenario at least once. And isn't trying to control a situation by pathologising a person's behaviour because you don't like it the opposite of love?'

Anxious-Avoidant Attachment

Attached was first published in 2010, and since then has sold over 2 million copies. It's widely regarded as a handbook for modern dating, a resource for making sense of other people's behaviour. On TikTok, videos explaining the core tenets of attachment theory abound. Armchair dating experts recount stories of chasing after a disinterested prospective partner, incessant thoughts of the person who was rejecting them, and an urgent feeling that they needed to rail against this. Watching these videos, it's easy to get sucked in, particularly if you're going through a confusing dating experience. I've certainly consumed this content and thought to myself, 'It all makes sense, I'm anxious and he's avoidant, end of story.'

But, is that really all there is to it? And is it really as simple as that?

Zara, 31 and straight, tells me she lived in a house where, at one point, there were more copies of *Attached* than inhabitants. Zara describes her attachment style as anxious-avoidant. 'I definitely used to be more anxious but then I had a bunch of really like more avoidant partners and weirdly that's made me more avoidant now. I would say that I probably err on the side of more avoidant than anxious these days.'

When it comes to how it impacts her love life, Zara says she forensically examines people's signals to try to figure out whether or not they like her and to try and read the situation. 'It makes me hypervigilant and hyperattentive to people's various different behaviours, and I'm constantly making a list of things that are for and against – whether or not they do or don't like me or how they might behave – to try and predict future behaviour or any different outcomes.'

Zara finds it difficult to predict how people are going to behave and it means she always prepares herself for the worst-case eventuality. 'I say to myself sometimes, okay, well if I never hear from him again, I never hear from him again.'

'Some of this I think is just having to date as a woman and prepare yourself and be detached from their [men's] behaviour,' she says. As an anxious-avoidant, she feels she is 'hyper push-me-pull-you', in the way she responds to people. She finds dating very tiring because she's constantly homing in on other people's behaviour in a romantic context.

'Because your brain is being used over time to accrue evidence and file it and categorise it based on: am I going to feel abandoned, or am I gonna feel trapped?' She feels she's always looking for evidence of two things: entrapment or abandonment.

Zara says she doesn't 'act anxious-avoidant'. 'I don't think people would know,' she says. 'But I do know from people that they find me very difficult to read, because another consequence of the attachment style, I think, is the hyper awareness which then leads to hypervigilance around your own behaviour.' She rarely makes the first move because, she says, 'the stakes feel too high'.

'When I first start liking somebody, I can feel quite stressed,' she says. 'I'm like, "Oh God, am I gonna get swept away by this? Is this going to be something that's going to cause me pain or distress or discomfort?" I have a deep sense of dread.' Having the language to describe this particular state of being is helpful for Zara because it gives her an awareness of what is happening, an understanding of her own emotions, and she's able to observe herself while it's going on.

'I'm very strict about doing anything that would make it seem like somebody else had got one over on me,' she says. 'I would never double text, I would never ask to see someone if they hadn't asked to see me the last time. If it's been two or three hours since the last message, I'll mirror their behaviour back. I would never be the first person to say "I like you".'

'It helps to try and understand yourself'

Attachment theory is helpful when it comes to identifying why we might have acted in a certain way, or perhaps why we keep falling into the same patterns. It's worth noting, of course, that attachment style isn't the only thing at play in these situations. So, while it's useful in some respects, it can also be reductive and not show you the entire picture of what's going on.

Sophie, 37 and straight, hasn't had a serious relationship for a few years, but has had a few casual situationships that have made her think she's an anxiously attached person. 'I tend to not like many people at all but when I do I become quite obsessed,' she says. 'It's usually a certain cliché type of male. I'm attracted to avoidant types and they never want to commit so this creates an environment for anxiety. I try to appear unbothered and super cool most of the time so I end up constantly anxious not knowing where I stand. I'm trying to learn to ask for a certain level of communication,' she says. But in her experience, expressing those needs hasn't had fruitful results. She feels she's always looking and analysing to see signs or patterns that the person might like her. 'And if I don't get those I assume the worst,' she says.

'My last situationship ended because he didn't want it to end badly. So, he ended it while we were good and it was crushing for me,' she says. 'I am trying to dig deep into these patterns and listen to people and also figure out what triggers certain things. But also I think I purposefully go for these casual situations,' she says. 'So I don't have to go through a full breakup in the long run.'

She says she wants to find a secure man to date, but she never finds herself attracted. 'It's just hard as the nice safe guys just don't appeal. How do we give these nice men a chance and not write them off after two dates with no chemistry? It helps to try and understand yourself,' she says. 'But it's all hard work. Trying to find dates, trying to find them when you feel good and not hormonal. Trying to find someone you even like.'

The relational skills gap

Just as I looked to horoscopes in my teens and twenties to find insights about whether my crush might fancy me back, attachment style discourse appeals to us because it allows us to categorise people who aren't meeting our needs into neat little boxes. Instead of accepting that someone might not be right for us, that they might not be interested, saying someone's avoidant feels less hurtful, less like we're being rejected, and we can lay the blame at the feet of the rejecter by making them the problem. In reality, it's probably just not a match, maybe they're emotionally unavailable, or you want different things. Ultimately, it's unlikely you'll ever truly know the 'why' and it's worth asking yourself if ruminating on the possibilities is worth the energy and time, particularly when the relationship is over.

Societally, we aren't taught about healthy relationships. If we're lucky, it might be a conversation our parents or guardians have with us. But that's not true of everyone. We're fed pseudoscience online because there's a market for it – largely because we're all feeling around in the dark, looking for answers as to why someone isn't texting us back, why someone might be pulling away.

Todd Baratz, a licensed therapist who posts on Instagram as @yourdiagnonsense says, 'not everyone is relationally skilled. And in fact, the majority of the population is pretty unskilled and it's not because they're toxic. It's because we live in a culture that teaches us literally nothing about relationships. So the result is oftentimes a mismatch in terms of emotional maturity, intelligence or awareness that we would really hope was there,' he says.

Perhaps knowing your attachment style is useful in helping you identify patterns in your behaviour. But that shouldn't come at the expense of pathologising yourself and minimising your emotional needs. Attachment theory is regarded as an important contribution to developmental psychology and our understanding of child development, but it is not without its criticisms from fellow psychologists. Some have questioned the universality of the theory and its lack of accounting for cultural differences. Other critics have taken issue with the emphasis on the mother-child bond in the theory – with some saying it could marginalise other caregivers, like fathers, siblings or other guardians. Others have challenged the idea that an attachment style is fixed and unchangeable, with some studies finding that attachment styles can change over time.

Judith Rich Harris criticised attachment theory for underestimating children's minds. 'The child's mind is more capacious and discerning than attachment theorists give it credit for,' writes Rich.[20] 'Early-appearing, long-lasting personality characteristics, often mistaken for the lingering effects of early experiences, are more likely due to genetic influences on personality.'

Attachment style shouldn't be an excuse for bad behaviour

Attachment style is also not a get-out-of-jail-free card for avoiding accountability in relationships. Just because one partner happens to be avoidant, for example, does not mean that they're off the hook when it comes to meeting their partner's emotional needs.

Kim, 33 and bisexual, spent her teens and twenties embroiled in 'a mess of back-to-back relationships with avoidant men'. At the time, Kim was anxiously attached, but she says that's now changed and she feels more avoidant. 'This manifested in my absolutely desperate need to be loved in a romantic relationship,' she says. 'I wanted to be rescued and would morph into whatever person I needed to be to make that happen – if I was a victim then surely I wouldn't be abandoned.'

Kim was cheated on in almost every single relationship, most of which she didn't end. 'In hindsight, they felt suffocated but I was basically too pathetic for them to walk away and they were too cowardly to leave anyway so they tried to hurt me as a way of escaping (we were all young, not bad people!),' she says. 'I made it my partner's choice to leave because I thought if I could just work hard enough, they might love me enough to change.'

Kim found that attachment styles were used against her by partners. 'Partners have treated me poorly and then blamed me for not accounting for their attachment style, as if it's written in stone and they don't have any accountability for it,' she says. 'I do think that labelling some of these issues helps but it's important that they're not used as an excuse.'

Kim started seeing a therapist who specialises in attachment theory in her mid-twenties, which helped her reflect on her own behaviour, and that of other people, and make sense of it. That understanding has been key in feeling less shame towards herself and less anger towards others. 'Other than my abusive ex-partner, I really do hold a lot of compassion for my partners in the past – we were young and all just doing our best despite living in a world that doesn't encourage healthy relationships,' she says.

Kim's words certainly ring true – when society doesn't encourage healthy relationships, we grow up not knowing how to behave or what to expect from our partners. We're all just trying to figure it out as best we can, but without a handbook to guide us through. Attachment theory isn't the problem per se. It's our over-reliance on this framework for making sense of other humans. Human beings are messy, relationships are messy, dating is messy.

Instead of trying to figure out the attachment style of the person you're talking to, a better use of your time might be to identify your emotional needs and how you can communicate them to ensure they're met. Perhaps instead of spending so much time thinking about attachment types, we could use that energy to build empathy and listening skills. Empathy *is* a skill and it requires work. As journalist Rebecca Ruiz writes, 'humans do inherit a genetic predisposition toward empathy and generosity,' but it is a mistake to assume that those traits are fixed at a particular level.[21] Actively practising empathy can help us see the humanity in the people we date. That doesn't mean tolerating treatment and behaviour that's out of step with our values. It means not viewing potential partners as the enemy and instead seeing them as human – flawed, imperfect individuals with complex and rich stories and personalities and, crucially, not a checklist of abstract traits and categories.

11

Moving On

You know you've got it bad when you're lurking on your FWB's housemate's Instagram page and you accidentally like a photo of his grandparents. I'd been trying to figure out why Sam, the guy I was casually hooking up with, wasn't replying to my texts. He had read receipts turned on, so I knew he'd seen the messages. That's when I decided to shapeshift into Hercule Poirot and engage in some highly ill-advised internet sleuthing. It never ends well. You find yourself scrolling through their mum's Facebook page, hoping and praying you don't accidentally like something. You trawl through their Twitter (or X) likes to see if you can find evidence that they're talking to someone else. You look through their Instagram followers to see if they've started following anyone new.

You're caught in a vicious circle and it feels terrible. Time and time again, I've witnessed my close friends doing the same. Discovering their exes have a new girlfriend by obsessively checking their tagged photos on Instagram. One friend even made me accompany her in walking past the flat of the guy she was seeing to see if he was home (they're now married). Another friend told me she couldn't stop Insta-stalking her fiancé's ex-situationship and couldn't figure out why. I'd wager that we all know someone – if not multiple people – who's acted in the way I've just described.

So, why do we stalk our ex's new partner? What's behind the social media sleuthing when we're obsessed with our situationship? Why do we look for online evidence when our FWB isn't texting us back? Why can't we stop overthinking our interactions? Why do we get hung up on people who just aren't that into us?

'Why am I stalking my ex?'

In March 2023, Yasmin, 28, met her now-boyfriend, 29, (both straight) on Hinge. They chatted on the app for about four days before swapping numbers. Their first messages were about a meme she'd put on her profile.

Two weeks later, they went out for drinks. 'I knew I liked him straight away but I get along with everyone so that's not much of a tell,' Yasmin explains. 'We got along really well and we ended up going on a night out to a rave together on the first date because we were having such a great time.'

They hung out the following night, and then the following weekend, they both went to an event and had a sleepover and she didn't leave his house until 9pm on the Sunday.

Yasmin says they clicked so well because they'd texted quite a lot and been quite open about what they were both looking for. 'I think we were both specifically not looking for a relationship, lol. So, I think it made us be a bit more authentic, and I am very open and I ask a lot of questions (maybe too many) so we'd spoken about a lot of things before we met.'

Early in the relationship, just after they'd both followed each other on Instagram, something happened which brought them closer together. 'This might sound weird, but this girl who he had been on a date with randomly followed me on Instagram the day after he followed me, and he was our only mutual so I asked who she was and then he realised she'd been following any new girls he followed,' Yasmin explains.

After that happened, they had a talk about it. 'I think it set the conversation to be less surface level which then allowed us to talk quite openly.'

'He said he'd noticed it with one other person but because they're both creatives he thought it could've been a work thing,' she says. 'But then with me there was no other explanation.'

There was no contact between Yasmin and the woman who'd followed her. It unnerved her to know that someone was watching his online behaviour so closely.

'I felt bad for her because I know what it's like to be obsessive,' she says. 'But also . . . sis. We both blocked her and she texted him like "Sorry I'll leave you alone now." '

Having that chat meant they could open up to each other and talk frankly about their emotional needs.

Journalist Olivia Petter, author of *Millennial Love* and host of 'Love Lives' podcast, wrote an article about her own experience of 'stalking' her boyfriend's exes. 'With my ex, I remember looking back at all of his ex-girlfriends, and just internalising all of the ways that we were similar and different and trying to create meaning out of each of those things,' Petter explains. She'd look at the pictures of the women and compare how they dressed to her own style and attempt to infer meaning from that difference. Her thought process would go like this: 'Maybe he doesn't like girls who dress like that and maybe he likes girls who dress like me or maybe I need to dress more like her and maybe I need to stop wearing these clothes?' Then her attention would turn to their makeup. 'I would be like: She didn't wear any makeup. Maybe I should stop wearing makeup. Maybe that's what he likes. Oh my god. What if he doesn't like me as much as the ex because I wear so much makeup. What if he thinks that I'm really superficial.'

So, why do we do this? Why are so many of us checking up on our exes' new partners? Why do we look back on new partners' former flames? Petter believes this habit is caused by internalised misogyny.

'I think, unfortunately, that women are raised with a lot of internalised misogyny. I think women who date men bear the brunt of that because you are constantly thinking about the other women that your partner has been with,' says Petter. 'If you have any modicum of self-esteem issues, or insecurities about your body or about the way you look or anything about you, which is most women, inevitably, at some point, particularly at a vulnerable moment, let's say you're hung over or tired, your brain is going to go to those dark places of self-doubt and rumination.' If you're having a moment with your partner where you don't feel completely secure, it's an easy trap to fall into. 'You will start creating all sorts of narratives in your head based on the information that you find and that's all they are – false narratives. They are fantasies, works of fiction, but the more information you discover, the harder it is to separate fact from fiction, I think, and that's the trap that I've been sucked into so many times.'

Socially, women who date men have been conditioned to regard each other as romantic threats, as competition for male attention. A 2023 study found that women are more likely to undergo appearance enhancements – such as cosmetic surgery, dieting, beauty treatments – when they perceive a threat to their relationship. The study found that romantic jealousy essentially prompts women to go through costly and risky procedures.[1]

In dating, a scarcity mindset means believing that you have limited romantic prospects and therefore you have to essentially take what you can get. Dating coach Hayley Quinn says: 'This often leads to you holding on to interactions too tight, meaning you don't walk away when you should. Even if someone isn't giving you the respect that you deserve.'[2] Petter says this is something she still struggles with now. She's conscious of it, but that doesn't stop the noise in her head. 'From the first second I meet someone new, I almost immediately start wondering about their exes,' she says. 'It's the same with when your ex moves on and you start looking at who they're moving on with and you start creating all sorts of meaning. Thoughts aren't facts, but it's very hard to see that in your lowest moments. I think it's a form of emotional self-harm to get sucked into that trap.'

This is what happened to me in early 2022 when scrolling through Facebook at bedtime.

I'd had a situationship with a guy I'd initially been good friends with. When things had fallen apart, I'd had to remove him from social media to remove the temptation to look at his profiles. But one thing I'd forgotten to do was unfriend him on Facebook. Just as I'm about to drift off to sleep, I see a photo of his new girlfriend in my feed alongside a caption full of heart and fire emojis. I went from feeling blissed out and ready for peaceful slumber, to my heart pounding and tears welling in my eyes.

I knew it would hurt me to look, but I did it anyway. I clicked on his Facebook profile and looked through photo after photo of his new girlfriend and compared myself to her. Was she prettier than me? Thinner than me? My inner critic, famously fond of fuelling my body image issues, clutched onto that detail. He'd told me he liked women with curves – was that just a line to get me into bed? I was the in-between girl, he'd tried me on for size and found me wanting.

For days I felt sad. I kept returning to the photos as if trying to find a secret hidden in them. What was I looking for? Proof that I wasn't good enough? Evidence of what she'd done differently? I'd fallen into the self-comparison trap and couldn't pull myself out.

In reality, love and attraction are so much more complex than that. And if I'd been compassionate with myself then, I'd have realised the photos didn't hold the answers I so desperately sought. There is no rhyme or reason to the situation. It was just a stick to beat myself with. No clarity, just pain.

'Why hasn't he texted me?'

In a recent talking stage with a guy I liked, I found myself feeling a little vulnerable and exposed after suggesting a date with him. He'd responded positively enough and we'd chatted for a decent amount of time afterwards, but it hadn't been enough to quell the anxieties I'd been feeling about this person. Were we ever going to meet up? Or did he just want to keep me on his bench, using me for validation and attention?

I sat back and watched as I surveyed who'd looked at my Instagram Stories – his name conspicuously absent from the list. I trawled my mind for an explanation. I checked local news – any storms? Power outages? Maybe his internet is down. Maybe he just has crap wifi? Perhaps he's taking a break from his phone. Maybe he has a sick relative and is visiting them in hospital. Maybe he's sick! Never-ending scenarios whirring in my mind.

I checked my Instagram viewed list so many times that I got a message saying: 'We limit how often you can do things on Instagram to protect our community.'

Bloody hell, I thought. How many times had I checked it? Certainly enough times for Instagram to think I was some kind of spammer or bot. Time to get a grip, girl. What was I even looking for, anyway? Confirmation that he still fancied me? A sign that he's not talking to someone else?

Overthinking

In those early stages of dating, we place so much importance on the frequency of texts. Akin to the 'if he wanted to he would' maxim, we say 'it takes a second to send a text'. We have a zero-tolerance policy to someone whose text messages aren't giving us the sense that they'd take a bullet for us.

I, for one, have got myself worked into a state when I've perceived a change in texting patterns. Questions will dominate my thoughts: Why hasn't he texted me? Is he taking longer than usual to reply to me? Did I say something wrong in my last messages? Is he dating other people? Perhaps he's on a date right now?

It's important to remind yourself that the frequency of a person's texts is not a failsafe barometer of their feelings for you. If you need constant messaging to make yourself feel reassured of their feelings, sit with that and ask yourself why? Maybe the question we should be asking on dates is: What's your texting style? If you're confused, ask for clarity. If they're not feeling it, you'll get your answer. If they're into you, they won't mind this question at all.

There are several ways you can do this – depending on how brave you're feeling. The first time I ever mustered the courage to do this, I did it in a very indirect way. 'I felt confused last night when we were talking, and I often feel that way, perhaps because when we slept together, we blurred the lines between friendship and something more. I guess I'm asking if you feel confused about that too.' More recently, I've felt braver: 'I would like to explore this connection, but I want to check that we're on the same page – if not, I'd rather know.' Just a few weeks ago (and feeling rather emboldened) I went with: 'The signals I'm getting are very hot and cold and it's hard not to interpret that as disinterest. Typically, I need more consistency in the early stages of dating to sustain my interest.'

'Why can't I move on?'

After someone's broken up with you, or a situationship has fizzled, have you found yourself wanting the person even more than before? You feel you want to pursue this person even more. You're experiencing 'frustration attraction' – a term coined by anthropologist Helen Fisher.

Scientists have theorised that there are two phases of rejection: protest and despair. In the protest stage, humans become consumed by the idea of regaining the lost lover and levels of the neurotransmitters dopamine and norepinephrine in the blood increase as the person searches for the person who's abandoned them. This is a stress reaction, but it mimics the feeling of being in love, which triggers the release of neurotransmitters.

As Fisher explains, 'frustration attraction may be a direct result of the protest response: As abandonment elevates the activity of central dopamine during protest, this rising catecholamine simply intensifies one's passion.'[3] Catecholamines are hormones produced by your adrenal glands in response to physical or emotional stress – the main types include dopamine, norepinephrine and epinephrine (also known as adrenaline). Fisher theorises that the brain's stress system may also play a significant role in frustration attraction. 'As stress increases, it triggers the production of dopamine (and norepinephrine) and suppresses serotonin activity, the cock-tail of neurotransmitters associated with romantic love,' writes Fisher. Fisher also identifies another brain response associated with frustration attraction: our reward system. 'Frustration attraction may also be due, in part, to another brain response associated with abandonment: the neural reaction to a delayed reward. When an expected reward is delayed in coming, reward-expecting neurons prolong their activities.[4] These neurons are central components of the brain's dopaminergic reward system, the pathways associated with romantic love.'

Just One More Dopamine Hit

The rush of lust is part and parcel of our brain's response to dating – the reward system, also known as the mesolimbic system, activates whenever we do anything rewarding, such as eating a nice meal, having sex, using an addictive drug. When positive stimuli (be it substances, social interaction, food, sex) are detected, the brain's dopamine pathways work to respond by releasing dopamine. As a neurotransmitter, dopamine is a kind of chemical messenger that helps us feel pleasure and forms part of the brain's reward system and pleasure centre.[5] This results in certain stimuli being associated with a feeling of reward or happiness, and as a result, people change their behaviour to keep eliciting those warm fuzzy feelings. These pathways are activated when we match with someone on dating apps and when we receive messages or likes from people we fancy. 'Dating apps are just big slot machines,' according to Dr David Greenfield, assistant clinical professor of psychiatry at the University of Connecticut School of Medicine.[6] 'First you have an anticipation of the possibility of something occurring, and that anticipated reward elevates dopamine by 100 percent. In other words, it's double the reward. When you actually check it and there's somebody of interest to you, you'll get another secondary hit of dopamine.'

Why Do You Want Them Back After They've Dumped You?

When you're dealing with romantic rejection, there are believed to be two phases: 'protest' and 'despair' (based on how infants respond to separation from caregivers).

As Fisher explains: 'During a protest phase, romantically rejected individuals often obsessively try to win back the beloved. As resignation sets in, they give up and slip into despair. However, these general phases of rejection grief are not yet substantiated.'[7]

One study by Fisher et al looked at fMRI brain scans of people who were still in love with someone who'd rejected them and found that 'looking at a romantic rejecter and cocaine craving have several neural correlates in common.'[8] This same study also found that people who were in love with their rejecters experienced the activation of the brain's reward system. In the study, Fisher explained that their hypothesis behind the activation of the reward system is 'partly because adversity tends to heighten feelings of romantic love and because when a reward is delayed in coming, reward-expecting neurons in the reward system prolong their activity.'

So, what does that protest phase look like? During this protest phase, you think about getting them back. You think to yourself, 'Perhaps if I could just change [insert insecurity] about myself, he/she/they will like me again.' The idea of the relationship being irredeemably over feels inconceivable.

According to Fisher, 'abandoned lovers are generally dedicated to winning their sweetheart back. They obsessively dissect the relationship, trying to establish what went wrong; and they doggedly strategize about how to rekindle the romance.'

The danger of the protest phase is that this obsessive refusal to accept the end of a relationship can lead to rejection violence, harassment, stalking.

Psychiatrists say the protest phase is a fundamental 'mammalian reaction' to the dissolution of a social connection.

Picture this. You go on a few dates with someone. You're attracted to them. You see potential in them. You start imagining what a relationship with them might be like. But those feelings aren't mutual. They might tell you in semi-explicit terms that it's 'not a match', that they 'don't see the connection progressing beyond friendship', or that they 'didn't feel a spark'. Or, they might say something that suggests the stars aren't quite aligning – which may be true, or it may be them trying to soften the blow. 'Hey, so I've really enjoyed getting to know you, but I'm just not sure I'm ready for a relationship,' or 'I'm not sure I'm over my ex.'

The danger with the second type of rejection is that it leaves too much room for hope.

It's a rejection, but softened. It's not me, it's just – they're not ready *right now*. Maybe once some time passes, they'll come back to me. Maybe they'll want me someday?

So, when you're typing out that paragraph to the person who just dumped you, trying to convince them that you can make it work, consider for a moment whether you might just be in the protest phase.

After the breakup – whether it was an LTR, a situationship, a couple of dates, whatever – if you find yourself checking for 'signs', it's worth paying attention to your own behaviour. Do you compulsively check who's viewed your Instagram Story to see if the person who's rejected you has viewed it? Do you get a little buzz when you see their name in the list of viewers? Do you find yourself posting more to your stories to get that nugget of validation, that nibble of dopamine, that reward. This is simply your brain's reward system.

You're not 'checking to see if your ex is still in love with you' or 'wondering if he wants you back yet'. No. Your brain just wants a nice dopamine-flavoured treat.

Much weight has been placed on the meaning of viewing a person's Instagram Story. The term 'orbiting' has been used to describe someone who ghosts a person, then regularly pops up in the 'viewed' list on Instagram. During my time reporting on tech's intersection with our dating behaviour, the Instagram Story has become a topic of much discussion. Imbuing meaning into the Instagram Story viewers can fuel this protest phase, lull you into a state of delusion where you convince yourself that they're obsessed with you and that they want you back. Looking at your story isn't enough. Step away from your phone. Take a break from Instagram. Or from posting on your story. Break the cycle. If a person wants to get back together, they'll probably text you or call you.

In the meantime, fill up your own cup.

12

Atypical Love

Dating hits differently when you're neurodivergent or experiencing mental illness. Traditionally, conversations surrounding the trials and tribulations of falling in and out of love have ignored neurodivergent people's lived experiences. Dating rules and advice often centre on the assumption that everyone in the dating realm is neurotypical, ignoring the nuanced ways in which neurodivergence impacts communication, emotional regulation, the way we process rejection, and much more.

This chapter is broken into four main sections, the first is ADHD (Attention Deficit Hyperactivity Disorder), the second is autism spectrum disorder (ASD), the third is Anxiety and the fourth is Borderline Personality Disorder (BPD).

'My whole life, I felt very different from other girls': ADHD and Dating

'I've always felt different and didn't know why.' This statement, in various iterations, was repeated to journalist Patrycja Boryka when she interviewed women for her BBC podcast 'That ADHD Story'. For Boryka, who has ADHD, that sentence really resonated with her own experience. She, too, had always felt a little bit atypical, but for a very long time, couldn't put her finger on the reason why.

'When you've got ADHD, you've got much lower self-esteem because of all the things that you do wrong throughout your life and especially when you're undiagnosed, you feel different and you don't understand why,' Boryka says.

That feeling of being set apart from other people profoundly impacted her first relationship. They'd been together since they were 15 and went to university together, eventually moving in together. But they broke up. 'I feel insecure because, my whole life, I felt very different from other girls,' says Boryka. This feeling of otherness made her view her boyfriend's female friends through an insecure lens.

'He'd have a female friend and I'd feel really insecure about that.' She would look at those friends and think, 'She's a normal girl,' and then look at herself and think, 'I'm not a normal girl. Obviously he's going to ditch me.' She would constantly compare herself to his friendship group of 'cool girls' and form a negative narrative about herself in doing so.

'All these insecurities that I would bring up in not a great way would then lead him to not tell me the truth about stuff,' she says. Boryka's boyfriend would hide the fact that his female friends messaged him because he knew she felt insecure about that.

At the time of their relationship Patrycja was undiagnosed and didn't know she had ADHD. A key symptom of ADHD is emotional dysregulation – a decreased ability to control emotional reactions. People with ADHD feel emotions more intensely. 'I look back and I'm like, wow, it's all my fault for not knowing,' she says. 'A lot of people with ADHD tend to go through that grieving process, especially if you didn't know you had it. You look back at your life and you're like, oh my god, if I knew I had ADHD, I would have done things very differently.'

ADHD is a deeply misunderstood and highly debated

disorder, and misconceptions and lazy stereotypes about the condition persist. One of the main stereotypes is that people with ADHD are always disruptive and hyperactive. This over-emphasis on hyperactivity has resulted in the under-diagnosis of girls, women and adults who didn't have visible signs of hyperactivity and whose ADHD manifested in other ways.[1]

It was as recently as 2000 that the *DSM* – the clinical handbook healthcare professionals use for the diagnosis of mental health conditions – recognised three different types of ADHD. Those three subtypes are: combined type ADHD, predominantly inattentive type ADHD, predominantly hyperactive-impulsive type ADHD.[2] As journalist Jess Joho writes, 'although that added much-needed nuance to capture the diversity of ways ADHD manifests, these additions still omitted a bevy of overlooked symptoms often more prominent in women and girls.'[3] One of those overlooked symptoms is Rejection Sensitive Dysphoria (RSD), which is a form of sensitivity that makes people react strongly when they are being (or sometimes just suspect they are being) rejected.

RSD and emotional dysregulation are symptoms Eleanor has struggled with throughout her dating life. She was diagnosed with ADHD in November 2021 after years of experiencing symptoms she couldn't explain. Rejection sensitive dysphoria certainly impacted her when she was dating. 'I would really struggle if someone had said something a certain way, or if they didn't want to go on another date, or hadn't texted me back. I would feel so emotionally rejected inside,' she says.

Eleanor has had a boyfriend for four and a half years and was diagnosed two years into that relationship. 'Before I was diagnosed, I had a lot of dating experiences that were very much like a flash in the pan,' says Eleanor. 'So, I'd match with someone on a dating app and then get really excited. I'd get the dopamine hit of meeting up with them, chatting to them, and it would go from zero to 100 really, really quickly. And then it would fizzle out because I would get bored.

'I think it's very indicative of the dopamine hit of when you first sort of start seeing someone and then it kind of wears off when that person isn't right for you,' she says. Eleanor was struggling with her mental health when she was dating and says she wasn't able to regulate her emotions because she hadn't yet developed the tools to know how to do that. She would go on dates that centred around alcohol because she was at university at the time, she says, but those dates would 'end in a messy way'. She describes the way she behaved while dating back then as 'scatty and difficult to tie down'. 'That's pretty much how I was before I met my boyfriend,' she adds.

Eleanor feels her ADHD shows up in her relationship with her boyfriend. 'He's autistic, so I think that's a very interesting duo that you probably do see quite a lot – one partner's got ADHD and the other partner's got autism,' says Eleanor. 'I think we kind of balance each other out quite well.' Her partner was with her when she went through the process of getting an ADHD diagnosis and getting the clarity and calm that brought her. 'That's very much something that we have navigated together,' she says.

Eleanor takes Elvanse for her ADHD, a medication currently experiencing UK and worldwide shortages.[4] She finds the medication helps her regulate her anxiety, sleep and emotions. 'I do struggle with my emotional regulation. This is definitely something that's been aided by medication but when I've not been on my medication, I've been very short, my temper is shorter, I can be quite fiery, and that's obviously something that we've both had to sort of balance out together,' she adds. 'I've learned to deal with that, being on my medication and having various therapies.'

She has found transparency helpful in her relationship. 'Together, we've developed tools for being transparent and honest with each other. Whereas before when I was dating people, because obviously I didn't know that I had ADHD, I couldn't be transparent with people and say, "Look, I have ADHD, this is how I feel about X, Y, Z and this might explain this behaviour in certain settings."'

Dopamine and ADHD share a close, yet complex link. Dopamine impacts mood, attention, learning, sleep, movement, the processing of pain, in addition to the function of the heart, kidneys and blood vessels. Scientists have been examining the connection between dopamine and ADHD and researchers don't agree over the biochemistry of the condition.

Brain imaging of patients with ADHD has resulted in no consistent findings on possible causes for the disorder.[5] It's believed, however, that a deficiency in dopamine diminishes executive function, impacting emotional regulation, attention and organisation. Dopamine deficiency hampers focus and impacts learning and memory and decreases motivation. This lack of dopamine means people with ADHD don't experience the same feeling of reward after finishing a task.[6]

Lala, the relationships expert who runs @Lalalaletmeexplain, has ADHD and finds it impacts her love life in a variety of ways, notably with hyperfixation. Hyperfixation refers to an intense focus on a particular topic or interest that causes you to spend huge amounts of time and energy on it, resulting in being fully immersed in it.

'There could be 10 things that I'm supposed to do today, but then suddenly, some story comes up and that is me for two days, I don't read anything else. I am completely fixated on that,' says Lala. 'And it's the same with people, which is where the limerence thing comes in. I will become hyperfocused on someone.' Lala also experiences limerence in her relationships, which she says is linked to the hyperfixation aspect of ADHD.

Impulsivity is another ADHD symptom which impacts her significantly while dating.

'I don't want to wait for anything,' she says. 'The problem is, when you bring that energy to dating, you don't take things slow, you're not like, oh we've only been talking a couple of days. Instead, I'm like, "No, we had a really great first date, come sleep over at my house tomorrow!" Let's do it all right now, there's no time to waste!'

'Another one for me is emotional dysregulation. I can get quite emotionally dysregulated pretty easily, it can take a little while to come back down,' says Lala. 'For example, if I'm sup-posed to meet a guy tonight for dinner and I haven't heard from him all day, and at 6pm an hour before the date then I message him and it's on one tick, the state that I'll get myself into with that is quite intense.'

To find out more, I spoke to Karen Doherty, a psychosexual therapist and relationship coach who specialises in working with couples who are impacted by ADHD or autism spectrum condition (ASC). She's worked with thousands of couples impacted by neurodiversity and spent thousands of hours talk-ing to couples impacted by ADHD. She's been working in this field since 2011, when neurodivergence wasn't being discussed to the extent it is today. She says that when she first started, she 'had a lot of pushback from therapists and psychotherapists, who were very resistant to that interpretation that something neurological could be at play rather than something mental health-related.'

When it comes to ADHD, Doherty says: 'The main issues

are around executive function, communication, and emotional dysregulation.' She adds: 'You do need to be a little bit careful because ADHD is really close to autism. There's loads of comorbidities. I work with both at the same time because a lot of the time there's usually both present, even if people are resistant to that.' A comorbidity refers to the simultaneous presence of two or more conditions. Research suggests that 80 per cent of adults with ADHD have at least one additional coexisting psychiatric condition, such as mood disorders or personality disorders.[7] Comorbidities can include, but are not limited to, anxiety, depression, OCD, bipolar disorder, substance use disorders and learning disabilities. She says that ADHD and autism are actually very similar. 'They manifest very similarly. So even the ADHD experts now are all talking about it in terms of neurodivergence, rather than just ADHD.'

If you're dating someone with ADHD, patience and compassion are key. Try not to criticise your partner – people with ADHD are highly self-critical and experience more perceived criticism from others.[8] When having difficult conversations, keep your language grounded in 'I feel' or 'I want' statements to ensure it doesn't come across as accusatory. Establishing coping strategies together can also help when your partner is experiencing emotional dysregulation – communication really helps here, so you can find out what your partner needs when they're feeling dysregulated.

Love on the Spectrum: Autism and Dating

Lydia Wilkins is the author of *The Autism-Friendly Cookbook* and a journalist specialising in disability and social issues. Wilkins is autistic and tells me masking is a common topic that comes up in conversations about dating and autism. 'Masking is a symptom of ASD [autism spectrum disorder] and I feel this is the most misunderstood thing. Masking is the suppression of autistic traits in order to appear as neurotypical as a coping mechanism,' explains Wilkins. 'This very often gets conflated with the idea that masking is to be liked. It is to cope in a world that is not meant for you.' Stimming – or self-stimulating behaviour – is a term that refers to repetitive body movements or the repetitive use of an object.

Neurotypical people moderate their behaviour in a dating context in order to shape themselves into a more desirable version of themselves and to maximise their chance of success. But it's important to note that this isn't the same thing as masking (aka camouflaging) which is hugely stressful for neurominorities and is carried out in order to avoid negative repercussions.

Masking manifests in several ways. 'If somebody stims with their hands, for example, they will stop doing that. It can mean mimicking other people,' says Wilkins.

Dr Hannah Belcher, lecturer, researcher, and author of *Taking Off the Mask,* explains that masking involves suppressing behaviours 'we find soothing but that others think are "weird".'

Belcher adds: 'It can also mean mimicking the behaviour of those around us, such as copying non-verbal behaviours, and developing complex social scripts to get by in social situations. With this comes a great need to be like others, and to avoid the prejudice and judgement that comes with being "different".'[9]

Natalie Roberts, a relationship coach for neurodivergent people, says, 'Masking is about who society's told them they need to be, who their family of origin has also told them to be, or who they think they should be. I think in dating, it's that we're showing up as who we think we should be.' She adds that 'if you're neurodivergent the chances are you're going to need to mask more and that will likely be to your mental and emotional detriment.'

Autistic people are routinely desexualised and assumed by neurotypicals to not be interested in sex. Wilkins has found that people have desexualised her because she's autistic and assumed that she's not sexual. 'The reactions of people around me have been very informative. There was an assumption that "She's just not interested, she's autistic." And also that I would only date somebody on the spectrum,' she says. She recalls talking to a friend about the Netflix series *Lucifer*, which she describes as having 'a lot of shirtless men'. When she told her friend about the show, Wilkins said the friend reacted in an unusual way. 'She was like, "Oh my god, you're interested in that? I had no idea! But you're autistic. You're not supposed to be saying things like this."' She goes on to say that her experience as an autistic woman has an additional gendered layer to it. 'I think as autistic women, we have to walk a tightrope that is not incumbent on autistic men. We are diagnosed later on in life, and that's because the diagnostic criteria were written for boys because there was an assumption that girls can't possibly be autistic. Why would they be?' This often results in autistic women masking more heavily than their male counterparts who, having been diagnosed earlier in life, haven't been expected to conform as heavily to social expectations.

Another challenge for Wilkins is interpreting other people's expressions – a common difficulty among autistic people.[10] 'I can't read faces,' says Wilkins. 'So unless it's the exaggerated happy or sad expressions, I can't read the in-between and people use this to their advantage.' Before the pandemic, Wilkins attended a course for autistic adults, which she says was the first time in her life she'd been given any support. The course covered life skills like budgeting, and featured a session which aimed to explain what flirting is – but Wilkins says, 'I can't say it was particularly helpful.'

In fact, it was so uninstructive that Wilkins had no idea how to interpret the behaviour of a guy she was spending time with. The man in question had shown an interest in her through various actions, but she wasn't 100 per cent sure of the intention behind his behaviour. 'I remember, for example, he seemed to kind of watch me if I ever left the room. He was always complimenting my clothes and all that sort of thing. If a guy's doing that, then he's probably showing some interest, unless you're friends,' she says.

Wilkins and the guy ended up going for coffee. In the lead-up to that meet-up, she enlisted the help of her friends to help decipher his messages. 'I've been sending screenshots to friends of mine to act as a translator,' she says. 'I've been asking: Can you read this for me? Is he flirting with me? I'm not sure about this.'

She told me that she really liked this person, and it turned out that he was also on the spectrum. 'To not have to talk about the world of ASD was such a relief, because I get asked questions about it all the time. People treat me frankly as a bit of a freak show sometimes. I'm just a person,' says Wilkins.

After meeting up, Wilkins received the following message: 'I had a nice time. To be honest, I think we should just be friends.' That message was immediately followed by: 'Have a nice rest of your life.' Understandably, these were confusing messages to receive. 'Two separate sentences that just contradicted each other,' says Wilkins. 'I wasn't even offended by this point. I just thought, like Nora Ephron says: "everything is copy." '

When she went to tell a friend the story of what happened, she was told, 'Oh, you're so brave.' 'What's brave about that? I mean, a war correspondent is brave for going into war zones.

I'm not brave for going for coffee with someone. It was some sort of hero narrative: "Oh, she's autistic, isn't it so crazy that people like that are doing normal stuff." '

Sophia is AuDHD, a term that describes a person who has both autism and ADHD. She found dating apps challenging because she couldn't discern whether people were genuine or not. Autistic people can have difficulty interpreting social cues, such as facial expressions, physical gestures, or the tone of someone's voice. This can lead to misunderstandings, like the misconstrual of people's feelings, intentions, or thoughts.[11] For Sophia, she found it challenging when she received mixed messages or someone's tone would change. This could be when a new match would spark a dopamine hit, only to be followed by the whiplash of disappointment and disillusionment when they started being overtly sexual or misogynistic right off the bat. 'But then I would have the other side of the coin where men would tell me what they wanted from a relationship and then be overly nice, maybe even love-bombing, for weeks, sometimes months. And then be like "Oh I'm not feeling it." Which sent my brain into overdrive,' she says.

Scientists have found that autistic people have altered dopamine signalling, which could impact social behaviour.[12] 'I really struggled with rejection, but I can always point to each case where I was strung along a bit,' she says. 'So the rejection probably always hit harder anyway.'

Neurotypical people's reactions to autistic people can reveal a great deal. Izzy is autistic with suspected ADHD, and is currently going through the diagnosis process. She has found that when she's disclosed that she's autistic, other people's reactions have been extremely telling, helping her see red flags in her love life. 'It helps weed out bad eggs when you communicate something and their reaction is

TERRIBLE . . . For example, I told my partner at the time that I felt too much for them and kept apologising and they said, "Yeah, you can be quite a lot. We should try to figure out how to work on that." ' That comment made her feel awful.

More broadly, autism manifests in other ways in her love life. 'I think this impacts my dating because I get REALLY attached to people really fast,' she explains. 'And because someone makes me feel happy, I decide that's my way of getting dopamine for a few months, so I very rarely get into actual relationships because they get a bit weirded out by how attached I get so fast. I've found that when my autism has resulted in a lot of burnout for me, someone boosting me up and making me feel good (even if it's really small like them just making me laugh or something like that) has made me feel obsessed and I've developed a micro-crush on them which sometimes stays just that, or other times it's gone on for months of my life.'

Izzy finds that communicating how she feels to her partners has been transformative. 'It's easy to feel like "too much" when you're dealing with "invisible" things like autism,' she says.

Getting an adult diagnosis of autism or AUDHD can be lifechanging and affirming, but it can also come with mixed emotions. People report experiencing relief at having an explanation for symptoms they'd been experiencing their whole life, a sense of finally making sense of the past. Making sense of an adult diagnosis can also bring feelings of grief for the past, imagining how different childhood and early adulthood could have been had one's neurodivergence been supported and understood. Faced with these emotions, some find it helpful to speak to therapists to make sense of – and attempt to heal from – the harm and trauma they experienced as an undiagnosed child or adolescent.[13]

When do I bring up my neurodivergence?

Knowing when to open up and share that you're neurodivergent in a relationship does not have a one-size-fits-all answer. Natalie Roberts, the relationship coach for neurodivergent people, says this is a question which comes up with her clients. 'I think it's a very individual choice,' she says. 'It will reflect how comfortable you are with those parts of yourself.'

She explains that the decision to disclose that you're neurodivergent boils down to feeling safe. 'We have to decide that for ourselves rather than when society says that it's safe. It comes back to how safe you feel. I think it's vulnerable to share any aspect of who we are. Neurodivergence is an important aspect of who we are,' says Roberts.

But at the very same time, she points out that this isn't a challenge that neurotypical people have to contend with or even consider. 'I don't think many neurotypical people have ever had to pause for a moment to weigh up whether it's safe to reveal that they're neurotypical. People who are neurotypical won't be thinking that they need to declare that.'

With sharing this kind of information, there can be an uncertainty as to how the other person will react. 'There are different ways to share this information and everyone's very different,' says Roberts. 'You will have no idea how somebody else will react to it. It comes down to what level of confidence you have to talk about it, whether a partner already has an understanding of it, or whether they're open to learning about it if they don't.'

If a neurotypical partner is curious and wants to ask questions, that also takes a level of comfort and vulnerability on the part of the neurodivergent individual.

So, how can neurotypical partners make their neurodivergent partners feel safe when they are sharing this information?

'The best thing you can do is to bring openness and curiosity,' says Roberts. Even if you have some degree of familiarity with neurodivergence, don't assume you know everything. 'I work in this space, but if somebody tells me that [they're neurodivergent], I don't then assume I know everything, because I don't know,' she says. 'I don't know where they're at with themselves. I don't know what it means for them. I don't know what words they use for it yet.'

Roberts works with people who might have only learned about their neurodivergence later in life and says that comes with unique experiences. 'Some have even been married for many years and then discover it and, for whatever reason, that relationship or marriage breaks down, and then they're now approaching new relationships with that information,' says Roberts. 'I speak to some people who have known they're autistic for 10 years and they sometimes still say, "I'm still working this out myself." We're all working ourselves out. I think that is a really helpful message to be sharing – we're all working ourselves out and discovering who we are for our whole life.'

Dating While Anxious

'Anxiety is the most common mental health condition seen in our society,' according to Danesh Alam, MD, medical director of Behavioral Health Services at Northwestern Medicine Central DuPage Hospital.[14] Researchers believe that anxiety symptoms are caused by a disruption to the emotional processing brain structures, which is known as the limbic system and consists of the hippocampus, amygdala, hypothalamus and thalamus.[15] People with anxiety disorders are thought to have heightened activity in these parts of the brain.

Gabriel, 35 and gay, had been WhatsApping a guy he'd met on a dating app and the two had been sending photos back and forth. While in the gym one day, the guy asked him what he was up to and asked for a pic. 'I went and surreptitiously took a photo of myself, it was just a full body pic in the mirror,' says Gabriel.

He felt pretty chill right after sending it, but after about 10 minutes or so, he hadn't received a reply to the photo and his anxiety started to bubble up. The more time went on, the more he panicked. 'I was like, maybe I don't have signal? But no, I had full signal, 5G, everything.'

By the end of the gym session, Gabriel had reached the belief that 'well, that's that then. I'm fucking ugly. I'm never gonna hear from him again,' he says. An hour and a half later, Gabriel had finished at the gym and was getting coffee and was in a state where he was constantly checking his phone. 'I felt really devastated. I was like, oh my god I'm ugly, I'm fat,' he says. The catastrophising had gone into overdrive.

'As I was driving home, I had accidentally put my phone on loud. And I saw his message come up and I basically nearly crashed the car reading it,' he says. 'It was a fire emoji and a heart and I was like, oh my God, thank God, I have value, I'm not nothing. It was the biggest euphoria relief I've ever felt in my entire life,' says Gabriel. 'I never look at texts or anything when I'm driving. I was fully possessed by it for two hours and felt worthless. And since then, that whole conversation just completely fizzled out, we spoke the next day and then I realised I wasn't really that interested in seeing that person anyway.'

Everyone experiences worry from time to time. But when anxious thoughts become a long-term experience, it could be caused by generalised anxiety disorder (GAD). GAD causes uncontrollable worrying about all aspects of your life, such as work, your health, dating, relationships, friendships, among many other things. The psychological symptoms of GAD include feeling perpetually 'on edge', experiencing feelings of dread or fear, finding it hard to concentrate, irritability and restlessness, per the NHS.[16] GAD also manifests in physical symptoms such as dizziness or light-headedness, trembling or shaking, palpitations, insomnia, excessive sweating, nausea, headache, muscle aches, to name a few.[17]

While GAD is the main anxiety disorder, there are several other anxiety disorders including (but not limited to) panic disorder, agoraphobia, social anxiety disorder, in addition to specific phobias.[18]

Anxiety and dating apps

When anxiety collides with dating, what is the impact? A 2020 study published in *Cyberpsychology, Behavior, and Social Networking* journal found that people with social anxiety and depression were found to use dating apps more often.[19] The authors of the study did not, however, establish whether social anxiety and depression cause people to turn to dating apps more frequently, or if high usage of the apps results in negative mental health outcomes. Further research is needed to establish whether there is a causal link. 'This study is the first to empirically demonstrate a positive correlation between dating app use and symptoms of social anxiety and depression,' says Ariella Lenton-Brym, a PhD student in clinical psychology at Ryerson University, and one of the authors of the study.[20] While increased use of apps was established, men with social anxiety and depression were also found to be less likely to start up a conversation with a match.

Another 2020 study found that users of swipe-based dating apps reported higher levels of anxiety, depression and distress, compared to those who don't use those apps.[21]

Socially anxious women are more likely to be interested in finding love on dating apps, the study found. 'With increased symptoms of social anxiety and depression, women may be even more likely to turn to technology for social connection, especially if alternative forms of social contact are reduced due to social avoidance,' says author Professor Martin Antony, from Ryerson University in Toronto, Canada.[22]

For people living with an anxiety disorder, avoidance behaviours are common. It makes sense, right? If something makes you feel dread, panic, stress, and makes you lightheaded and dizzy, chances are you'll probably avoid doing it. A 2021 study found that people with higher social anxiety were less likely to have a romantic partner.[23]

For me, my love life and my anxiety have been very close bedfellows, leading me to have long periods of dating avoidance. I've held my phone out in front of me, watching those three grey dots appear in a conversation, feeling panic surge through my body. My heart has raced when I've mustered up the long-overdue courage to send a message expressing how I feel to someone I like. A red blotchy rash spreads across my chest as I sit on a first date, hoping that he won't notice (in fact, typically I choose high-necked outfits or scarves to cover up!). My hands have trembled as I've waited for my situationship to show up at my flat.

There have been times when this anxiety was completely debilitating. I've dated men who made me so anxious, I would throw up after seeing them. I've had panic attacks before second dates because I knew I wasn't that interested in the person and I was stressed about the prospect of that person trying to kiss me. I have felt like a freak, like I'm 'too sensitive', like I'm not mentally capable of handling the emotions involved with finding love, feeling ill-equipped for the ups and downs and the uncertainties of courtship.

Dating is a major trigger for my anxiety and because of the deeply unpleasant symptoms and emotional impact, I've opted many times to simply avoid dating, to opt out for a while. Usually it's to protect myself, to keep myself on an even keel. But while I'm wrapped up in the safety of my no-dating security blanket, 1 also feel like I'm letting my anxiety win. I don't believe I should have to sacrifice my own mental wellbeing for the sake of finding a partner, but I also don't want to rule out finding love because my mental health has made me avoid doing so. It's a double-edged sword.

In early 2020, I decided it was high time I spoke to someone – I had been putting it off for years and telling myself that nothing was wrong. I remember that first therapy session so well – I sat down in her armchair and instantly burst into floods of tears. I hadn't realised the weight of what I'd been carrying around with me, how much it was pressing on me. Even now, in dating contexts, I can sense the anxiety rearing its head from time to time, like a rising water level in a river prone to flooding.

Anxiety around dating can cause us to look for patterns in others' behaviour, to look for signs that we're about to be rejected or broken up with, rendering us in a constant state of hypervigilance. Rebecca has depression, anxiety and OCD. Her OCD manifests through perfectionism and obsessive thoughts. 'Since being single, my anxiety and OCD have got so much worse, which I think modern dating culture has really contributed to,' she says. 'I'm in my mid 30s and I would still like to have children one day. Having that biological clock ticking away has turned swiping on dating apps into an obsession, and I spend more time than I like to think about swiping away hoping to find "the one" . . . A couple more years and I'll be looking at having a baby with a donor. Still keeping my fingers crossed of meeting someone first though,' she says.

Rebecca gets very anxious about saying no to people, or choosing to stay home instead of going on a date with someone – 'just in case that's the one night when I'm going to meet Mr Right.' As a result, she eventually felt completely burned and is now finally having to learn how to put herself first.

She's found that she questions everything to the nth degree when she meets someone who claims they're looking for a relationship. 'I'm always on red alert for them wanting to leave or not being trustworthy or questioning whether I've made the right decision or whether I should still be looking for someone more suited to me,' she says. 'The anxiety dominates any relationships and I can't just relax and see how things go! So much advice online is to follow your gut feeling, but I can't really trust my gut feeling as it's driven by the anxiety and the OCD.'

What's 'dating anxiety'?

We know that dating is particularly anxiety inducing. But there's actually a psychological term that's used to describe the specific type of anxiety that comes with the process of finding a partner. Dating anxiety has been described as 'distress associated with interactions with potential romantic partners prior to the development of a full-fledged relationship'.[24]

Professor Viren Swami has researched the phenomenon of dating anxiety, which is different from social anxiety, and its relationship to appearance-related factors. As Swami notes in his research, dating anxiety may be a normative part of emerging adulthood. But at the same time, it can 'hinder one's ability to form intimate romantic relationships', and to initiate sexual relationships.[25] In the long term, it can impact one's behaviour and mental wellbeing, resulting in 'diminished self-esteem, fewer sexual experiences, feelings of loneliness, a lack of confidence or assertiveness, and poorer self-rated social skills.' In my research for this book, I spoke to lots of people who experience dating anxiety and found that it can take several iterations. Some experience anxiety about putting themselves out there, but for others the very process of using dating apps can be a trigger.

Oli, a 31-year-old straight man, tells me he 'gets incredibly anxious on a first date'. His anxiety also impacts the way he uses dating apps. 'When dates aren't happening, sometimes a little depression, feeling like I'll be alone for the rest of my life,' he says. 'My friends are great but they're mostly pairing off and getting married so it just makes me feel lonely sometimes.' He says that he's 'slow to open up to people, and also just kind of a weird, nerdy guy, with an understated sense of humour, so I just feel like I'm boring when I meet new people . . . Add to that that I'm an ex-Mormon, and there's some baggage there that makes it more complicated, particularly around drinking (extremely common first date, but I don't like doing that as a first date) and sex.' He feels that there is a real lack of public spaces where single people can go to try and meet new people – 'things other than bars and clubs and churches that will attract different kinds of people. No easy answer as to what that might look like.'

Kaya, is a 29-year-old bisexual woman, who describes the current dating scene as 'complete shit but can't work out how to leave it'. She says, 'The anxiety that comes from overthinking unwritten rules e.g. when to respond, when to sleep with someone, when to divulge certain bits of information, these are things I actively try to unlearn but it still feels that they are inescapable especially when everyone else on the apps is abiding by them.' She says that her mental health has been negatively affected by the apps over time, and she blames the apps for the anxiety she feels while dating. 'First dates usually go well, sometimes second dates too, but the minute attachment styles etc come into play there is instant overthinking and me and the other person end up going either too avoidant or too clingy.' When Kaya experiences rejection, she feels 'shit', even when it's not someone she particularly cared about. 'Even if I don't like someone it leads to overthinking of why didn't they like me? Never used to be as sensitive to criticism in all areas of my life but it has hugely increased since starting dating two years ago.' Kaya finds it difficult to find people she's attracted to, who she shares similar interests with, and who want the same things she wants. 'I think it is basically impossible to get the pacing correct with dating apps as opposed to meeting someone naturally and falling in love over a period of time,' she says. Kaya wants an ENM relationship (ethically non-monogamous) but struggles to find what she's looking for on apps. 'I don't just want to date an existing couple who only want a shag or a unicorn and that's basically 90 per cent of poly people on apps,' she says. She worries that there's nobody out there for her who she's compatible with, that perhaps she's too fussy, and it makes her regret leaving her 'miserable' long-term relationship 'because at least I don't have to deal with the insecurity of dating'.

Dan, a 34-year-old straight man, suffers from social anxiety. 'I'm frequently unsure or worried about how I'm conducting myself and if I am sufficiently providing or reciprocating as a participant or partner,' he says. 'It's challenging, but it's always been that way. Meeting new people, getting to know them in a meaningful way, and finally getting comfortable enough to be vulnerable around them is a lot to ask for numerous folks. My biggest emotional challenge is I've been a loner my entire life and I'm wary of giving up my independence/freedom for someone who's less than satisfactory while also recognising there is no perfect match: people are complicated, they have their own baggage and have their own stuff going on.'

What to do when anxiety is impacting your dating experiences

As an anxious person, the balance of wanting to find love while also wanting to protect my mental wellbeing is tough. Surely love shouldn't come at the expense of my mental peace?

Opening up to others about your anxiety can help, research shows. According to a 2016 study, increasing self-disclosure can help lessen social anxiety and motivate people to connect again.[26] So, that could mean talking candidly to a close friend about how you're feeling or, if you feel comfortable, sharing with the person you're dating and expressing your emotional needs.

'Break the avoidance cycle,' advises Dr Eric Goodman, author of *Your Anxiety Beast and You*, who has a doctorate in counselling psychology. 'Lean into the anxiety. Because when you behave as if your anxiety is your enemy, you're telling your brain to treat whatever is causing the anxiety as a real threat,' says Goodman. 'You're teaching your brain to unleash its fight or flight response.' As journalist Jess Joho writes: 'Avoidance is how these cycles of social anxiety often perpetuate themselves if left unchecked. The more we can sit with and confront our discomfort, though, the more our brains realize that nothing too bad happens when we do the things that are making us anxious.'[27]

When I'm in the eye of the storm with my anxiety, I find it helpful to ask myself what it is I'm so afraid of. If it's rejection that I'm fearing, I trace this fear to the consequences. If I'm rejected, what will happen? My life will not be materially changed. I'll feel a bit wounded in the aftermath, but my life will be unchanged. My family will still love me, my friends will still be there, I'll still have a job, my bank balance will remain the same, my heart will keep beating, the world will keep turning. And I will still be me.

Don't take off your emotional armour too soon. Take things really slow and try not to put too much pressure on the outcome of a connection. As Goodman says, 'you don't want to put a whole lot of emotional weight into any one connection at the beginning . . . Eventually over time, if things are going well, that's when we invite more emotional attachment. But people do need to reserve a little emotional armor during those superficial stages of online dating.'[28]

Pay attention to how dating apps make you feel – if this is a stressor that exacerbates your anxiety, consider setting some digital boundaries. If you notice your anxiety spiking during or after you engage in this activity, consider taking a short break, or giving yourself a time limit for a 'swiping session' – no more than 15 minutes in one sitting, for example, as Dr Jess Carbino, Bumble's in-house sociologist, recommends. If you find that your anxiety manifests in moving an online connection into a real-life meet up, you could also impose a deadline or limit on yourself – perhaps no more than one or two weeks of texting before setting a date for an in-person meet-up.

If you're speaking to someone and feel invested in that connection, you might find anxiety bubbling up at times. Ask yourself: What do I need right now? Am I anxious because I'm not sure of this person's intentions? Am I looking for signs that I'm going to be rejected? What is triggering my anxiety right now?

If your anxiety is stemming from feeling uncertain about

another person's intentions towards you, or a lack of clarity as to what they're looking for, consider taking action to find an answer. Anxious people are prone to people pleasing and prioritising other people's comfort over their own. If you need clarity, ask a question. For example: 'Hey, I've enjoyed chatting to you lately. Just wanted to ask for a bit of clarity. Are you looking for a relationship?' Or perhaps: 'I'm enjoying talking to you and I'd like to explore this connection in person. How do you feel?'

Self-compassion is key in these situations. Remember that putting yourself out there is a universally uncomfortable act. Even non-anxious people find it hard. Celebrate yourself for embracing your vulnerability, for doing a hard thing, and if it doesn't work out, at least you tried. And you'll know for next time, that you can get through it. What's the worst that can happen?

BPD and Dating

Rejection is Cassie's (26 and bisexual) biggest trigger. She has borderline personality disorder (BPD), a mood disorder which impacts how a person manages their emotions.

The symptoms of BPD, according to the NHS, fit into four categories: affective dysregulation, cognitive distortions, impulsive behaviour, 'intense but unstable relationships'.[29]

Having BPD causes Cassie to have an intense fear of abandonment, exacerbating any experiences of rejection. 'I immediately equate rejection to me being the worst person to ever walk this planet, and naturally, someone who will die alone with nobody to love them,' she says.

A year before her diagnosis, Cassie heard that someone she'd been intimate with had told their mutual friend that they didn't want their relationship to progress beyond sex, and that they weren't interested in dating her. 'I had been planning to ask this person out on a date and I remember finding out this information being quite literally a painful experience for me,' she says.

'I immediately felt like my body was on fire and that my chest was falling in on itself, almost like someone was crushing it with their foot,' Cassie says. 'I could feel myself sweating and burning up. I felt my face fill with hot, prickly tears. I forgot how to breathe and slowly started to hyperventilate.' Cassie could hear her brain screaming at her, telling her that she was right, that she is a 'horrible, unlovable woman'.

She felt that this person had 'sussed her out', that it was inevitable now that everyone else would too, and that she'd be 'alone and miserable' forever.

'You know what's crazy? I really wasn't invested in this person at all,' Cassie adds. 'But rejection to me feels personal, it feels like a knife straight in my heart, no matter who it comes from. Rejection is basically confirmation of how worthless and unlovable I am. I've been waiting to find someone to tell me I was right about myself and now that I have, my world is over.'

Cassie's rejection sensitivity rears its head when she senses 'a hint of rejection from someone in any capacity', causing her to 'spiral and split'. 'I will cry for hours about how I am incapable of functioning like a normal person. Why am I not likeable? Why can't I maintain a relationship? Why do I do this? I'm annoying, I'm pathetic, people are embarrassed to know me, everyone in my life pities me, my parents are disappointed in the person I am, it would be better for everyone if I wasn't here,' she says. These negative thoughts spiral quickly. 'That route to rock bottom is a quick one,' says Cassie. 'The shame will swallow me whole and I will often spend a whole evening dissecting past relationships and friendships, analysing their downfalls and taking mental note of how I ruined them,' she says.

These days, Cassie feels she's better at dealing with these feelings. She's learned to be open and honest with people about her BPD.

Before she met her girlfriend, when she was actively dating, Cassie had to be careful not to become infatuated with someone quickly. The pressure to be the 'cool girl' when dating is at odds with the nature of BPD. 'We're told that in order to be attractive to people, especially women to men, we have to be chill, relaxed and to be able to go with the flow. But I can't do that a lot of the time. My BPD doesn't allow room for me to be chill about my emotions, I wish it did,' she says.

Now that she's in a long-term relationship, she often hyper-focuses on possible signs that her partner isn't happy. 'I often just blurt out, "You want to leave me don't you? You've fallen out of love with me haven't you?" Just because she didn't greet me with enthusiasm. I will sometimes convince myself that she's going to break up with me, so I will make plans in my head about how I'm going to cope when she goes,' says Cassie.

Cassie works every day to control her BPD. 'Some days I succeed and some days I fail,' she says. 'I'm incredibly lucky to have a partner who took steps to learn about BPD and my triggers and who loves me all the same.'

When rejection happens, Cassie finds it helpful to not focus on her thoughts. 'If I let them in I know I will start to spiral and eventually split,' she says. 'I find that moving my body helps a lot, I'll go for a walk or a run or I'll tidy the flat. Something that takes my mind off the bad thoughts.'

When she perceives rejection, she finds it helpful to take things back to basics and think about the concept of individual preference and taste. 'I'll write a list of foods I despise and then next to them write the name of a friend who loves that food. It helps remind me that there's nothing wrong with me not liking salmon, and there's nothing wrong with Charlie for loving salmon,' she says. 'And there certainly isn't anything wrong with the salmon itself. People have different tastes and preferences and sometimes that's all it is. It doesn't have to be deeper than that.' Doing this helps Cassie to realise that if she's not 'someone's cup of tea', that doesn't mean she's bad, it's simply a case of personal preference. It does not mean she's 'the devil incarnate who deserves a loveless life'.

As one of the most stigmatised mental health conditions, many hold misconceptions about what the condition entails. Writer Zuva Seven states in an article about dating with BPD: 'The emotional instability of those with BPD creates a vicious cycle whereby actions to cope with the burden of stigma exacerbate the condition.'[30] This means they might close themselves off and isolate themselves, perhaps neglecting treatment or not taking their medication.

Iris was diagnosed with BPD or emotionally unstable personality disorder (EUPD) when she was 22. She's now 29. 'I'm not sure I appreciate either label, to be honest,' she says. 'Although I have this label, I really don't identify with it so much anymore and I really feel like there's a need to de-pathologise and de-stigmatise that.'

Iris sees her BPD as related to attachment trauma, or relational trauma. 'There's a lot of fear in relationships and I tend to attach quite quickly to people and value them highly and then maybe get quite disappointed when they don't live up to those expectations,' she says. 'I am currently single and have been single my whole life really. As much as I do a lot of work on myself. I've done a lot of therapy. I'm also four years sober. I find it very difficult to be in relationships with other people.' Through four years of recovery and lots of therapy, Iris feels a lot more able to voice what she needs, to seek out people who are more emotionally intelligent and secure. 'I have full faith that I will find a partner, I just haven't had that yet.' She hasn't found a person who she's able to 'unpack all of this stuff and be myself with' and someone who 'has the capacity and the knowledge and the depth to go there with me'. But she feels optimistic about the prospect of meeting someone who has the capacity to understand BPD and go on that journey with her.

Iris has found it helpful to do somatic therapy – a treatment which focuses on how trauma and emotions appear in the body.[31] There's less of a focus on diagnoses, and instead a focus on the ways in which our emotions manifest in our body. 'Somatic therapies posit that our body holds and expresses experiences and emotions, and traumatic events or unresolved emotional issues can become "trapped" inside,' explains Amanda Baker, clinical psychologist in the Department of Psychiatry at Massachusetts General Hospital.[32] Iris says, 'Somatic work helps me understand the sensations in the body, rather than like being like, "Oh, it's this diagnosis, or it comes from this trauma."'

She still experiences a lot of fear around rejection, which can be destabilising to her daily routine. 'I'm actually experiencing that right now with someone that I'm interested in in a romantic context,' she says. 'How that shows up is: They won't message me back and I will be convinced that I've done something wrong. I've said something wrong, even if I haven't done anything wrong.'

In the past, Iris found this extremely difficult, and it would make her angry, and she'd find herself lashing out. She no longer does that. 'I have a lot more awareness of things and I have a lot more tools to cope.'

She's developed coping strategies for dating too. Somatic work encourages her to be present in her body and to 'understand that what I'm experiencing is not necessarily true, it's just what I'm feeling in my body and I can actually pivot to places in my body that are feeling safety and go into those'. Consciously separating her feelings from the situation helps her gain perspective. 'Whether it's fact or just feeling, I don't feel like I've ever been truly not rejected in terms of dating,' she says. She's starting to not internalise that and to remember that she's being rejected because she's not compatible with the person for various reasons. Those reasons, Iris explains, could be because she's sober or because she's spiritual – 'Not a lot of people vibe with that.'

She wants to destigmatise the BPD diagnosis. 'I feel like there needs to be a lot more done to make women who've experienced trauma and sexual violence seem less hysterical and to instead view this as a genuinely rational reaction to the experiences they've been in.'

When you are dating or in a relationship with someone with BPD, empathy and understanding are imperative. BPD carries a stigma, so it's important to educate yourself on the condition and how it manifests, in case you may be harbouring any misconceptions about it. An intense fear of abandonment is a significant part of BPD, so reassuring your partner that you care, that you're going nowhere, that you love them, are crucial in making them feel safe.

13

New Beginnings

It's easy to feel defeated in the dating game. I've often sat swiping endlessly wondering if I'll ever meet someone. I ask myself: Is this working?

The reality is: Dating apps do work for some people. Determined to find out why dating apps work for some but not others, I posted on social media asking for online dating success stories. Within a few hours, my phone was inundated with people's love stories. I must have had around 50 people in my Instagram DMs.

As a life-long nosy person, asking people about their love lives is one of my favourite topics. There were a few things I wanted to know, the first of which were: How long did they message for? Did they skip the messaging part and head straight to IRL? Or did they take a little time to get to know each other before taking the leap? And, crucially, how was that first date? Was the connection there straight away? Was there instant attraction or did it grow over time?

We're fed so many rules about dating – don't sleep with them on the first date, don't drink too much, don't be late, don't wait forever before meeting up. But in reality, love doesn't work like that. You don't just follow a long list of rigid instructions and, once you've followed all these rules, you get presented with your one true love. If only it were that simple.

That's why I wanted to speak to people who fell in love and broke the rules as they did so.

Holly, 40, met her partner, 44, on Tinder in 2021. 'We didn't really chat much before we met – maybe a few messages back and forth for a week,' she tells me. 'He just seemed really lovely,' says Holly. They went for a walk around Alexandra Palace in London.

'I didn't fancy him at first,' she says. 'We kept walking and I kept making the walk slightly longer as I started to quite enjoy his company.'

'He asked to kiss me when we sat on a bench and I said no,' says Holly. 'But we did at the end of the date. I thought it was going to be more of a friends thing, I wasn't sure.'

After that date, Holly told him she really liked him, but that she wasn't sure if she wanted to be just friends. 'He then video called me and totally put me at ease and basically said I think there's something more than friendship and I have enough friends.'

They then met up again for another walk and Holly says, 'We just totally hit it off.'

Her attraction to this man quickly grew. 'I had some big trust issues so it took me time to let my guard down,' she says. 'He just kept being consistent and kind and so interesting.'

Holly knew this man was worth the 'slow burn'. It was through interrogating her own attachment style that she decided to break with old dating patterns after reading *Attached*. 'I was worried at first that I didn't think he gave me enough "butterflies", that I didn't think there was enough spark!'

'He was secure, he was grounded, he knew who he was and just let it build and grow and probably three months in, I was like, shit I am in love with this man. He was in love with me too!'

'He actually restored my faith in men. I did a lot of dating and sleeping around using dating apps after the breakdown of my marriage,' says Holly. 'Funny story though: I once said to my partner, "Can you believe we met each other and of all the places in London we are only like a few miles away, it's just mad and meant to be!" He goes: "Well, I put a five miles radius on my Tinder.'

Sometimes it's not fate. It's just your app settings. Holly and her partner are now married. 'We are so happy,' she tells me, after sending me a photo of the two of them beaming with joy. 'It took some time, but we found each other.'

Diya, 39 and straight-ish ('80:20 straight:bi'), met her partner on Hinge during the pandemic. They're now married with two daughters. They texted for about a week before going on a picnic in Greenwich Park in London. 'I was impressed that he said he fancied smoked mackerel pate and would make some, so I did mushroom and pink peppercorn tarts and a coconut raspberry cake, and he brought this amazing salad with fresh peaches, feta, and dressing in a tiny glass jar that def impressed me!'

'We were having such a nice time that we got through three bottles of white wine and a bottle of San Pellegrino, but because lockdown had just ended and I hadn't been out properly for three months, I then threw up on one side of the picnic blanket.'

Diya says she was excessively apologetic 'in the way drunk people are', and told him she needed a lie-down before going home. 'So we lay on the blanket (me facing away obvs) and I was, even in that state, impressed again that he asked, "Can I put my arm 'round you?" So we had a bit of a snooze-spooning, then he walked me to the station and I was v. aware there might have been – ahem – vom in my hair, but he said he'd had a lovely time and would I like a second date, dinner the following week?!'

'He proposed in the same spot in Greenwich Park a couple of months ago,' she says.

Kelly, 35 and pansexual, tells me she didn't prioritise her partner when they first met on an app. 'I wanted something casual. He wanted a long-term relationship. So basically, I wasn't really prioritising him, but it was when he was really caring, really consistent, really good at communicating that I decided actually let's just meet up and see what happens,' she tells me.

They'd been chatting for a few weeks before meeting up. They met on the Thursday 'just to make sure we were both real . . . And then we saw each other Friday, Saturday, Sunday, and then from there every week, we saw each other on Wednesdays and Sundays. So it progressed really quickly, actually, after we did meet each other.'

That first date, they met in a carpark and chatted for about half an hour before she had to go and pick up her son from nursery. 'It was a very unconventional first date, but I didn't want him to meet my son or anything like that until I was absolutely sure,' Kelly adds.

'Another thing I really liked was his communication because he texted me as soon as he got back. Then I was quite worried because I've been out of the dating scene for a long time. I was thinking: Am I going to play the game, like what do I have to do? What are the rules, but he mitigated all that because he just texted me first, so that was really nice.'

She felt she had an instant connection and found him really attractive. 'I thought that he was a really nice person. I definitely saw him and thought oh yeah, he's exactly as I imagined,' Kelly says. They started talking more deeply over the following weeks. He was consistent and made sure they chatted every night. She says she always felt comfortable with him.

Katrina, 29 and pansexual, meanwhile, had just broken up with a man she was seeing. 'I was determined to have a fun summer. I just thought if I put the energy out there I was bound to meet some people. So I was just constantly swiping and making sure that I was asking questions and stuff. But then I kind of found myself running out of steam,' she says. She says she said yes to everyone to keep her options open. 'I'm a really big believer in chatting to people to find out who they are.' I actually got overwhelmed with the app and deleted it. I was kind of having lots of mini conversations with people. She ended up talking to someone whose profile photo showed he'd been to the same music festival she'd gone to that summer – Green Man in Wales.

'I asked him to chat to me on the phone actually because I think meeting someone is a big commitment of your time and I wanted to chat on the phone because I know that if he's not got good chat, then we're not gonna get on in real life,' she explains. 'We ended up talking on the phone for hours. And then after that, I was like, yeah, you've passed the test. We decided to meet at a pub in Camden. And he proceeded to be 45 minutes late, but I stayed – turns out he got locked out of his house. He just kept saying, "I'll be there soon. I'll be there soon,"' she says. 'I'm glad I stayed. And we went on a sort of pub crawl around Camden.'

They went on their second date two days later. And they then went on four dates in one week. Katrina says it was very quick. 'I'm quite a straightforward, blunt person, and I was like, "Look, I fancy you, do you fancy me?" He was like, "Yeah." So I was like, "Let's just keep seeing each other."' They eventually moved in together and now they're married.

Katie, 32 and bisexual, says she and her partner (33, straight) were talking back and forth for ages before meeting up.

'First date was perfect. We met at Voodoo Rays in Peckham and shared a 22-inch pizza and a couple of pints then walked to Peckham Levels and had a couple of cocktails,' she says.

They hit it off, she says, so she invited him to come back to her place. 'We stayed up listening to music for hours and hours. I remember thinking – is he going to kiss me? And then FINALLY he did. One thing led to another and we ended up breaking the couch.'

'I knew that Pete was my person the minute we started chatting, but it took us six months to let our guard down and fully commit to it,' she says. 'Five years later, we've bought a house, got through a pandemic, have a gorgeous puppy and are about to take the biggest step with IVF. I don't know what it was about him but I just knew he was going to be my person. He was kind, gentle, but so much fun and exciting. He was everything I always hoped for. We've had our moments and things haven't been perfect but we go from strength to strength each year.'

Danielle, 32 and heterosexual, met her boyfriend on Hinge in June 2021. 'I dated on the apps for YEARS and honestly it was horrible,' says Danielle. There was very little messaging before they took things to a real-life setting. 'We met up probably 2–3 days after matching.'

'First date was amazing. I could relive it to this day,' she says. On their first date, when her now-boyfriend was away from the table, the waitress said to her, 'Wow this is your first date?! You guys seemed like you've been dating for years.' There was an instant connection between Danielle and her boyfriend. 'I walked up, he was wearing a purple polo, smiling, and I knew that moment he was my person, it was like a tug and all there was in that moment was him, like I knew him in a previous life. We saw each other that night, and the next day and the next day and it just felt right,' she continues.

Hearing these stories gives me hope for love and I hope they do the same for you. Granted, it's not always helpful to hear success stories when you're having a terrible time. What strikes me in hearing them is that all of them tug at something I've been thinking about: vulnerability. What so many of the people I spoke to have in common is that many of them 'broke the rules' of dating – they had sex on the first date, they got drunk, they threw up in front of their date, they waited ages before meeting up, they were direct and they didn't play it cool. What they did instead was pay attention to how they felt during the date, how the person made them feel, they trusted their instincts and communicated with each other. There was far less focus on dating rules and maxims, but instead an emphasis on what felt right to them in that moment and on trusting one's instincts. These are stories where vulnerability, authenticity and honouring one's needs reigned supreme. The rest, as they say, is history.

Conclusion
Finding intimacy in a disconnected world

Is dating beyond hope? Is the system irreparably broken? I don't think it is. Fixing love is going to take work and change. It'll involve difficult conversations, discomfort, self-reflection and a greater effort to understand one's own emotional needs.

Get Comfortable With Being Alone

Romantic love is still prized as an aspirational state. One is not complete until one finds a partner. My father isn't marrying me off to a local landowner anytime soon, but at the same time, I'm continually asked why I don't have a partner. Our societal scripts around what relationships should look like are evolving.

Remember, also, the systemic issues and economic problems at play that make the 'married with babies' ideal an unattainable fantasy in today's society. Politicians call childfree women 'narcissistic' and they are blamed for the UK's falling birth rate, but as journalist Vicky Spratt points out, our politicians should look to the economic picture of our country to understand the reason why we're not having kids: 'Average living standards are lower than 15 years ago; excluding London, the UK is one of the poorest countries in north-west Europe; in London, historically high housing costs now offset much of the advantage of increases to people's earnings in recent years; the UK is also one of the most unequal countries in north-west Europe.'[1]

Re-imagine Your Own Timeline

I want to address a period that author Nell Frizzell calls 'the panic years', when many women and AFAB people begin to feel intense pressure in their twenties and thirties to make a decision about whether or not they want children. This is not a universal experience, so this section may not feel relevant to all readers and you may want to skip to the next section if mentions of fertility treatment are triggering or upsetting for you.

Our biological clocks can make us feel like we need to find the right partner before time runs out in order to become parents. Coping with that intense pressure (which often feels amplified by society, family, friends, social media) is tough and something I've struggled with for years. In March 2024, I took the decision to freeze my eggs – an experience which I can only describe as an emotional and physical rollercoaster. Egg freezing isn't a failsafe 'backup plan' but I feel empowered and fortunate that I have possible options up my sleeve, should I need them.

I have been so inspired to see people taking control of their own destinies and forging their own paths to becoming parents. One of my best friends made the decision shortly before her 40th birthday to conceive a baby using donor sperm and she now has a beautiful baby daughter. Journalist Nicola Slawson was 39 and single when she took the decision to have a baby with her gay best friend Tom – they now have a baby daughter.[2]

When the spectral figure of parenthood looms large in your mind, when you can't escape the noise of the time pressure, what do you do? Step one: Stop imposing arbitrary deadlines and timelines on yourself. Life isn't a to-do list. Step two: Make a plan. If you don't meet someone, would you still want to have a baby? What options are available to you to make that happen? Step three: Read up on the science of fertility, speak to doctors, and do not listen to societal bullshit. If you can afford to, consider getting a fertility test so you know what you can plan accordingly. Step four: Be proud of yourself for living life on your terms.

Anti-Oppression Dating

Dating does not exist in a vacuum. And many of the emotionally exhausting obstacles we face stem directly from systems of oppression that operate within society, shaping people's attitudes and behaviours.

While some of the experts I spoke to are hesitant about placing the onus on us as individuals to fix the problems that exist in dating culture, that doesn't mean we must blithely accept the status quo, nor should we sink into pessimist mentalities and the belief that nothing will ever change. The only way we can dismantle these power structures is by taking action, by educating ourselves, and examining the ways in which we may have contributed to these power structures during our lives. It's on us to embody the social justice values we claim to hold, to turn words into deeds in our daily lives, to treat others as we would want to be treated.

Unpacking who we find attractive and why is the first step in this. Ask yourself: If you were presented with all the photos of every dating profile you've ever rejected, what would it reveal about you? Would you feel comfortable with people in your life seeing that list of people you've rejected? Or would you feel ashamed? We need to interrogate our own 'preferences' and sit in the discomfort. Statements like 'I don't date Brown chicks,' or 'I don't like Black guys,' or 'Asian guys aren't my type,' feed into these ideologies that simply claiming you have a preference is entirely justifiable and definitely not rooted in racism. These statements aren't 'just preferences' – they are benevolent racism, in which people hide behind a mask of colour-blindness or racial neutrality to dodge acknowledging their discriminatory beliefs.[3,4]

Self-education begins at home. Our education doesn't stop when we leave school or graduate from university. We should regard educating ourselves as a continuous, life-long commitment and something that enriches our lives, and those of the people around us. Learning about the systems of oppression that exist around us can help us do a little more to dismantle every day by being more considerate of others and overcoming our internalised biases.

Intuitive Dating

It's easy to get drawn into a rules-based approach to dating. When we're feeling anxious or uncertain about a romantic interaction, many of us look for clarity in these rules and the myriad taglines that accompany them.

Viewing dating as a generalised, rigid set of behaviours is an attempt to bring order to the disordered, to homogenise the human experience. Love – and human beings – cannot be simplified and flattened in such a way.

Instead of relying on generalisations and scripts, we should instead look inward and become attuned with our own instincts and gut feelings. 'Intuitive dating involves checking in with your "gut" – what is your gut feeling about a person? What does your gut say to do before or after a date?' says relationship coach Carrie Jereslow.[5]

So, what does that look like when applied in real life? Say, for instance, you've been on a great date, the person seems into you, and you have a strong urge to text them. Rules-based dating would tell you it's unwise to message because it'd come across as 'too keen'. Intuitive dating would mean following that feeling and sending the damn text. If that person likes you, appearing 'too interested' won't put them off – quite the contrary.

A prime example of one of the 'shouldn'ts' is asking for clarity. We are encouraged not to express our emotional needs or to ask what the other person is feeling out of fear that we'll 'come on too strong' or scare them off. So, we go with the flow, find ourselves in ill-defined situationships when we've wanted something long-term, and spend our energy fretting about whether the person likes us.

If there's one lesson I've learned in my thirties, it's to ask for clarity.

To avoid dating burnout, we should become more intentional about our swiping on apps.

What if we slowed down our swiping and took the time to look at everything in a person's dating profile? Yes, they're hot, but have they listed their relationship or family preferences in the profile? Are their preferences in line with yours? Are they looking for ENM when you want monogamy? Do they want kids, but you don't? Are they looking for something casual when you're not? Look at their bio – does this seem like a person you'd get on well with? Have they written negative statements like 'no drama, please', or 'looking for someone who doesn't take themself too seriously'?

Emotionally Intelligent Dating

Why do we feel the way we feel? Why did I react like that?

I set out to write *The Love Fix* to answer these questions and to examine the difficult emotions that come with our quest for love and connection.

Being aware of the 'why' of an emotion or reaction can move us closer to identifying our own needs in romantic contexts. Knowing what you need is half the battle, the other half comes in asking for what you need and setting your expectations.

That can be really difficult in the early stages of dating when you're only just getting to know someone. If you've identified that you get anxious if the person you're dating doesn't text you often enough, you could ask: 'What's your texting style?' 'What's your communication style?'

Step back. When something triggers you or if someone does something to upset you, take a moment to pause and reflect. Is this a trigger that's come up before? Maybe it has a name that you've given it. Take a walk, call a friend, do something that will take you away from the situation and give you a moment of breathing space.

Pause before sending the paragraph-text. We all know the feeling – the person you've been spending time with is acting in a way that feels disrespectful, downright rude, perhaps. You want to give them a piece of your mind, you've got a paragraph prepared in your notes app.

Take a breath and don't do anything in a flash of rage. Wait until you feel calmer, re-read the paragraph and see if you still want to send it in its current state. If it's a rage-fuelled message, you might want to leave it in the Notes app forever, or perhaps you might choose to re-write it in non-combative language. Say what you need to say but do it eloquently. The honey will be so sweet, they won't taste the poison.

Honest Dating

Researcher and author Brené Brown writes that 'Clear Is Kind. Unclear Is Unkind.'[6]

We should approach dating with honesty and respect towards others. Dating has evolved rapidly and we are still figuring out what we owe one another, but just because there isn't an established set of expectations for situationships and talking stages doesn't mean you're off the hook. Always remind yourself of your values and what you'd expect if you were in the other person's position.

Choose the people who choose you. I spent years of my life chasing after and yearning for people who didn't want me. I viewed their lack of interest in me as something I could change. Perhaps through making changes to my physical appearance to be deemed worthy. If I just acted a certain way, they'd want me again.

After breakups, I would struggle to detach because I wanted the person to change their mind, to like me the way I liked them. It took me a very long time to realise that I shouldn't want people who don't want me. It took a considerable mindset shift for this message to finally stick. Now, if someone is making it clear that they don't want to be with me, or that they can't commit to dating me, that's my cue to leave the situation and not look back.

You don't fancy me? Cool, I don't fancy you, then. You don't see me as girlfriend material? Fine – I now feel the same about you. If it helps, view their disinterest as an ick. Let it turn you off. View their indifference as a trait that makes you lose attraction to them.

Walk away with your head held high, keep your communication non-combative, do a Gwyneth Paltrow and wish them well.

Romantic love isn't the be-all-and-end-all. If romantic love isn't in your life, you're not deficient in any way. Love comes in so many beautiful forms: familial, platonic, self-love. Friendships are love stories too. Not everyone has a great relationship with their parents or family, but if you do, cherish those relationships. Your relationship with yourself will be the longest one of your life. You don't have to love yourself in order to be loved. But be a friend to yourself, treat yourself well, and remind yourself constantly of the worth you hold.

As someone who's been single for 15 years, I have learned that being alone is better than being in a bad relationship. Do not let fear dictate your decision-making in matters of the heart. Get comfortable with your own company and take time to decide what you want in a partner and relationship. Think about your dating values – how am I going to conduct myself while I look for love? If I experienced XYZ, how would I feel?

Let me leave you with these final thoughts: Whatever may have happened in the past, please know you are worthy of love. You deserve clarity and compassion. You are worthy of being treated with respect and kindness. Do not let anyone else's behaviour towards you define your worth.

Acknowledgements

Writing *The Love Fix* has been such a joy. I'm thankful to each and every one of my readers for picking up this book.

To Florence Rees, my wonderful agent at AM Heath, thank you for always believing in me and being my champion. I feel blessed to have such a supportive, honest and trustworthy agent. I always feel I'm in safe hands and you've got my back.

To Marianne Tatepo, my brilliant editor at Square Peg, thank you for commissioning *The Love Fix* and seeing value in this book. From those early conversations when *TLF* was a kernel of an idea, to shaping the manuscript into the best version it could be, your creativity and strategic thinking has been invaluable in this process.

To Emily Martin, thank you for your attention to detail, your thoughtful edits and your helpful suggestions during the editing process. It's been a delight to bring another book into the world with the Square Peg imprint. It really does take a village: Special thanks to Yeti Lambregts for creating such a stunning cover for *TLF*. My thanks to Ellie Auton, Amelia Rushen, Fiona Brown, Rhiannon Roy, Ali Thompson, Morgan Dun-Campbell, and the entire Square Peg and Vintage team for working on this book.

I'd like to thank everyone who shared their experiences with me for this book. Your stories have helped me illustrate the current state of our dating culture and without your generosity, I couldn't have brought these stories to light. Thank you also to the many experts, academics, therapists, and journalists who kindly gave their time to share their insights and talk about their findings. Your input has helped bring clarity to a murky and oft-confusing aspect of our lives.

Grateful, as ever, to my Mashable colleagues, in particular my boss Shannon Connellan and my colleagues Sam Haysom and Anna Lovine for their unwavering support and generous time off to write the manuscript.

I'm lucky to have such an encouraging group of friends who kept me sane, supported and supplied with copious G&Ts during this time. Shannon Kephart, Lizzie Isherwood, Gianluca Mezzofiore, Liza Hearon, Maya Robert, Sean Blyth, Beth Ashley, Gigi Engle, Amber Fahrner. Thank you to my two besties: Elisha Hartwig and Fraser Draycott, you've both been by my side through the ups and downs and you've cheered me on throughout this entire process (not to mention holding my hand through the myriad dating disasters over the years).

To my wider family: my gorgeous super-smart cousins (honorary sisters, really) Ellen and Freya, my Auntie Lisa and Uncle Alan, thanks for always being in my corner. I'm so excited to celebrate with you all. I'm grateful to have indomitable role models in my life: Auntie Margaret, single and fabulous and a fellow recipient of the 'you're too picky' remark, thanks for being a pillar of strength for all of us. Auntie Eileen: thankful to have you as my cheerleader, you are such a supportive aunt. Jenny Johnson, thanks for the gorgeous 'hugs in the post'. Rebecca McRandal: a fellow lover of romance fiction, thanks for always being there with the recommendations, along with emotional support. Thank you to the Cross-Watson family for their kindness and generosity over the past few years.

To my lovely brother Jamie, I truly couldn't ask for a better, more loving, sweet-natured brother. And Alice, my sis-in-law, you're not just my brother's wife, you're one of my closest friends. Thank you for all you do. To both of you: the bond the two of you have as a couple is truly something to aspire to. That's the bar!

Mum and Dad: you're truly the best parents a girl could ask for. Dad, I love that your Apple Watch wallpaper is our family photo from my book launch for *Rough*. I feel so fortunate to have had your support in pursuing my dreams. I've never been in any doubt that you're proud of me. Mum, thank you for always being the very first reader of my manuscripts. You keep me sane in those final weeks of writing when I have no clue if the words I've been typing into 20+ Google Docs amount to anything resembling a book. Thanks for always being a reassuring voice and a sounding board when I need it. You once wrote 'I believe in you' on the bottom of a china teddy and I've held those words dear ever since.

Endnotes

Introduction

1 Pheby, C. (2023, December 12). 'The good, the bad, and the ugly of dating apps in Britain'. https://business.yougov.com/content/48146-the-good-the-bad-and-the-ugly-of-dating-apps-in-britain

2 Shepherd, T. (2024, January 14). 'Love story: Australian researchers becoming world leaders in the study of romantic love'. *Guardian.* https://www.theguardian.com/lifeandstyle/2024/jan/15/love-story-australian-researchers-becoming-world-leaders-in-the-study-of-romantic-love

3 Bolu Babalola on X (formerly Twitter) (n.d.). https://twitter.com/BeeBabs/status/1720083980480114774

1 First Encounters

1 'Dating App Revenue and Usage Statistics (2023)'. *Business of Apps* (2023, May 2). https://www.businessofapps.com/data/dating-app-market/

2 Bandinelli, C. (2022). 'Dating apps: towards post-romantic love in digital societies'. *International Journal of Cultural Policy*, 28(7), 905–919. https://doi.org/10.1080/10286632.2022.213715

3 Singleton, L. 'By 2037 half of babies likely to be born to couples who met online, says report' (2019, November 27). *Imperial News.* https://www.imperial.ac.uk/news/194152/by-2037-half-babies-likely-born/

4 'Activity on dating apps has surged during the pandemic' (2021, February 12). *Fortune*. https://fortune.com/2021/02/12/covid-pandemic-online-dating-apps-usage-tinder-okcupid-bumble-meetgroup/

5 Noor, P. (2019, December 6). 'What Tinder's biggest 2019 trends reveal about how people are dating'. *Guardian*. https://www.theguardian.com/technology/2019/dec/06/tinder-trends-dating-app-2019-kombucha-elizabeth-warren-woke

6 'Tinder Revenue and Usage Statistics (2024)'. *Business of Apps*. (2024, February 20). https://www.businessofapps.com/data/tinder-statistics/

7 'Hinge's first Gen Z report reveals top dating trends and tips to find a relationship in 2024' (n.d.). *Hinge*. https://hinge.co/press/2024-GenZ-Report

8 Prendergast, C. (2024, July 16). 'Forbes Health Survey: 79% of Gen Z report dating app burnout'. *Forbes Health*. https://www.forbes.com/health/dating/dating-app-fatigue/

9 'A short history of dating' (2021). BBC Bitesize. https://www.bbc.co.uk/bitesize/articles/ztrptrd#:~:text=Dating%20%2D%20the%20term%20can%20fill,or%20a%20mixture%20of%20both.&text=The%20first%20use%20of%20the,getting%20turned%20by%20other%20men

10 Esther (2021, February 14). 'The OKCupid of 100+ Years Ago: Matrimonial Ads from Old Newspapers'. *My Heritage*. https://blog.myheritage.com/2021/02/the-okcupid-of-100-years-ago-matrimonial-ads-from-old-newspapers/

11 Matthews, M. (2016, January 4). 'Alternative Courtship: Matrimonial advertisements in the 19th century'. *Mimi Matthews*. https://www.mimimatthews.com/2016/01/04/alternative-courtship-matrimonial-advertisements-in-the-19th-century/

12 TBS (2020, May 23). '*Friends*: Chandler Tries Online Dating' (Season 2 clip). *YouTube*. https://www.youtube.com/watch?v=Jk9gUzo2AV8

13 Singh-Kurtz, S. (2023, January 11). 'How Tinder changed every-thing'. *The Verge.* https://www.theverge.com/23549905/tinder-swipe-creation-dating-app-revolution-land-of-the-giants

14 Ibid.

15 'Swipe right this Valentine's Day: Top 10 online dating services revealed' (2024, February 14). www.ofcom.org.uk. https://www.ofcom.org.uk/media-use-and-attitudes/online-habits/swipe-right-this-valentines-day-top-10-online-dating-services-revealed/

16 Wilson, R. (2024, February 14). 'Tinder downloads are falling but the dating app era isn't over yet'. CNN. https://edition.cnn.com/2024/02/14/business/dating-apps-2024-hinge-tinder-dg/index.html

17 Ibid.

18 Pheby, C. (2023, December 12). 'The good, the bad, and the ugly of dating apps in Britain'. https://business.yougov.com/content/48146-the-good-the-bad-and-the-ugly-of-dating-apps-in-britain

19 Tierce, M. (2023, February 14). 'The End of Love'. *The Paris Review.* https://www.theparisreview.org/blog/2023/02/14/the-end-of-love/

20 'The rise of ebabies and the online family' (n.d.). *eharmony.* https://www.eharmony.co.uk/labs/the-rise-of-ebabies/

21 Ibid.

22 Rosenfeld, M., Thomas, R. J., & Hausen, S. (2019). 'Disintermedi-ating your friends: How online dating in the United States displaces other ways of meeting'. *Proceedings of the National Academy of Sciences of the United States of America*, 116(36), 17753–17758. https://doi.org/10.1073/pnas.1908630116

23 Kelley, L. (2024, April 11). 'America is sick of swiping'. *The Atlantic.* https://www.theatlantic.com/technology/archive/2024/04/dating-apps-are-starting-crack/678022/

24 Chavda, J. (2024, April 14). 'Key findings about online dating in the U.S.'. *Pew Research Center.* https://www.pewresearch.org/

short-reads/2023/02/02/key-findings-about-online-dating-in-the-u-s/

25 Strubel, J., & Petrie, T. A. (2017). 'Love me Tinder: Body image and psychosocial functioning among men and women'. *Body Image*, 21, 34–38. https://doi.org/10.1016/j.bodyim.2017.02.006

26 Stacey, L., & Forbes, T. D. (2021). 'Feeling Like a Fetish: Racialized Feelings, Fetishization, and the Contours of Sexual Racism on Gay Dating Apps'. *The Journal of Sex Research*, 59(3), 372–384. https://doi.org/10.1080/00224499.2021.1979455

27 Vinter, R. (2023, October 28). ' "It's quite soul-destroying": how we fell out of love with dating apps'. *Guardian*. https://www.theguardian.com/lifeandstyle/2023/oct/28/its-quite-soul-destroying-how-we-fell-out-of-love-with-dating-apps

28 Bahemia, N. (2021, January 1). 'To swipe or not to swipe: the decision-making process behind online dating'. *LSE*. https://blogs.lse.ac.uk/psychologylse/2021/01/07/to-swipe-or-not-to-swipe-the-decision-making-process-behind-online-dating/

29 'Swipe right this Valentine's Day: Top 10 online dating services revealed' (2024, February 14). www.ofcom.org.uk. https://www.ofcom.org.uk/media-use-and-attitudes/online-habits/swipe-right-this-valentines-day-top-10-online-dating-services-revealed/

30 Gionet, A. (2023). 'How Many Swipes Does It Take to Find a Significant Other?' *The Loupe*. https://www.shaneco.com/theloupe/articles-and-news/how-many-swipes-does-it-take/

31 Lebowitz, S. (2018, May 10). 'A scientist who's worked at Tinder and Bumble has seen many people make the same mistake with their dating apps'. *Insider*. https://www.insider.com/tinder-bumble-scientist-time-spent-on-dating-apps-2018-5

32 Fellizar, K. (2018). 'Millennials Spend an Average Of 10 Hours A Week On Dating Apps, Survey Finds, But Here's What Experts Actually Recommend'. *Bustle*. https://www.bustle.com/p/millennials-

spend-average-of-10-hours-a-week-on-dating-apps-survey-finds-but-heres-what-experts-actually-recommend-8066805

33 Government Digital Service (2015). 'Maximum weekly working hours'. *GOV.UK*. https://www.gov.uk/maximum-weekly-working-hours/calculating-your-working-hours

34 Zhang, J. (2016, July 12). 'What Happens After You Both Swipe Right: A Statistical Description of Mobile Dating Communications'. *arXiv.org*. https://arxiv.org/abs/1607.03320

35 Chavda, J. (2024, April 14). 'Key findings about online dating in the U.S.'. *Pew Research Center*. https://www.pewresearch.org/short-reads/2023/02/02/key-findings-about-online-dating-in-the-u-s/

36 Ashley, B. (2024, April 18). 'Dating culture has become selfish. How do we fix it?' *Mashable*. https://mashable.com/article/selfish-dating-app-culture

37 'Rising cost of dating brings money conversation to the table'. (n.d.). *Experian*. https://www.experianplc.com/media/latest-news/2023/rising-cost-of-dating-brings-money-conversation-to-the-table/

38 Lufkin, B. (2022, February 25). 'Do "maximisers" or "satisficers" make better decisions?' *BBC Worklife*. https://www.bbc.com/worklife/article/20210329-do-maximisers-or-satisficers-make-better-decisions

39 Schwartz, B., Ward, A., Monterosso, J., Lyubomirsky, S., White, K., & Lehman, D. R. (2002). 'Maximizing versus satisficing: Happiness is a matter of choice'. In *Journal of Personality and Social Psychology* (Vols. 83–83, pp. 1178–1197). https://doi.org/10.1037//0022-3514.83.5.1178

40 Poorna Bell on X (formerly Twitter) (2020, January 26). https://twitter.com/poornabell/status/1221409634369646592?s=20

41 Stanford University (2020, February 5). 'Online dating is the most popular way couples meet'. *Stanford News*. https://news.

stanford.edu/2019/08/21/online-dating-popular-way-u-s-couples-meet/

42 Bandinelli, C. (2022). 'Dating apps: towards post-romantic love in digital societies'. *International Journal of Cultural Policy*, 28(7), 905–919. https://doi.org/10.1080/10286632.2022.2137157

2 Crush

1 'Rejection and Physical Pain Are the Same to Your Brain'. *Forbes* (25 December 2015). www.forbes.com/sites/nicolefisher/2015/12/25/rejection-and-physical-pain-are-the-same-to-your-brain.

2 Joyce, Carolyn. 'How to Deal With Rejection: Try These Powerful, Personal Strategies!' *PsychAlive* (24 February 2022). www.psychalive.org/how-to-deal-with-rejection.

3 Kross, E., Berman, M. G., Mischel, W., Smith, E. E., & Wager, T. D. (2011). 'Social rejection shares somatosensory representations with physical pain'. *Proceedings of the National Academy of Sciences*, 108(15), 6270–6275. https://doi.org/10.1073/pnas.1102693108

4 DeWall, C. N., MacDonald, G., Webster, G. D., Masten, C. L., Baumeister, R. F., Powell, C., Combs, D., Schurtz, D. R., Stillman, T. F., Tice, D. M., & Eisenberger, N. I. (2010). 'Acetaminophen Reduces Social Pain'. *Psychological Science*, 21(7), 931–937. https://doi.org/10.1177/0956797610374741

5 Pronk, T. M., & Denissen, J.J.A. (2019). 'A Rejection Mind-Set: Choice Overload in Online Dating'. *Social Psychological and Personality Science*, 11(3), 388–396. https://doi.org/10.1177/1948550619866189

6 Ruiz, R. (2022, April 22). 'What is SEL?' *Mashable*. https://mashable.com/article/sel-curriculum-what-is-sel-in-education

7 Ferrier, G. (2021, May 18). 'Social-emotional learning standards in the UK & US'. CASCAID. https://cascaid.co.uk/social-emotional-learning/standards/

8 'Shameful statistics show a mental health crisis that is spiralling out of control as demand far outweighs capacity, warns BMA'. *BMA* media centre (n.d.). The British Medical Association Is the Trade Union and Professional Body for Doctors in the UK. https://www.bma.org.uk/bma-media-centre/shameful-statistics-show-a-mental-health-crisis-that-is-spiralling-out-of-control-as-demand-far-outweighs-capacity-warns-bma

9 'Men's Health Week: Men's changing attitude to mental health and therapy'. (2022, June 16). https://www.bacp.co.uk/news/news-from-bacp/2022/16-june-mens-changing-attitude-to-mental-health-and-therapy/

10 Team, S., & Eloise, M. (2021, September 24). 'Why are we all adopting therapy-speak?' *Stylist*. https://www.stylist.co.uk/health/mental-health/rise-in-therapy-speak/568865

11 Seresin, A. (2019, October 9). 'On Heteropessimism'. *The New Inquiry*. https://thenewinquiry.com/on-heteropessimism/

12 Lothian-McLean, M. (2022, December 12). 'Framing men as the "villains" gets women no closer to better romantic relationships'. *Guardian*. https://www.theguardian.com/commentisfree/2022/dec/11/men-villains-women-romantic-relationships-victimhood

13 'From Swiping to Sexting: The enduring gender divide in American Dating and Relationships'. *The Survey Center on American Life* (2023, November 9). https://www.americansurveycenter.org/research/from-swiping-to-sexting-the-enduring-gender-divide-in-american-dating-and-relationships/

14 Sussman, A. L. (2023, November 24). 'Opinion: Why aren't more people getting married? Ask women what dating is like'. *The New York Times*. https://www.nytimes.com/2023/11/11/opinion/marriage-women-men-dating.html

15 Townsend, C. (2023, January 21). 'Who is Andrew Tate? And why is the controversial figure taking over TikTok?' *Mashable*. https://mashable.com/article/andrew-tate-hustlers-university

16 Novara Media. (2023, January 22). 'Vogue Dating columnist on 'The Sexual Marketplace', incels and Narcissists' [Video]. YouTube. https://www.youtube.com/watch?v=1It1PdTEKH4

17 'Masculinity and women's equality: study finds emerging gender divide in young people's attitudes'. King's College London (2024, April 18). https://www.kcl.ac.uk/news/masculinity-and-womens-equality-study-finds-emerging-gender-divide-in-young-peoples-attitudes

18 Wellings, K., Palmer, M. J., Machiyama, K., & Slaymaker, E. (2019). 'Changes in, and factors associated with, frequency of sex in Britain: evidence from three National Surveys of Sexual Attitudes and Lifestyles (Natsal)'. *BMJ*, l1525. https://doi.org/10.1136/bmj.l1525

19 Porter, A. (2023, November 27). 'Blind dating in the online age: Does it really work?' *Mashable*. https://mashable.com/article/blind-dates-online-dating

20 Holden, L. (2023, August 21). 'Pear Ring: Can singles jewellery help me find The One?' *Evening Standard*. https://www.standard.co.uk/lifestyle/singles-pear-ring-help-dating-relationship-find-the-one-b1101919.html

21 The Kinsey institute is best known for the Kinsey Scale, a spectrum created in 1948 to chart one's heterosexuality or homosexuality.

22 'Singles In America: Match releases largest study on US single population for 12th year'. (2022, November 15). Match.com MediaRoom. https://match.mediaroom.com/2022-11-15-Singles-in-America-Match-Releases-Largest-Study-on-US-Single-Population-for-12th-Year

23 Thompson, R. (2023, May 22). 'Gen Z is challenging the way we date, says Tinder report'. *Mashable*. https://mashable.com/article/tinder-future-of-dating-2023-gen-z

24 Iovine, A. (2022, December 7). 'Top 8 dating trends of 2022'. *Mashable*. https://mashable.com/article/8-dating-trends-2022

25 Hsieh, C. (2021, November 1). 'Is the "Situationship" Ruining Modern Romance?' *Cosmopolitan.* https://www.cosmopolitan.com/sex-love/a9566889/what-is-a-situationship/

26 Narr, G., & Luong, A. (2021). 'Bored Ghosts in The Dating App Assemblage: How Dating App Algorithms Couple Ghosting Behaviors With a Suffuse Mood of Boredom'. *SSRN Electronic Journal.* https://doi.org/10.2139/ssrn.4233502

3 Sparks

1 'Chemistry Between People: A Sum of Their Connections' (2021, December 29). Association for Psychological Science – APS.https://www.psychologicalscience.org/observer/chemistry-relationships

2 Reis, H. T., Regan, A., & Lyubomirsky, S. (2021). 'Interpersonal chemistry: what is it, how does it emerge, and how does it operate?' *Perspectives on Psychological Science*, 17(2), 530–558. https://doi.org/10.1177/1745691621994241

3 Styx, L. (2022, February 17). 'What Happens When We Feel Romantic Chemistry, and How Much Does It Matter?' *Verywell Mind.* https://www.verywellmind.com/whats-happening-when-we-feel-romantic-chemistry-with-someone-and-how-much-does-it-matter-5217953

4 'Love tips from an expert: shaky bridges and electric shocks'. *CBC Radio* (2019, April 26). ttps://www.cbc.ca/radio/tapestry/love-in-the-lab-1.5112420/love-tips-from-an-expert-shaky-bridges-and-electric-shocks-1.5112525

5 *APA PsycNet DoiLanding page.* (n.d.). https://psycnet.apa.org/doiLanding?doi=10.1037%2Fh0037031

6 Dean, J. (2016). 'What "The Love Bridge" Tells Us About How Thoughts and Emotions Interact'. *PsyBlog.* https://www.spring.

org.uk/2012/04/what-the-love-bridge-tells-us-about-how-thoughts-and-emotions-inte–ract.php

7 Doyle, G. (2023, June 15). 'We can do hard things' episode 219: 'How to Make a Friend & Find a Date with Logan Ury'. https://momastery.com/blog/we-can-do-hard-things-ep-219/

8 Petak, T. (2021, October 12). 'Why Dating Experts Say You Should Stop Looking for an Instant Spark – and Start Simmering'. *InStyle*.https://www.instyle.com/lifestyle/relationship-simmering-versus-sparks

9 De Klerk, A. (2017, October 11). 'This is the percentage of men who believe in love at first sight'. *Harper's BAZAAR*. https://www.harpersbazaar.com/uk/culture/culture-news/news/a40735/percentage-of-men-who-believe-in-love-at-first-sight/

10 Zsok, F., Haucke, M., De Wit, C. Y., & Barelds, D. P. H. (2017). 'What kind of love is love at first sight? An empirical investigation'. *Personal Relationships*, 24(4), 869–885. https://doi.org/10.1111/pere.12218

11 Park, W. (2023, March 14). 'The dark side of believing in true love'. *BBC Future*. https://www.bbc.com/future/article/20190211-the-dark-side-of-believing-in-true-love

12 Thortful. (2022, August 9). 'Brits meet their soulmates when they're twenty six!' https://www.thortful.com/blog/the-age-we-meet-our-soulmate/

13 Ballard, J. (2021). 'Do Americans believe in the idea of soulmates?' *YouGov*. https://today.yougov.com/society/articles/34094-soulmates-poll-survey-data?redirect_from=%2Ftopics%2Fsociety%2Farticles-reports%2F2021%2F02%2F10%2Fsoulmates-poll-survey-data

14 Bishop, K. (2022, February 25). 'Why people still believe in the "soulmate myth"'. *BBC*. https://www.bbc.com/worklife/article/20220204-why-people-still-believe-in-the-soulmate-myth

15 Ibid.

16 Springer, S. H., PhD (2012, August 4). '"Destiny" beliefs can threaten long-term marital success'. *Psychology Today*. https://www.psychologytoday.com/gb/blog/the-joint-adventures-well-educated-couples/201207/destiny-beliefs-can-threaten-long-term

17 Ibid.

18 Park, W. (2023, March 14). 'The dark side of believing in true love'. *BBC Future*. https://www.bbc.com/future/article/20190211-the-dark-side-of-believing-in-true-love

19 Editorial team (2021). 'What are the odds of love? Rachel Riley reveals all'. *eharmony*. https://www.eharmony.co.uk/dating-advice/attraction/odds-of-love/

20 eharmony UK (2017, August 3). 'Rachel Riley reveals the Odds of Love' [Video]. YouTube. https://www.youtube.com/watch?v=hUGEcoCtwfw

21 Doac. (2024, February 22). 'Moment 150: The REAL (& Usually Unseen) Reason You're Struggling With Love & Relationships!: Logan Ury'. Apple Podcasts. https://podcasts.apple.com/gb/podcast/moment-150-the-real-usually-unseen-reason-youre/id1291423644?i=1000646482664

22 Fry, H. (n.d.). 'The mathematics of love' [Video]. TED Talks. https://www.ted.com/talks/hannah_fry_the_mathematics_of_love/transcript?language=en

23 'Peter Backus – Why I don't have a girlfriend: An application of the Drake equation to love in the UK' (n.d.). University of Warwick. https://warwick.ac.uk/newsandevents/podcasts/upload/?podcastItem=peterbackus.m4v

24 'Beating the odds' (n.d.). Department of Economics, the University of Warwick. https://warwick.ac.uk/fac/soc/economics/news/2013/6/beating_the_odds/

25 Wakin, A., Vo, D. B. 'Love-variant: The Wakin-Vo IDR Model of Limerence'. In: Inter-Disciplinary – Net. 2nd Global Conference: *Challenging Intimate Boundaries*, 2008.

26 Keller, K., MA (2023, October 13). 'Limerence: When is it more than heartbreak?' *Psychology Today*. https://www.psychologytoday.com/gb/blog/the-young-and-the-restless/201109/limerence-when-is-it-more-than-heartbreak

27 Apple Podcasts Preview. (2023, June 14). '219. How to Make a Friend & Find a Date with Logan Ury'. https://podcasts.apple.com/gb/podcast/we-can-do-hard-things-with-glennon-doyle/id1564530722?i=1000617093627

28 Peskin, M. F., & Newell, F. N. (2004). 'Familiarity breeds attraction: effects of exposure on the attractiveness of typical and distinctive faces'. *Perception*, 33(2), 147–157. https://doi.org/10.1068/p5028

29 Pyke, R. E. (2020). 'Sexual Performance Anxiety'. *Sexual Medicine Reviews*, 8(2), 183–190. https://doi.org/10.1016/j.sxmr.2019.07.001

30 Maxwell, J. A., Muise, A., MacDonald, G., Day, L. C., Rosen, N. O. & Impett, E. A. (2017). 'How implicit theories of sexuality shape sexual and relationship well-being'. *Journal of Personality and Social Psychology*, 112(2), 238–279. https://doi.org/10.1037/pspi0000078

4 Just My Type

1 Lorde, A. (1984). 'Sister Outsider: Essays and speeches'. http://ci.nii.ac.jp/ncid/BA01234259

2 Wade, T. J., & Dimaria, C. (2003). 'Weight Halo Effects: Individual Differences in Perceived Life Success as a Function of Women's Race and Weight'. *Sex Roles*, 48(9/10), 461–465. https://doi.org/10.1023/a:1023582629538

3 De Lise, J. (2022, June 28). 'We're losing our LGBTQ+ spaces: Where do we go from here?' *BRICKS Magazine – If you have a voice, use it*. https://bricksmagazine.co.uk/2022/06/28/were-losing-our-lgbtq-spaces-where-do-we-go-from-here/

4 https://ww3.rics.org/uk/en/modus/built-environment/urbanisation/queer-venues-crisis.html

5 Kelleher, P. (2022, February 5). 'Debate rages over whether straight, cis people should be allowed in queer bars, clubs and spaces'. *PinkNews*. https://www.thepinknews.com/2022/02/05/lgbt-gay-bar-queer-spaces-straight-cis-debate/

6 Nadeem, R. (2023, February 2). 'Online Dating: The Virtues and Downsides'. Pew Research Center: Internet, Science & Tech. https://www.pewresearch.org/internet/2020/02/06/the-virtues-and-downsides-of-online-dating/

7 Bandinelli, C. (2022). 'Dating apps: towards post-romantic love in digital societies'. *International Journal of Cultural Policy*, 28(7), 905–919. https://doi.org/10.1080/10286632.2022.2137157

8 Bradley, S. (2022, September 23). 'How to flirt when you've just come out as bisexual'. *Mashable*. https://mashable.com/article/flirting-guide-freshly-out-bisexual

9 Rich, A. (1980). 'Compulsory heterosexuality and lesbian existence'. *Signs*, 5(4), 631–660. https://doi.org/10.1086/493756

10 Salle, K. (2023, October 30). 'Black women share how they navigate dating'. https://www.stylist.co.uk/relationships/dating-love/black-women-dating-disappointment-how-to-navigate/835815

11 Brown, A. (2018, January 9). '"Least Desirable"? How racial discrimination plays out in online dating'. *NPR*. https://www.npr.org/2018/01/09/575352051/least-desirable-how-racial-discrimination-plays-out-in-online-dating

12 (Deleted by author) (n.d.). *Medium*. https://theblog.okcupid.com/race-and-attraction-2009-2014-107dcbb4f060

13 Aldana, A. A., & Salazar, L. (2024). 'Racial preferences in dating apps: an experimental approach'. *The History of the Family*, 1–21. https://doi.org/10.1080/1081602x.2024.2352547

14 Holt, B. (2021, February 8). 'Racism thrives in the online dating world'. *Mashable*. https://mashable.com/article/racism-online-dating

15 Mineo, L. (2024, June 12). 'How dating sites automate racism'. *Harvard Gazette*. https://news.harvard.edu/gazette/story/2024/04/how-dating-sites-automate-sexual-racism/

16 Peck, A., Berkowitz, D., & Tinkler, J. E. (2021). 'Left, right, Black, and White: how White college students talk about their inter- and intra- racial swiping preferences on Tinder'. *Sociological Spectrum*, 41(4), 304–321. https://doi.org/10.1080/02732173.2021.1916663

17 Ibid.

18 'Dating while Black: Online, but Invisible'. (n.d.). UC Press Blog. https://www.ucpress.edu/blog/54733/dating-while-black-online-but-invisible/

19 Ibid.

20 Anderson, M. (2023, February 22). 'OP-ED: How dating apps can leave Black women feeling fetishized, appropriated and haunted'. *EBONY*. https://www.ebony.com/op-ed-dating-apps-black-women-fetishized-appropriated-and-haunted/

21 Wayne State University (2020, September 1). 'The "Obama effect": Research explores how Black women internalize and conceptualize beauty standards'. *Graduate School*. https://gradschool.wayne.edu/news/the-obama-effect-research-explores-how-black-women-internalize-and-conceptualize-beauty-standards-53586

22 Raymundo, J. (2021). 'The Burden of Excellence: A Critical Race Theory Analysis of Perfectionism in Black Students'. *The Vermont Connection*, 42(1). https://scholarworks.uvm.edu/tvc/vol42/iss1/12

23 https://www.essence.com/culture/report-black-women-work-harder-for-less/

24 'Black women face more bias and get less support'. (n.d.). *Lean In*. https://leanin.org/article/women-in-the-workplace-black-women#!

25 Yeboah, A. *VIEW: Perfectionism—the fight I will never win*. (2023, March 20). Minnesota Women's Press. https://www.womenspress.com/view-perfectionism-the-fight-i-will-never-win/

26 Dubey, S. (2023, March 4). 'Body Shaming Is Now Spreading On Dating Apps – Give Us A Break'. *HuffPost UK*. https://www.huffingtonpost.co.uk/entry/body-shaming-is-now-spreading-on-dating-apps-can-we-just-live_uk_640076ace4b05f1e793da8c3#:~:text=According%20to%20some%20statistics%20released,dating%20app%20or%20social%20media.

27 Dinic, M. (2021). 'Physical appearance and sexual attractiveness'. *YouGov*. https://yougov.co.uk/topics/health/articles-reports/2021/08/05/physical-appearance-and-sexual-attractiveness

28 Hughes, L. (2023, May 18). 'Weight Stigma Study: Exploring weight discrimination in society & the gym'. *OriGym*. https://origympersonaltrainercourses.co.uk/blog/weight-stigma-study

29 'Facts & Factors (Industry Trends, Revenue, Statistics, Segmentation, Report)'. *GlobeNewswire News Room* https://www.globenewswire.com/en/news-release/2023/02/09/2604662/0/en/Latest-Global-Weight-Loss-and-Weight-Management-Market-Size-Share-Worth-USD-405-4-Billion-by-2030-at-a-6-84-CAGR-Growing-obesity-rate-to-propel-market-growth-Facts-Factors-Industry.html

30 'Google's year in search'. (n.d.). *Google Trends*. https://trends.google.com/trends/yis/2023/GB/

31 *Piers Morgan Uncensored*. (2022, October 8). 'Andrew Tate: "Women belong to men in marriage!" on women being "Property"' [Video]. YouTube. https://www.youtube.com/watch?v=ScpdoAVkRVo

32 'Tate thinks the world's problems would be solved if women had body counts on their forehead'. Andrew Tate. (n.d.). PodClips. https://podclips.com/c/tate-thinks-the-worlds-problems-would-be-solved-if-women-had-body-counts-on-their-forehead

33 Oppenheim, M. (2023, May 22). 'One in four young men agree with Andrew Tate's views on women, poll finds'. *The Independent*. https://www.independent.co.uk/news/uk/home-news/andrew-tate-women-masculinity-romania-b2342084.html

34 Smith, M. (2023, September 27). 'One in six boys aged 6–15 have a positive view of Andrew Tate'. *YouGov*. https://yougov.co.uk/society/articles/47419-one-in-six-boys-aged-6-15-have-a-positive-view-of-andrew-tate

35 'What is considered a high body count for a female?' (n.d.). *Quora*. https://www.quora.com/What-is-considered-a-high-body-count-for-a-female

36 Ibid.

37 Engle, G. (2023, August 3). 'What is purity culture and how does it impact sex?' *Mashable*. https://mashable.com/article/purity-culture-impact-sex

5 Putting Yourself Out There

1 Holland, G., & Tiggemann, M. (2016). 'A systematic review of the impact of the use of social networking sites on body image and disordered eating outcomes'. *Body Image*, 17, 100–110. https://doi.org/10.1016/j.bodyim.2016.02.008

2 Gilmour, P. (2021, June 15). 'Is it time to reconsider everything we think we know about orgasms?' *Cosmopolitan*. https://www.cosmopolitan.com/uk/love-sex/sex/a36518203/orgasm-report-results/

3 'Body Insecurities: America's ultimate cockblock' (2023). *Pure*. https://pure.app/content/en/journal/us-american-bodypoz

4 Grabe, S., Ward, L. M., & Hyde, J. S. (2008). 'The role of the media in body image concerns among women: A meta-analysis of experimental and correlational studies'. *Psychological Bulletin*, 134(3), 460–476. https://doi.org/10.1037/0033-2909.134.3.460

5 Helmore, E. (2020, March 26). '"Heroin chic" and the tangled legacy of photographer Davide Sorrenti'. *Guardian*. https://www.theguardian.com/fashion/2019/may/23/heroin-chic-and-the-tangled-legacy-of-photographer-davide-sorrenti

6 Nash, A. (1997, September 7). 'The model who invented Heroin chic'. *The New York Times*. https://www.nytimes.com/1997/09/07/arts/the-model-who-invented-heroin-chic.html

7 Helmore, E. (2020, March 26). ' "Heroin chic" and the tangled legacy of photographer Davide Sorrenti'.

8 Demopoulos, A. (2022, November 21). 'The term "heroin chic" needs to die – even if skinny-worship rages on. *Guardian*. https://www.theguardian.com/fashion/2022/nov/20/heroin-chic-fashion-skinny-worship

9 Bassi, I. (2023, July 11). 'Toxic Fat-Phobic moments in 2000s celebrity culture'. *BuzzFeed*. https://www.buzzfeed.com/ishabassi/toxic-fat-phobic-moments-celebrity-culture-2000s

10 Lucy Huber on X (formerly Twitter). (n.d.). https://twitter.com/clhubes/status/1395061523274506242?ref_src=twsrc%5Etfw%7Ctwcamp%5Etweetembed%7Ctwterm%5E1395061523274506242%7Ctwgr%5Eff29ea8f7500e972a47907a710196c067a82fc5a%7Ctwcon%5Es1_&ref_url=https%3A%2F%2Fwww.fridaythings.com%2Frecent-posts%2Fbody-image-diet-culture-millennials-gen-z

11 Hare, B. (n.d.). 'Reality TV breeds new body ideals' *CNN*. https://edition.cnn.com/2010/SHOWBIZ/06/01/kardashian.body.types/index.html

12 McComb, S. E., & Mills, J. S. (2022). 'The effect of physical appearance perfectionism and social comparison to thin-, slim-thick-, and fit-ideal Instagram imagery on young women's body image'. *Body Image*, *40*, 165–175. https://doi.org/10.1016/j.bodyim.2021.12.003

13 Clark, K. (2022, December 22). 'Supply and demand: How surgeons are navigating the BBL boom'. *Connect*. American Society of Plastic Surgeons. https://www.plasticsurgery.org/news/articles/supply-and-demand-how-surgeons-are-navigating-the-bbl-boom

14 Kale, S. (2019, July 19). 'Gym, eat, repeat: the shocking rise of muscle dysmorphia'. *Guardian.* https://www.theguardian.com/lifeandstyle/2019/jul/17/gym-eat-repeat-the-shocking-rise-of-muscle-dysmorphia

15 Nagata, J. M., Murray, S. B., Bibbins-Domingo, K., Garber, A. K., Mitchison, D., & Griffiths, S. (2019). 'Predictors of muscularity-oriented disordered eating behaviors in U.S. young adults: A prospective cohort study'. *International Journal of Eating Disorders,* 52(12), 1380–1388. https://doi.org/10.1002/eat.23094

16 Filice, E., Raffoul, A., Meyer, S. B., & Neiterman, E. (2019). 'The influence of Grindr, a geosocial networking application, on body image in gay, bisexual and other men who have sex with men: An exploratory study'. *Body Image,* 31, 59–70. https://doi.org/10.1016/j.bodyim.2019.08.007

17 National Eating Disorders Association. (2018, February 21). 'Identity & eating disorders'. https://www.nationaleatingdisorders.org/identity-eating-disorders

18 Knight, R., Carey, M., Jenkinson, P. M., & Preston, C. (2022). 'The impact of sexual orientation on how men experience disordered eating and drive for muscularity'. *Journal of Gay & Lesbian Mental Health,* 1–23. https://doi.org/10.1080/19359705.2022.2118921

19 Parker, L. L., & Harriger, J. A. (2020). 'Eating disorders and disordered eating behaviors in the LGBT population: a review of the literature'. *Journal of Eating Disorders,* 8(1). https://doi.org/10.1186/s40337-020-00327-y

20 Calzo, J. P., Blashill, A. J., Brown, T. A., & Argenal, R. L. (2017). 'Eating disorders and disordered weight and shape control behaviors in sexual minority populations'. *Current Psychiatry Reports,* 19(8). https://doi.org/10.1007/s11920-017-0801-y

21 Knight, R., Carey, M., Jenkinson, P. M., & Preston, C. (2022). 'The impact of sexual orientation on how men experience disordered eating and drive for muscularity'. *Journal of Gay & Lesbian Mental Health,* 1–23. https://doi.org/10.1080/19359705.2022.2118921

22 Drummond, M. (2005). 'Men's bodies'. *Men And Masculinities*, 7(3), 270–290. https://doi.org/10.1177/1097184x04271357

23 Webb, H. J., Zimmer-Gembeck, M. J., Waters, A. M., Farrell, L. J., Nesdale, D., & Downey, G. (2017). ' "Pretty pressure" from peers, parents, and the media: A Longitudinal Study of Appearance-Based Rejection Sensitivity'. *Journal of Research on Adolescence*, 27(4), 718–735. https://doi.org/10.1111/jora.1231

24 Korteling, J., & Toet, A. (2022). *Cognitive Biases*. In Elsevier eBooks (pp. 610–619). https://doi.org/10.1016/b978-0-12-809324-5.24105-9

25 Lee, E. (2023). 'The State of the Union: How Gen Z and millennials view marriage, according to data'. *theknot.com*. https://www.theknot.com/content/thoughts-on-marriage-statistics

26 Defino, J. (2024, January 9). 'Ask Ugly: now that I'm a mother, I'm mourning my old, "pretty" self. Is this normal?' *Guardian*. https://www.theguardian.com/lifeandstyle/2023/dec/07/balancing-motherhood-beauty-identity-ask-ugly?utm_source=substack&utm_medium=email

6 DTR (Defining the Relationship)

1 Denby, A., & Van Hooff, J. (2023). ' "An emotional stalemate": cold intimacies in heterosexual young people's dating practices'. *Emotions and Society*, 1–17. https://doi.org/10.1332/263169021x16740853641050

2 'Hinge's first Gen Z report reveals top dating trends and tips to find a relationship in 2024'. (n.d.). Hinge. https://hinge.co/press/2024-GenZ-Report

3 Hinds, R., Garwood-Cross, L., Moore, K., Hakim, J., Katz, R., Light, B., Mercer, J., & Upton, M. (2021). 'COVID sex lives: survey 1 report'. https://salford-repository.worktribe.com/output/1476682/covid-sex-lives-survey-1-report

4 Thompson, R. (2023, May 22). 'Gen Z is challenging the way we date, says Tinder report'. *Mashable.* https://mashable.com/article/tinder-future-of-dating-2023-gen-z

5 Maclean, K. (2019, December 10). *Research: Pressure Points Study 2019.* The Blog. https://blog.pof.com/2019/09/research-pressure-points-study-2019/

6 Ibid.

7 Cavender, E. (2022, August 17). 'BeReal promised authenticity online. That doesn't exist'. *Mashable.* https://mashable.com/article/bereal-app-authenticity

8 De C. Hamilton, A. F., & Lind, F. (2016). 'Audience effects: what can they tell us about social neuroscience, theory of mind and autism?' *Culture and Brain,* 4(2), 159–177. https://doi.org/10.1007/s40167-016-0044-5

9 Duguay, S. *Dressing up Tinderella: interrogating authenticity claims on the mobile dating app Tinder.* Taylor & Francis. https://www.tandfonline.com/doi/abs/10.1080/1369118X.2016.1168471?journalCode=rics20

10 Brown, B. (2017). *Braving the wilderness: The quest for true belonging and the courage to stand alone.* Random House.

7 It's Raining Men!

1 Thompson, R. (2017, November 14). 'Why heterosexuals are so obsessed with height in online dating'. *Mashable.* https://mashable.com/article/height-online-dating

2 'Size matters' (2018, July 20). *University of St Andrews News.* https://news.st-andrews.ac.uk/archive/size-matters/

3 Brada, B. T. (2020, December 5). 'Leg-lengthening: The people having surgery to be a bit taller'. *BBC News.* https://www.bbc.co.uk/news/world-55146906

4 'The Big Lies People Tell In Online Dating' (2021, August 10). OkCupid Dating Blog. https://theblog.okcupid.com/the-big-lies-people-tell-in-online-dating-a9e3990d6ae2

5 'Gender roles and identity in children'. *Pregnancy Birth and Baby*. Australian Government Department of Health and Aged Care. https://www.pregnancybirthbaby.org.au/gender-roles-and-identity-in-children

6 'How do revenge porn laws work in England & Wales?' (2022, January 11). McAllister Olivarius. https://mcolaw.com/for-individuals/online-reputation-and-privacy/revenge-porn-laws-england-wales/

7 Oppenheim, M. (2023, June 27). 'Revenge porn laws to be over-hauled to help victims'. *Independent*. https://www.independent.co.uk/news/uk/home-news/revenge-porn-law-change-victims-b2364459.html

8 'Sharing nudes and semi-nudes: advice for education settings working with children and young people' (2021, August 3). GOV. UK. https://www.gov.uk/government/publications/sharing-nudes-and-semi-nudes-advice-for-education-settings-working-with-children-and-young-people/sharing-nudes-and-semi-nudes-advice-for-education-settings-working-with-children-and-young-people

9 Thompson, R. (2021). *Rough: How violence has found its way into the bedroom and what we can do about it*. Random House.

10 Owen, C. (2023, March 27). '#Men4Change toolkit launched to support young men in talking about masculinity, gender inequalities and sexual violence'. *University of Liverpool News*. https://news.liverpool.ac.uk/2023/03/27/men4change-toolkit-launched-to-support-young-men-in-talking-about-masculinity-gender-inequalities-and-sexual-violence/

11 Nasir, R., John, E. & Mais, D. (2022, September 5). 'Suicides in England and Wales'. Office for National Statistics. https://www.

ons.gov.uk/peoplepopulationandcommunity/birthsdeathsand-marriages/deaths/bulletins/suicidesintheunitedkingdom/2021r egistrations

12 'Latest suicide data' (n.d.). Samaritans. https://www.samaritans. org/about-samaritans/research-policy/suicide-facts-and-figures/latest-suicide-data/

13 'Why are suicides so high amongst men?' (n.d.). Priory. https:// www.priorygroup.com/blog/why-are-suicides-so-high-amongst-men

8 The Rules of Love

1 Smith, S. (2023, August 16). 'Unpacking our growing obsession with rules-based dating'. *Dazed*. https://www.dazeddigital.com/life-culture/article/60590/1/the-pitfalls-of-rules-based-dating-tiktok-relationship-advice

2 Borresen, K. (2022, November 23). 'The truth about the "Three-Date rule"'. *Yahoo Sports*. https://sports.yahoo.com/truth-three-date-rule-015616799.html?guccounter=1&guce_referrer=aHR0cHM6 Ly93d3cuZ29vZ2xlLmNvbS88&guce_referrer_sig= AQAAAG7AOyv72jSDnEg9p3PWvzTvDigHewU95GKN YUow4Rzc8cEoYP12rCmDlUATKD2UH-G4ghep BGWbQpWIR0WNK74vvnLSZOmbBXGKKK_DJPEfR-z69T7NiyDv_W4OynRC_zyuEHAyAHjKHGV7je5AkM nlNIxgsXBmGjdXoDJRFjxng

3 Endendijk, J. J., Van Baar, A. L., & Deković, M. (2019). 'He is a Stud, She is a Slut! A Meta-Analysis on the Continued Existence of Sexual Double Standards'. *Personality and Social Psychology Review*, 24(2), 163–190. https://doi.org/10.1177/1088868319 891310

4 Alba, B., Hammond, M. D., & Cross, E. J. (2023). 'Women's Endorsement of Heteronormative Dating Scripts is Predicted by

Sexism, Feminist Identity, A Preference for Dominant Men, and A Preference Against Short-Term Relationships'. *Sex Roles*, 89(7–8), 442–457. https://doi.org/10.1007/s11199-023-01405-6

5 #LaidBarePodcast. 'Ladies . . . is it really this bad in the streets??? Was my friend wrong by asking her date to pay for her uber? Tell me! I wanna know.' (n.d.). X (formerly Twitter). https://twitter.com/LaidBarePodcast/status/1633749660194963458

6 Ibid.

7 Daniels, E., & Leaper, C. (2011). *Gender issues*. In Elsevier eBooks (pp. 151–159). https://doi.org/10.1016/b978-0-12-373951-3.00017-x

8 Porter, A. (2023, May 5). 'All-expenses-paid dates are on the rise, but are they really a good idea?' *Mashable*. https://mashable.com/article/all-expenses-paid-dates

9 FeminineClips on TikTok. (n.d.). https://www.tiktok.com/@feminineclips/video/7213560649576746283?_r=1&_t=8ipgPUzjlpY

10 McIntosh, K. (2023, August 10). '"The female Andrew Tate": the new influencer dating doctrine is extreme – but I can see why it's popular'. *Guardian*. https://www.theguardian.com/commentisfree/2023/aug/09/female-andrew-tate-influencer-dating-debt-man-bills

11 Sprinkle_sprinkle on TikTok. (n.d.). https://www.tiktok.com/@shera_sprinkle_sprinkle/video/7320436163611823403?_r=1&_t=8iph1UCOCf3

12 Varina, R. (2023, October 20). 'Let's discuss hypergamy: the oldest dating technique in the book'. *Cosmopolitan*. https://www.cosmopolitan.com/uk/love-sex/relationships/a45592448/hypergamy-definition/

13 Upton-Clark, E. (2022, April 21). 'High value dating is a highly problematic concept'. *Refinery29*. https://www.refinery29.com/en-gb/2022/04/10935439/high-value-dating-tiktok

14 Stepek, J. (2023, February 17). 'UK houses haven't been this unaffordable since 1876'. *Bloomberg.com*. https://www.bloomberg.

com/news/newsletters/2023-02-17/uk-houses-haven-t-been-this-unaffordable-since-1876

15 Vicky Spratt (@vicky.spratt) Instagram photos and videos. (n.d.). https://www.instagram.com/p/C8FXeKvI3Ja/?img_index=1

16 Alba, B., Hammond, M. D., & Cross, E. J. (2023). 'Women's Endorsement of Heteronormative Dating Scripts is Predicted by Sexism, Feminist Identity, A Preference for Dominant Men, and A Preference Against Short-Term Relationships'. *Sex Roles*, 89(7–8), 442–457. https://doi.org/10.1007/s11199-023-01405-6

17 De Geus, R., Ralph-Morrow, E., & Shorrocks, R. (2022). 'Understanding Ambivalent Sexism and its Relationship with Electoral Choice in Britain'. *British Journal of Political Science*, 52(4), 1564–1583. https://doi.org/10.1017/s0007123421000612

18 Thompson, R. (2021). *Rough: How violence has found its way into the bedroom and what we can do about it*. Random House.

9 Endings – Reframing Rejection

1 Miller, K., & Champion, L. (2021). '5 Signs You're Dealing With Mixed Signals in a Relationship–And How To Deal With Them Effectively'. *Well+Good*. https://www.wellandgood.com/mixed-signals/

2 Van Der Veen, F. M., Burdzina, A., & Langeslag, S.J.E. (2019). 'Don't you want me, baby? Cardiac and electrocortical concomitants of romantic interest and rejection'. *Biological Psychology*, 146, 107707. https://doi.org/10.1016/j.biopsycho.2019.05.007

3 Iovine, A. (2022, November 29). 'Tinder's Year in Swipe identifies "situationships" as a valid relationship status'. *Mashable*. https://mashable.com/article/tinder-situatonships-year-in-swipe

4 Thompson, R. (2023, July 12). 'The lonely state of getting over someone you never dated'. *Mashable*. https://mashable.com/article/getting-over-someone-you-never-dated

5 Ibid.

6 Powell, D. N., Freedman, G., Jensen, K., & Preston, V. (2021). '"Talking" as a romantic interaction: Is there consensus?' *Journal of Couple & Relationship Therapy*, 20(4), 384–404. https://doi.org/10.1080/15332691.2020.1867684

7 Freedman, G., Powell, D. N., Le, B., & Williams, K. D. (2018). 'Ghosting and destiny: Implicit theories of relationships predict beliefs about ghosting'. *Journal of Social and Personal Relationships*, 36(3), 905–924. https://doi.org/10.1177/0265407517748791

8 Pancani, L., Aureli, N., & Riva, P. (2022). 'Relationship dissolution strategies: Comparing the psychological consequences of ghosting, orbiting, and rejection'. *Cyberpsychology*, 16(2). https://doi.org/10.5817/cp2022-2-9

9 LeFebvre, L. E., & Fan, X. (2020). 'Ghosted?: Navigating strategies for reducing uncertainty and implications surrounding ambiguous loss'. *Personal Relationships*, 27(2), 433–459. https://doi.org/10.1111/pere.12322

10 Freedman, G., Powell, D. N., Le, B., & Williams, K. D. (2018). 'Ghosting and destiny: Implicit theories of relationships predict beliefs about ghosting'. *Journal of Social and Personal Relationships*, 36(3), 905–924. https://doi.org/10.1177/0265407517748791

11 Ibid.

12 Timmermans, E., Hermans, A., & Opree, S. J. (2020). 'Gone with the wind: Exploring mobile daters' ghosting experiences'. *Journal of Social and Personal Relationships*, 38(2), 783–801. https://doi.org/10.1177/0265407520970287

13 Bates, L. (2019, March 25). '"Being a woman is scary": the unspoken danger of declining a man's advances'. *Guardian*. https://www.theguardian.com/world/shortcuts/2019/mar/25/being-a-woman-is-scary-the-unspoken-danger-of-declining-a-mans-advances

14 Baumeister, R. F., Wotman, S. R., & Stillwell, A. M. (1993). 'Unrequited love: On heartbreak, anger, guilt, scriptlessness, and

humiliation'. *Journal of Personality and Social Psychology*, 64(3), 377–394. https://doi.org/10.1037/0022-3514.64.3.377

10 Too Sensitive

1 Acevedo, B., Aron, E., Pospos, S., & Jessen, D. 'The functional highly sensitive brain: a review of the brain circuits underlying sensory processing sensitivity and seemingly related disorders' (2018, April 19). *Philosophical Transactions of the Royal Society Lond B: Biological Sciences* 373(1744): 20170161. Royalsocietypublishing.org/doi/10.1098/rstb.2017.0161

2 Hsieh, C. & Norris, R. (2024, July 22) 'Why Am I So Sensitive? Here's What the Experts Say'. https://www.wellandgood.com/why-am-i-so-sensitive/

3 Saner, E. (2021, November 15). '"They could be the visionaries of our world": do "overemotional" people hold the key to happiness?' *Guardian*. https://www.theguardian.com/lifeandstyle/2021/nov/15/visionaries-overemotional-people-happiness-sensitivity-smells-sounds

4 'The highly sensitive person' (n.d.). https://hsperson.com/

5 'Why being a highly sensitive person is actually a strength, according to a neuropsychologist'. (n.d.). https://www.stylist.co.uk/health/mental-health/highly-sensitive-person-strengths/607195

6 Acevedo, B. P., Santander, T. et al. 'Sensory Processing Sensitivity Predicts Individual Differences in Resting-State Functional Connectivity Associated with Depth of Processing.' *Neuropsychobiology*, 80, no. 2, 2021, pp. 185–200. https://doi.org/10.1159/000513527.

7 Aron, Elaine. *The Highly Sensitive Person: How to Thrive When the World Overwhelms You.* Thorsons, 1999

8 Thompson, R. (2020, September 16). 'How to set boundaries in the early stages of dating'. *Mashable.* https://mashable.com/article/setting-boundaries-dating-relationship

9 Sumter, S. R., Vandenbosch, L., & Ligtenberg, L. (2017). 'Love me Tinder: Untangling emerging adults' motivations for using the dating application Tinder'. *Telematics and Informatics*, 34(1), 67–78. https://doi.org/10.1016/j.tele.2016.04.009

10 Thomas, M. F., Binder, A., Stević, A., & Matthes, J. (2023). '99 + matches but a spark ain't one: Adverse psychological effects of excessive swiping on dating apps'. *Telematics and Informatics*, 78, 101949. https://doi.org/10.1016/j.tele.2023.101949

11 NYU (2021, February 26). 'Social media use driven by search for reward, akin to animals seeking food, new study shows'. https://www.nyu.edu/about/news-publications/news/2021/february/social-media-use-driven-by-search-for-reward--akin-to-animals-se.html

12 'Reward learning' (n.d.). National Institute of Mental Health (NIMH). https://www.nimh.nih.gov/research/research-funded-by-nimh/rdoc/constructs/reward-learning

13 Skinner, B. F. 'Two types of conditioned reflex: a reply to Konorski and Miller'. *J. Gen. Psychol.* 1937;16:272–79

14 NYU (2021, February 26). 'Social media use driven by search for reward, akin to animals seeking food, new study shows'. Ibid.

15 Thompson, R. (2023, January 20). 'How to improve your self-esteem'. *Mashable.* https://mashable.com/article/self-esteem-tips

16 'Attachment Theory and Practice'. (2017, January 1, updated 2023, 11 April). Education Scotland. https://education.gov.scot/resources/attachment-theory-and-practice/

17 Thompson, R. (2021, February 25). 'What is attachment theory and how does it impact sex and relationships?' *Mashable.* https://mashable.com/article/attachment-theory-explained

18 Stefanou, C., & McCabe, M. P. (2012). 'Adult Attachment and Sexual Functioning: A review of past research'. *The Journal of Sexual Medicine*, 9(10), 2499–2507. https://doi.org/10.1111/j.1743-6109.2012.02843.x

19 Spratt, V. (2023, October 17). 'Has attachment theory gone too far?' *Refinery29*. https://www.refinery29.com/en-gb/2022/06/10771935/attachment-theory-problems

20 Rich Harris, J. (2009). 'Attachment theory underestimates the child'. *Behavioral and Brain Sciences*, 32(1), 30. https://doi.org/10.1017/S0140525X09000119

21 Ruiz, R. (2019, June 7). '5 ways to be a more empathetic person'. *Mashable*. https://mashable.com/article/how-to-develop-empathy

11 Moving On

1 Arnocky, S., MacKinnon, M., Clarke, S.C.T., McPherson, G. E., & Kapitanchuk, E. (2023). 'Women's romantic jealousy predicts risky appearance enhancement effort'. *Evolutionary Psychology*, 21(3). https://doi.org/10.1177/14747049231185782

2 Quinn, H. (2023). 'Scarcity – the mindset keeping you single'. *Hayley Quinn*. https://www.hayleyquinn.com/men-blog/scarcity-the-mindset-keeping-you-single/

3 Fisher, H. (2006). *Broken Hearts: The nature and risks of romantic rejection*. Psychology Press.

4 Schultz, W. (2000). 'Multiple reward signals in the brain'. *Nature Reviews. Neuroscience*, 1(3), 199–207. https://doi.org/10.1038/35044563

5 Watson, S. (2021, July 20). 'Dopamine: The pathway to pleasure'. *Harvard Health*. https://www.health.harvard.edu/mind-and-mood/dopamine-the-pathway-to-pleasure

6 Thorpe, J. (2019, September 22). 'What happens in your brain when you get a match on a dating app'. *Bustle*. https://www.

bustle.com/p/what-happens-in-your-brain-when-you-get-a-match-on-a-dating-app-18735535

7 Fisher, H., Brown, L. L., Aron, A., Strong, G., & Mashek, D. (2010). 'Reward, addiction, and emotion regulation systems associated with rejection in love'. *Journal of Neurophysiology*, 104(1), 51–60. https://doi.org/10.1152/jn.00784.2009

8 Ibid.

12 Atypical Love

1 Joho, J. (2020, August 17). 'What is ADHD: Explaining everything you don't understand about ADHD'. *Mashable*. https://mashable.com/article/what-is-adhd-myths-stigma

2 Holland, K. (2021, October 28). 'The History of ADHD: A Timeline'. *Healthline*. https://www.healthline.com/health/adhd/history#1987

3 Joho, J. (2020, August 17). Ibid.

4 Direct, A. (2023, November 2). *UK-wide and Global shortage of Elvanse and Atomoxetine*. ADHD Direct. https://adhddirect.co.uk/blog/uk-wide-and-global-shortage-of-elvanse-and-atomoxetine/

5 Magnus, W. (2023, August 8). *Attention deficit hyperactivity disorder*. StatPearls - NCBI Bookshelf. https://www.ncbi.nlm.nih.gov/books/NBK441838/

6 Villines, Z. (2023, June 28). 'How to increase dopamine with ADHD'. *Medical News Today*. https://www.medicalnewstoday.com/articles/how-to-increase-dopamine-adhd#other-causes-of-adhd

7 Katzman, M. A., Bilkey, T. S., Chokka, P., Fallu, A., & Klassen, L. J. (2017). 'Adult ADHD and comorbid disorders: clinical implications of a dimensional approach'. *BMC Psychiatry*, 17(1). https://doi.org/10.1186/s12888-017-1463-3

8 Beaton, D. M., Sirois, F., & Milne, E. (2020). 'Self-compassion and Perceived Criticism in Adults with Attention Deficit Hyperactivity Disorder (ADHD)'. *Mindfulness*, 11(11), 2506–2518. https://doi.org/10.1007/s12671-020-01464-w

9 National Autistic Society. (n.d.). 'Autistic people and masking'. https://www.autism.org.uk/advice-and-guidance/professional-practice/autistic-masking

10 Tohoku University 'Why people with autism read facial expressions differently'. *Neuroscience News*. (2021, August 5). https://neurosciencenews.com/aans-asd-facial-expression-19065/

11 University of Kansas (2001, December 25). 'Social difficulties in autism spectrum disorder'. *KU SOE*. https://educationonline.ku.edu/community/social-difficulties-in-autism-spectrum-disorder

12 Mandić-Maravić, V., Grujičić, R., Milutinovic, L., Munjiza-Jovanovic, A., & Pejović-Milovančević, M. (2022). 'Dopamine in Autism Spectrum Disorders–Focus on D2/D3 partial agonists and their possible use in treatment'. *Frontiers in Psychiatry*, 12. https://doi.org/10.3389/fpsyt.2021.787097

13 Pryal, K.R.G., JD, PhD. (2023, July 22). 'Making Sense of the Past as a Late-Diagnosed Autistic Adult. A Personal Perspective: Understanding the past when diagnosed in later life'. *Psychology Today*. https://www.psychologytoday.com/us/blog/living-neurodivergence/202307/making-sense-of-the-past-as-a-late-diagnosed-autistic-adult

14 'The Science of Anxiety (Infographic)' (2020, June 8). *Northwestern Medicine*. https://www.nm.org/healthbeat/healthy-tips/emotional-health/the-science-of-anxiety

15 Martin, E., Ressler, K. J., Binder, E. B., & Nemeroff, C. B. (2009). 'The Neurobiology of Anxiety Disorders: brain imaging, genetics, and psychoneuroendocrinology'. *Psychiatric Clinics of North America*, 32(3), 549–575. https://doi.org/10.1016/j.psc.2009.05.004

16 'Symptoms – Generalised anxiety disorder in adults' (2022, October 13). NHS. https://www.nhs.uk/mental-health/conditions/generalised-anxiety-disorder/symptoms/

17 Ibid.

18 Mayo Clinic staff. 'Anxiety disorders – Symptoms and causes'. (2018, May 4). *Mayo Clinic.* https://www.mayoclinic.org/diseases-conditions/anxiety/symptoms-causes/syc-20350961

19 Lenton-Brym, A. P., Santiago, V. A., Fredborg, B. K., & Antony, M. M. (2021). 'Associations between social anxiety, depression, and use of mobile dating applications'. *Cyberpsychology, Behavior, and Social Networking*, 24(2), 86–93. https://doi.org/10.1089/cyber.2019.0561

20 Yurcaba, J. (2020, November 9). 'Social anxiety and depression linked to dating app usage, study finds'. *Verywell Mind.* https://www.verywellmind.com/dating-app-usage-linked-to-social-anxiety-and-depression-study-finds-5086454

21 Holtzhausen, N., Fitzgerald, K. C., Thakur, I., Ashley, J., Rolfe, M., & Pit, S. (2020). 'Swipe-based dating applications use and its association with mental health outcomes: a cross-sectional study'. *BMC Psychology*, 8(1). https://doi.org/10.1186/s40359-020-0373-1

22 Berman, R. (2020, November 11). 'Social anxiety, depression, and dating app use: What is the link?' *Medical News Today.* https://www.medicalnewstoday.com/articles/social-anxiety-depression-and-dating-app-use-what-is-the-link#The-studys-findings

23 Doyle, F. L., Baillie, A., & Crome, E. (2021). 'Examining whether social anxiety influences satisfaction in romantic relationships'. *Behaviour Change*, 1–13. https://doi.org/10.1017/bec.2021.18

24 Hope, D. A., & Heimberg, R. G. (1990). 'Dating anxiety'. In *Springer eBooks* (pp. 217–246). https://doi.org/10.1007/978-1-4899-2504-6_8

25 Swami, V., Barron, D., & Furnham, A. (2022). 'Appearance Orientation and Dating Anxiety in Emerging Adults: Considering the

Roles of Appearance-Based Rejection Sensitivity, Social Physique Anxiety, and Self-Compassion'. *Archives of Sexual Behavior*, 51(8), 3981–3992. https://doi.org/10.1007/s10508-022-02367-8

26 Plasencia, M. L., Taylor, C. T., & Alden, L. E. (2016). 'Unmasking one's true self facilitates positive relational outcomes'. *Clinical Psychological Science*, 4(6), 1002–1014. https://doi.org/10.1177/21677 02615622204

27 Joho, J. (2021, February 7). 'How online dating impacts people with anxiety (and how to deal with it)'. *Mashable*. https://mashable.com/article/online-dating-anxiety

28 Joho, J. (2021, February 7). Ibid.

29 'Overview – Borderline personality disorder' (2023, January 12). NHS.UK. https://www.nhs.uk/mental-health/conditions/borderline-personality-disorder/overview/

30 Seven, Z. (2022, January 24). 'How to navigate dating when you have borderline personality disorder (BPD)'. *Mashable*. https://mashable.com/article/dating-with-borderline-personality-disorder-bpd

31 Salamon, M. (2023, July 7). 'What is somatic therapy?' *Harvard Health*. https://www.health.harvard.edu/blog/what-is-somatic-therapy-202307072951

32 Ibid.

Conclusion

1 Spratt, V. (2024, January 3). 'Don't blame "narcissistic" women for the UK's falling birth rate'. *inews.co.uk*. https://inews.co.uk/opinion/dont-blame-narcissistic-women-for-the-uks-falling-birthrate-2827854

2 Slawson, N. (2024, January 6). 'Two single friends, one radical plan: why I'm having a child with my gay best mate'. *Guardian*. https://www.theguardian.com/lifeandstyle/2024/jan/06/

two-single-friends-one-radical-plan-why-im-having-a-child-with-my-gay-best-mate

3 Esposito, L., Romano, V. 'Benevolent Racism: Upholding Racial Inequality in the name of Black empowerment'. *Western Journal of Black Studies, Pullman* 38,2 (Summer 2014) 69–83. https://www.proquest.com/docview/1612357759?sourcetype=Scholarly%20Journals

4 Esposito, L., Romano, V. 'Benevolent Racism and the Co-Optation of the Black Lives Matter Movement'. *Western Journal of Black Studies; Pullman* 40,3 (Fall 2016). 161–173. https://www.proquest.com/docview/2049976066?pq-origsite=gscholar&fromopenview=true&sourcetype=Scholarly%20Journals

5 Hogan, B. (2022, December 27). 'You should try "Intuitive dating"'. *Lifehacker*. https://lifehacker.com/you-should-try-intuitive-dating-1849754708

6 Brown, B. (2018, October 15). 'Clear Is Kind. Unclear Is Unkind'. *BreneBrown*. https://brenebrown.com/articles/2018/10/15/clear-is-kind-unclear-is-unkind/

About the author

Rachel Thompson is a journalist specialising in reporting on sex, dating, and relationships. Thompson is the Features Editor at *Mashable*, and has written for the *Sunday Times, Guardian, Telegraph, GQ, Stylist, Refinery29*, British *Glamour, Stylist, ELLE* and many more. Her first book *Rough: How Violence Has Found Its Way Into the Bedroom And What We Can Do About It*, a non-fiction investigation into sexual violence, was published by Square Peg in August 2021. *Stylist* magazine called *Rough* '2021's most important book about sex'. Thompson is originally from Warwickshire and now lives in London.